Taxonomies of the
School Library Media Program

Taxonomies of the
School Library Media Program

DAVID V. LOERTSCHER

Illustrated by
Mark Loertscher

LIBRARIES UNLIMITED, INC.

Englewood, Colorado   1988

LIBRARIES UNLIMITED, INC.
P.O. Box 3988
Englewood, Colorado 80155-3988

Library of Congress Cataloging-in-Publication Data

Loertscher, David V., 1940-
    Taxonomies of the school library media program / David
V. Loertscher ; illustrated Mark Loertscher.
    xvi, 336 p. 22x28 cm.
      ISBN 0-87287-662-4
    1. School libraries. 2. Media programs (Education)   I. Title.
Z675.S3L68   1988
027.8'223--dc19   87-35367
                                                    CIP

Libraries Unlimited books are bound with Type II nonwoven material that meets and exceeds National Association of State Textbook Administrators' Type II nonwoven material specifications Class A through E.

To the many library media specialists throughout the country who have encouraged me, contributed to my ideas, pointed to shortcomings, and put these ideas to work with teachers and young people.

And to my wife, Sandra, seven sons, and two daughters who make life worth living.

Contents

Illustrations

Figure

Table

Introduction

The story is told of a wealthy British nobleman, Joseph Benthan, who amassed a considerable fortune during his lifetime. He was generous with his means, and upon his death left most of his large estate to a London hospital on whose board of directors he had served. In an interesting stipulation in his will, however, he specified that his skeletal remains were to be preserved and brought into all the meetings of the hospital board. It was the secretary's responsibility to bring the skeleton, decked out in the robes representing Benthan's earthly status, to the meetings and duly record in the minutes, "Joseph Benthan, present, but not acting."[1]

In the latest U.S. government survey, 95 percent of American schools claim to have a school library. That figure is at least a 90 percent increase over what would have been the case in 1950. But, are these libraries contributing to education, or like Joseph Benthan are they present, but not acting?

When this book was nearing completion, the author carried the manuscript everywhere and would edit a page if the opportunity presented itself. At an Explorer Scout meeting one evening, all the junior and senior aged boys saw the four-inch D-ring binder and wanted to know what I was working on. I replied that I was just finishing a book about school libraries. They were aghast! "School libraries? You've got to be kidding!" I suppose my image decreased 150 points in their estimation. What, on earth, could you write about school libraries? Aren't they just places you go to get stuff? Don't you just stick stuff on shelves and check it out? Anyway, who in his right mind would be interested in school libraries enough to buy this book? So much for ten years' thinking and a year of writing.

Obviously, there are plenty of people around who don't know what the function of the school library media center is. In fact, school librarians are not sure how they are supposed to "act" in the educational process. As the 1980s draw to a close, educators, particularly administrators, are questioning the investment in school libraries. "If I invest $500,000 in a library media center, what should I get out of it?" "What should the teachers expect?" "What difference in the students' education will result?"

The purpose of this book is to explore a role for the modern school library media center, to provide a method for pursuing that role, and to provide some hints for evaluation to check on progress toward that goal. While school library media specialists are the principal audience, the author believes that administrators, teachers, and other interested persons may benefit from its pages, particularly from its recommendations on both self-evaluation and the evaluation of the LMC program.

This book has evolved over a ten-year period, and audiences in twenty-six states have heard the author expound on bits and pieces of it. All of these people have shaped the author's ideas and the direction of the recommendations included here. So many have been encouraging and helpful. Special thanks to Marian Colclasure who read and re-read the manuscript for errors.

NOTES

1. Retold in "Church News Section," *Deseret News*, September 5, 1987, 16.

The Emerging Concept of the School Library Media Center

If you were alive in 1979, you have lived the entire history of the microcomputer. Likewise, if you were alive during World War II, then you have lived almost the entire history of the school library media center. True, school libraries, particularly high school libraries, existed at the turn of the century, but their development was limited.

Like the microcomputer, the school library media program has undergone a radical change in philosophy and conception since its beginning. Like any other rapid change in ideas, the development of school libraries is unbalanced. Many centers are indispensable to the educational program, others are peripheral to it. Some centers have moved with the times, others are moving, and still others have remained unchanged.

In order to understand the current philosophical definition of the role that a library media center should play in a school, a short historical tour of library development is necessary.[1] Three developmental stages have taken place. These may be titled the three revolutions.

THE FIRST REVOLUTION

The first revolution began just after World War II, when a number of leaders in the library and audiovisual world conceived a revolutionary idea for school libraries. These revolutionaries challenged the idea that a school library should be a repository for books designed to supplement a child's reading. In the place of a warehouse, these leaders dreamed of a center in each school, staffed by a trained professional educator, which would contain not only printed materials but a wide range of audiovisual materials and equipment as well. The function of that center would be not only to house a vast range of material but to interpret that collection to the teachers and students of the school.

Our first revolutionary soldiers consisted of professors in university library science and audiovisual departments, state library supervisors, district level library supervisors, and visionary building level personnel. People such as Mary Gaver, Bob Brown, Frances Henne, Carolyn Whitenack, Margaret Rufsvold, Mary Peacock Douglas, Harvey Frye, and James Finn were but a few of the brilliant minds who lent their strength to the cause. What did they do? What did they advocate?

Classroom collections were merged to form centralized collections, and audiovisual media and equipment were purchased. Print collections were improved and made more appealing. Facilities were constructed and remodeled. Professional and clerical staff were employed. Public relations programs were fostered. And most important, leaders encouraged and succeeded in getting local, state, and federal governments to spend money to create these new organizations within the school.

At first, there was some parallel development of libraries containing only print media and audiovisual centers containing audiovisual materials and equipment. The most influential leaders, however, encouraged a merging and blending of all media into a comprehensive center with the appropriately trained personnel to handle the entire spectrum of media services. Practically, most schools could afford to hire only one specialist and so looked for a single and broadly educated professional who was knowledgeable about all the media.

Today, there is still a long way to go to establish the library media center idea—a place with a rich collection of media and a full staff of professional, technical, and clerical personnel in every school. The first revolution is not over. It will not be over until the target is reached. Revolutionaries of the first order will be needed for some time to come.

THE SECOND REVOLUTION

Often, so much effort is expended in creating the library media center of the first revolution that when it is complete, the question of what to do next is often uncertain and sometimes embarrassingly absent. Everyone seems to agree that there is great potential in the library media center program for education, but the question of how to ensure that teachers and students use it properly and to capitalize on that potential becomes a stumbling block. The old saying, "out of sight, out of mind," applies to library media centers, since a teacher and a student must make a concerted effort to leave the learning environment of the classroom and go to a separate location in the building for media services. Many fine facilities, stocked with plenty of books, audiovisual materials, and computer equipment, are underused. In such cases, administrators become rightfully anxious about the situation, and in the absence of evidence of worth begin to cut back on the rate of investment in a facility and program which do not carry their own weight.

In the last ten years, a new concept, instructional development or resource-based teaching, has emerged from the fields of educational psychology and instructional technology.[2] Resource-based teaching is the opposite concept of textbook-based teaching. Teachers and library media specialists work together to systematically create sound instructional modules or units for learners using the full resources of the library media center. This new role is a natural extension of the role of the library media specialist and of the center. The person who knows materials in all the modern formats and who understands how to use these materials to make an impact on instruction is the logical partner to the teacher.

Adopting a program of resource-based teaching thrusts the library media center into the very heart of the instructional program. The center becomes accountable for progress in every facet of the school's curriculum. Thus, the library media specialist is just as interested in student achievement as is the teacher. If achievement is low in any area of the curriculum, the library media specialist and the teacher review ways to improve student performance by using materials and educational technology more meaningfully.

But have these second revolutionary ideas worked? Have they been embraced by school library media specialists, teachers, and administrators and adopted into the operational plans of the school? Yes and no. Some library media specialists and districts have adopted second revolution methodologies and are excelling. Others have accepted the philosophical concepts but seem to be going through an identity crisis. These are the people who have learned the rudiments of resource-based teaching but have not been able to practice it. They feel that their present program of services is already so pressing that there is little time to think about resource-based teaching, let alone do it. So they feel guilty. They feel a gap between what they think they should be doing and what they are able to do. Still others do not grasp the new view of library media programs because they have not been able to coordinate all the philosophical ideas of the last forty years into a coherent pattern—an overall look at what ought to and should be done. Many research studies done in the last ten years show that the roles being followed by library media specialists are not consistent across the country.

THE THIRD REVOLUTION

Revolutionaries of the third kind include administrators, library media specialists, and teachers who decide that an evolutionary pattern of change for the library media program is unacceptable. These people are too impatient to wait while the library media center evolves gradually from a passive warehouse facility into an active participant in instruction. These are the people who demand an immediate payoff in the investment made in the library media center. They want a return on the half-million or million dollars, NOW!

These revolutionaries review the current concept of the library media program, see where it must be, and reevaluate every policy and every practice that have gone on in the past. Throwing out much of the past, these people ask, "What will it take to make resource-based teaching the number one activity and service of the library media program? What will it take to see that direct services and warehouse support are present but do not impede the instructional component of the center program?" These persons launch a major reorientation, and the library media center is held accountable to perform.

Radical change is not easy to implement in any organization. But sometimes it is the only way to make progress. Often, the change can be implemented as an experiment to be tried and evaluated after a period of time. Several examples might illustrate this type of revolutionary change.

The principal and the teachers note that the library media specialist in an elementary school has no time to work with units of instruction since scheduled classes of library skills instruction take up the bulk of the specialist's time. The goal is to replace the library skills time with resource-based teaching services. The administrators and teachers do away with scheduled library time and replace it with resource-based teaching time scheduled as needed by the faculty. The units taught cooperatively are tracked and evaluated for their effectiveness.

The principal of a high school notes that the library is being used for term paper use by the English and social studies departments but not by any other departments. Most teachers in the building are getting some materials and equipment from the center and individual students are receiving help, but the center is largely empty and is not contributing to many of the departments of the school. With the encouragement of the library media specialists and department heads, the principal assigns a specialist to be a functioning part of each department. A program of joint planning with departments is instituted. Summer planning days are held with teachers who have not previously worked with the LMC. These teachers and the library media staff plan resource-based units of instruction, carry them out during the school year, and report their progress to the administration. One by one, each department in the school takes on such a planning session until the library is a part of the total curriculum.

NOTES

1. The bulk of this chapter is a revision of David V. Loertscher, "School Library Media Centers: The Revolutionary Past," *Wilson Library Bulletin* 56 (February 1982): 415-16. The article is revised and reprinted by permission from the February 1982 issue of *Wilson Library Bulletin*.

2. The term "resource-based teaching" is a Canadian term. It is explained clearly in the publication *Partners in Action: The Library Resource Centre in the School Curriculum*, Toronto, Canada: Ontario Ministry of Education, 1982. The related term "instructional development" is a U.S. creation and is developed well in the book, Walter Dick and Lou Carey, *The Systematic Design of Instruction*, 2nd ed. Scott, Foresman, 1985.

ADDITIONAL READINGS

Bowie, Melvin, comp. *Historic Documents of School Libraries*. Fayetteville, Ark.: Hi Willow Research and Publishing, 1986.
     Bowie has collected in photoreproduction form a number of important early documents of school libraries, including the 1877 history of school libraries, the C. C. Certain Standards, and the Cecil and Heaps history of school libraries.

Branyan, Brenda M. *Outstanding Women Who Promoted the Concept of the Unified School Library and Audiovisual Programs, 1950 through 1975*. Fayetteville, Ark.: Hi Willow Research and Publishing, 1981.
     This dissertation documents many of the accomplishments of the early pioneers of school libraries, but concentrates on Eleanor Ahlers, Elenora Alexander, Cora Paul Bomar, Esther Burrin, Leila Ann Doyle, Ruth Ersted, Sara Fenwick, Mildred Frary, Mary V. Gaver, Frances Hatfield, Sue Hefley, Frances Henne, Phyllis Hochstettler, Mary Frances Johnson, Mildred Krohn, Helen Lloyd, Alice Lohrer, Jean Lowrie, Alice Brooks McGuire, Virginia McJenkin, Marie McMahan, Mary Helen Mahar, Marilyn Miller, Margaret Nicholsen, Mildred Nickel, LuOuida Phillips, Elnora Portteus, Lillian Shapiro, Sara Srygley, Peggy Sullivan, Mary Ann Swanson, Lorraine Tolman, Carolyn Whitenack, and Elinor Yungmeyer.

Gillespie, John T., and Diana L. Spirt. *Creating a School Media Program*. New York: R. R. Bowker, 1973.
     See chapter 1, "School Library to Media Center," for an excellent brief history of the school library media center.

Lembo, Diana L. [now Diana Lembo Spirt]. "A History of the Growth and Development of the Department of Audiovisual Instruction of the NEA from 1923 to 1968." Ph.D. diss., New York University, 1970.

Lembo, Diana L., and Carol Bruce. "The Growth and Development of the Department of Audiovisual Instruction: 1923-1968." *Audiovisual Instruction* 16-17 (September 1971-June/July 1972): in 10 pts.
A summary of Diana Lembo's dissertation, listed above.

Pond, Patricia Brown. "The American Association of School Librarians: The Origins and Development of a National Professional Association for School Librarians, 1895-1951." Ph.D. diss., University of Chicago, 1982.

Pond, Patricia. "Development of a Professional School Library Association: American Association of School Librarians." *School Media Quarterly* 5 (Fall 1976): 12-18.
A summary of the author's dissertation.

Pond, Patricia B. "The History of AASL: Origins and Development, 1896-1951." In *School Library Media Annual*, edited by Shirley L. Aaron and Pat R. Scales. Littleton, Colo.: Libraries Unlimited, 1983, 113-31.
A summary of the author's dissertation.

Pond, Patricia B. "Seeking Recognition for Early Leaders in School Library Service." *Interchange* 16, no. 2 (Winter 1987): 18-21.
This brief article contains some good character sketches of early school library pioneers, including Martha Wilson, Harriet Wood, Martha Pritchard, Lucile Fargo, and Mary Hall.

Saettler, Paul. *A History of Instructional Technology*. New York: McGraw-Hill, 1968.
This long out-of-print history will be published in a second edition by Libraries Unlimited in 1988.

Spirt, Diana L. "Best Wishes for the Next Fifty: A Brief Overview of the AECT from 1923 to 1973." *LJ/SLJ Previews* 1 (April 1973): 5-10.
A summary of the Diana Lembo dissertation listed above.

Woolls, Blanche. *Managing School Library Media Programs*. Englewood, Colo.: Libraries Unlimited, 1988.
See the first chapter for an interesting and informative view of the history of school libraries.

What Is a Library Media Program?

Building an exemplary library media program is like building a magnificent structure. Each component part of the structure must be in its proper place if the building is to be functional and permanent. Figure 2.1 illustrates the components of the library media program.

The model illustrates three basic foundation stones of a school library media program. The first is a solid foundation of warehousing services which should provide easy access to the storehouse of materials, equipment, and facilities.

Direct services to students and teachers provide individual attention, reference work, gathering of materials, public relations, and support of teaching units upon request.

Resource-based teaching is the most important foundation stone of the three. Being the opposite concept of textbook-based teaching, resource-based teaching describes units of instruction which exploit or capitalize on the resources of the library media center. Such units require that the library media program have a direct impact on learning, whether the topic of the unit is dinosaurs, Victorian literature, or differential equations.

The entire base of the model can be divided into two triangles, the lower right one depicting the clerical role and the upper left one describing the professional role. In terms of time and energy spent, the clerical role assumes the major responsibility for warehousing functions, some role in direct services, and a small role in resource-based teaching. The professional, on the other hand, invests a major portion of each working day in the creation, execution, and evaluation of resource-based teaching units in a cooperative venture with teachers. The professional spends considerable time providing individualized services and supervises warehousing functions.

Building upon the foundation of warehousing, direct services, and resource-based teaching, the library media specialist creates vertical program features. These program features can be a K-12 continuum

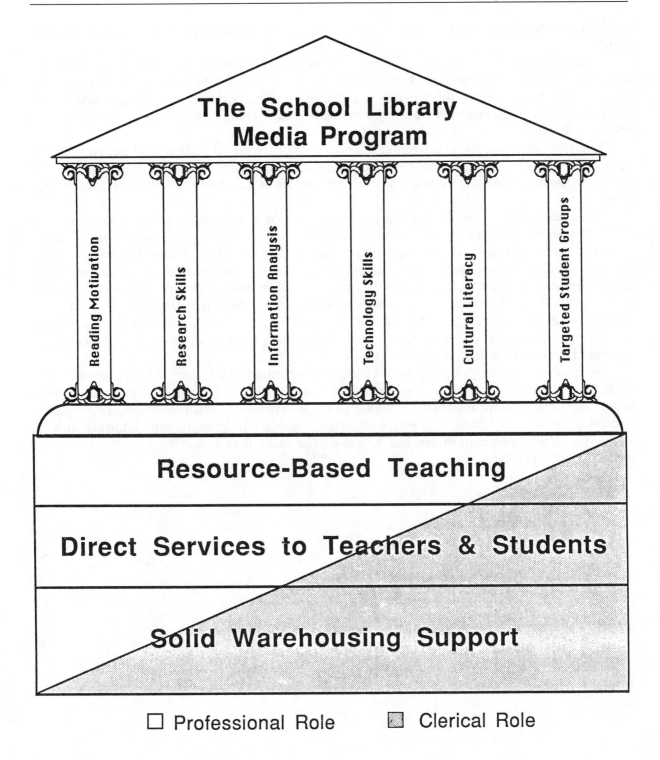

Fig. 2.1. The school library media program.

within an entire district, or they may be program features for a single school spanning all the grade levels.

The choice of vertical program features is a function of the talent of the library specialist, the educational goals of the school or district, or of direct negotiations with the faculty and administration of the school. Thus, the program features of one library media center might be different from any other, or the program features of one school district might be different from those of a neighboring district.

Whatever program focus the center adopts, the library media staff is held accountable for achieving excellence in that particular focus. However, a program focus must be integrated into the curricular structure of the school, not independent from it. A few examples will illustrate this point.

In an elementary school, the reading motivation program might be an integral part of the reading skills program of the school and might be incorporated into a whole-language arts program, one that combines reading, writing, and oral expression into an integrated whole. Reading teachers, classroom teachers, and library media specialists work in a concerted and cooperative program to ensure that there is a sustained silent reading program, that every child is read to every day, that parents are involved in promoting reading, that books are "shoveled" at students, that reading is made a "fashionable" thing to do, that fiction and informational books are used with or instead of basal readers, and that reading in the content areas and writing are integrated into every aspect of the curriculum.

An information analysis program may include the traditional library skills program, but is much broader in scope. Such a program would include skills which teach children and young adults how to handle information. Thinking skills, interpretive skills, recognizing propaganda, discerning accuracy of facts, drawing conclusions, making judgments, and knowing how to handle too much information are just a few of the skills that would be integrated into the curriculum of the school.

The Role of the Library Media Specialist

The potential for building partnerships between teachers and librarians is no accident. State certification rules in the United States require that the school librarian be educated first as a teacher and then as a library media specialist—the latter usually being a part of a master's degree program. In the majority of cases, librarians have had background as a classroom teacher. In Canada, teacher-librarians must have experience as classroom teachers before becoming a teacher-librarian. In both countries, the requirements create the idea of a teaching librarian, a colleague with the classroom teacher in the instructional process, one who is sympathetic to and supportive of the teacher's role.

The first responsibility of the school library media specialist is to set in place the three foundation stones of a successful program: warehousing, direct services, and resource-based teaching. This is no small task. Combining both clerical and professional skills, the three principal services are put in place with the resource-based teaching services being the focal point of the program. This means that a beginning library media specialist builds a program starting at the top, not the bottom. Resource-based teaching is put in place before direct services and warehousing services.

Building the three foundation stones of the library media program can be done by following the eleven steps of the library media center taxonomy.[1] Each level of the taxonomy is an important piece of the total program, but each can have its drawbacks. The library media specialist can become so involved in any level of the taxonomy that other levels are excluded or simply ignored. The best program is one that has a healthy mix of all the levels of the taxonomy.

Levels 1 and 2 of the taxonomy constitute the warehouse building block. Levels 3-7 concentrate on direct services to students and teachers. Levels 8-11 are the building blocks of resource-based teaching. (See figure 3.1, page 10.)

The Library Media Specialist's Taxonomy

1. **NO INVOLVEMENT**
    The library media center is bypassed entirely.

2. **SELF-HELP WAREHOUSE**
    Facilities and materials are available for the self-starter.

3. **INDIVIDUAL REFERENCE ASSISTANCE**
    Students or teachers retrieve requested information or materials for specific needs.

4. **SPONTANEOUS INTERACTION AND GATHERING**
    Spur-of-the-moment activities and gathering of materials occur with no advance notice.

5. **CURSORY PLANNING**
    Informal and brief planning with teachers and students for library media center involvement—usually done in the hall, the teachers' lounge, the lunchroom, etc. (Here's an idea for an activity and new materials to use. Have you seen...? Can I get you a film?)

6. **PLANNED GATHERING**
    Gathering of materials is done in advance of class project upon teacher request.

7. **EVANGELISTIC OUTREACH**
    A concerted effort is made to promote the philosophy of the library media center program.

8. **SCHEDULED PLANNING IN THE SUPPORT ROLE**
    Formal planning is done with a teacher or group of students to supply materials or activities for a previously planned resource-based teaching unit or project.

9. **INSTRUCTIONAL DESIGN, LEVEL I**
    The library media specialist participates in every step of the development, execution, and evaluation of a resource-based teaching unit. LMC involvement is considered as enrichment or as supplementary.

10. **INSTRUCTIONAL DESIGN, LEVEL II**
    The library media center staff participates in resource-based teaching units where the entire unit content depends on the resources and activities of the LMC program.

11. **CURRICULUM DEVELOPMENT**
    Along with other educators, the library media specialist contributes to the planning and structure of what will actually be taught in the school or district.

Fig. 3.1. The library media specialist's taxonomy.

THE LIBRARY MEDIA CENTER
TAXONOMY EXPLAINED

The Solid Warehousing Services Building Block

Level 1—No involvement: The library media center is bypassed entirely.

Here the library media specialist, for whatever reason, makes no attempt to be involved in a particular sequence of instruction. Not every unit can be plugged into the center during the school day. A problem occurs, however, if nonuse is a habitual pattern for either teachers or students. Not all the teachers will ever be reached, nor will the students, but these nonusers should be in the minority. The library media specialist must never give up trying to work with the nonuser even though successes will be difficult to achieve.

Level 2—Self-help warehouse: Facilities and materials are available for the self-starter.

Level 2 is basic to the complete program of library media services. At this level, the library media specialist has organized materials and equipment for the browser. The center is inviting and attractive. Patrons can find the materials or equipment they need, know how to use them, and can check them out for use at home or in the classroom. This level involves the selection, acquisition, presentation, and maintenance of the collection. Services at this level are the kind that no one notices when they are running smoothly, but about which everyone complains when things go wrong.

The major problem with this level is that warehousing services expand to fill the time available. It is very easy to get stuck in the warehouse and never really progress beyond level 2. The warehouse is never finished. Books must get shelved, burned-out projection lamps replaced. An entire day can be filled with exhausting warehousing functions and will be unprofitable in terms of a solid contribution to education.

The Direct Services to Teachers and
Students Building Block

Level 3—Individual reference assistance: Students or teachers retrieve requested information or materials for specific needs.

Here the library media specialist assumes the magician's role: the ability to know where to locate important and trivial information and materials from a vast array of sources, whether these be in the LMC's collection, in a neighboring LMC, from the district LMC, from the public library, from an academic library, or from a national network or database. Level 3 includes reading, viewing, and listening advisory services for students and teachers.

Movement toward the "information society" adds another dimension to level 3. Students will need to learn how to handle information from sophisticated databases and high technology sources. This level assumes that the library media specialist may at times deliver the information directly to the user, but will continually work to help patrons gain the skills they need to find and use information themselves.

Level 3 services can often dominate the time of the library media specialist, and because this level of service is particularly interesting and stimulating, other levels of service can easily be pushed into the background.

Level 4 — Spontaneous interaction and gathering: Spur-of-the-moment activities and gathering of materials occur with no advance notice.

During many instructional periods, a teacher and/or student will discover a new direction that is not in the instructional plan, yet is too exciting to neglect. The library media specialist might respond at a moment's notice with materials, resource people, production activities, research projects, games, or any other activity that capitalizes on the unique teaching moment. These instant projects might last a few minutes in a single class or might grow to involve the whole school for a semester or even a year.

✔ Spontaneous services, however, might become an excuse for a lack of planning by teachers or turn into a babysitting service. For students, this spontaneous need and subsequent interaction can spark a lifelong interest and even direct career choices.

Level 5 — Cursory planning: Informal and brief planning with teachers and students for library media center involvement — usually done in the hall, the teachers' lounge, the lunchroom, etc. (Here's an idea for an activity and new materials to use. Have you seen...? Can I get you a film?)

When the teacher accepts the library media specialist as a source of ideas and the specialist blooms in this role, all kinds of great things can occur. Library media specialists collect bags of tricks: ideas that have worked from other teachers or other library media specialists, from principals, from conventions attended, from professional journals, and from their own creative minds. The library media specialist knows the sources for help — people, materials, and equipment — and knows where and how to get them. Teachers learn to depend on the library media specialist to generate solutions and end stagnation. Similar services are provided to individual students and groups of students.

Problems can develop at this level if the library media specialist is perceived as a pest rather than a source of ideas.

Level 6 — Planned gathering: Gathering of materials is done in advance of class project upon teacher request.

When there is time to communicate with the teacher about the topic of an upcoming unit, the library media specialist can assemble materials from many sources. Materials from the LMC can be gathered before the "eager beaver" students have time to raid the cache; neighboring schools can lend their materials; public libraries can be put on notice of an impending demand; materials from other libraries, rental sources, and free materials from agencies and businesses can be assembled. Given enough lead time, the library media specialist can flood the teacher with materials.

Gathering the right things at the right time for the right uses is no small task. Problems can develop if the library media specialist collects too much — on the wrong levels — for the wrong objectives. A clear idea of exactly what is needed is essential if success is to be achieved.

Level 7 — Evangelistic outreach: A concerted effort is made to promote the philosophy of the LMC program.

Here one thinks of a library media specialist who enthusiastically preaches the gospel of media through promotion, cultivation, stimulation, testimonial, recommendation, and selling, all with the concerted purpose of gaining converts among the students, the teaching staff, and the administration. This might include teaching in-service workshops to promote audiovisual production and/or use of audiovisual materials, showing teachers the various uses of equipment and materials and explaining how a medium can suit various ability and interest levels, promoting the usefulness of high interest/low reading-level books, or encouraging the use of interdisciplinary materials. For students, motivational campaigns are conducted to involve them in media experiences.

As with other types of evangelistic movements, the inattentive, the antagonistic, and the backsliders will be a problem. Promotional campaigns can backfire or be ineffective.

The Resource-Based Teaching Building Block

Level 8 — Scheduled planning in the support role: Formal planning is done with a teacher or group of students to supply materials or activities for a previously planned resource-based teaching unit or project.

At this level the library media specialist has an opportunity to sit down with a teacher (twenty minutes is usually required) and see exactly what that teacher has in mind for a resource-based teaching unit of instruction. The library media specialist assumes a "servant" role; the teacher is the "master." The library media specialist accepts without question the unit objectives formulated by the teacher and is willing to gather any material or perform any service or activity desired by the teacher (within reason, of course). The advantage of this level over level 6 is that the library media specialist thoroughly understands what will happen in a unit and is able to provide focused services rather than rely on guesswork or intuition, which a level 6 gathering effort might entail.

On occasion, students have independent projects in mind which need level 8 planning. Students served at this level are encouraged to take a leadership role, and the library media specialist demonstrates the support services of a library media center. The objective here is to promote responsibility, planning, creativity, and organizational skill in the individual or group of students who are working on a project.

The library media specialist on this level not only is able to discern needs but is also adept at drawing up activities, preparing materials, assigning responsibilities, and producing audiovisual or computer materials which would contribute to the success of the learning objectives.

The servant/master role of level 8 is satisfying at its best, but it neglects a true collegial relationship between the teacher and the library media specialist.

Level 9 — Instructional design, level I: The library media specialist participates in every step of the development, execution, and evaluation of an instructional unit. LMC involvement is considered as enrichment or as supplementary.

At this level, the library media specialist goes beyond the servant/master role and becomes a true colleague and educator with the teacher as a partner. Together, these two persons plan carefully for a successful educational experience. Formal planning for resource-based teaching begins far in advance and will require a number of preparatory planning sessions, planning while the unit is underway, and a formal evaluation session at the end. Here we think of a team approach, where neither partner exploits the other. It should be pointed out, however, that level 9 service does not necessarily require the library media specialist to spend major blocks of time in the classroom. Neither does it mean that the unit will be taught in the library media center. LMC activities are considered supplemental and enriching to the unit objectives. Learning experiences extend unit content and become growth opportunities for students. Often, individual student interests are explored, creative talents expressed, or discovery and inquiry learning fostered.

While supplementary and enriching experiences can be marvelous features of the LMC program, the central core of learning may not be addressed.

Level 10—Instructional design, level II: The library media center staff participates in resource-based teaching units where the entire unit content depends on the resources and activities of the LMC program.

At level 10, the teacher and the library media specialist design and carry out the unit so that the LMC activities form the core of the unit and are not supplementary to it. The library media specialist becomes as interested in learning as the teacher. All activities focus on the learning of unit content. If teaching an information skill or a production skill is planned, it is integrated into the unit, but the real focus of the unit is upon the subject-oriented concepts to be learned. At this level, the library media center is the heart of the instructional effort. Without the LMC's cooperation, the unit would be inferior.

Level 10 experiences are those which library media specialists point to when they say "this LMC is the heart of an instructional program." A problem might occur, however, if the partnership of teacher and library media specialist breaks down. The teacher can transfer the burden of instruction to the library media specialist and lose the advantage of joint participation. At level 10, the library media specialist still does not spend the same amount of time in the teaching mode as does the teacher. Some learning activities are conducted by the teacher alone, some by the team, and some by the library media specialist alone.

Level 11—Curriculum development: Along with other educators, the library media specialist contributes to the planning and structure of what will actually be taught in the school or district.

Curriculum development is more than just an invitation to attend curriculum meetings; it means that the library media specialist is recognized as a colleague and contributes meaningfully to planning. The knowledge of materials, sources, technology, present collections, and teaching/learning strategies makes the library media specialist a valuable asset as curricular changes are considered and implemented. The library media specialist will not be able to attend all of the curriculum committee meetings in all the disciplines on a regular basis, but can serve as a consultant to the committee. When a textbook is being adopted, the library media specialist can give the committee a clear idea of how the present library media center collection can support the philosophy and the daily requirements of that textbook. Advance planning for collection development can be done before the preferred text is adopted rather than trying to play a game of collection catch up.

ADDING VERTICAL PROGRAM FEATURES

Building upon the foundation of the taxonomy, the library media specialist may add vertical program features or threads which can run through a program. Each program feature is negotiated with administrators and teachers, and combines the talent of the library media specialist with the needs of the curriculum of the school.

The model in chapter 2 pictured six program features, but these features were arbitrarily chosen as just a few of the possibilities. Dependent on the size of the staff, one, several, or many features are planned. Each may span the grade levels in the school and may interlock with other schools to form a pattern for the entire district. All are integrated into classroom instruction.

Achieving excellence with a vertical program feature will depend not only on the resourcefulness of the library media specialist, but on how well teachers accept and integrate that feature into their own agendas.

THE PERSONAL QUALITIES OF THE LIBRARY MEDIA SPECIALIST

One of the questions most often asked about the emerging role of the school library media specialist is whether the model demands too much of any single person to accomplish. Are we expecting too much of one person to be an expert in books, audiovisual and computer media, resource-based teaching, the reference process, and management strategies? The answer is probably yes if there is not an adequate sized staff in the library media center. Research indicates that when the staff of any library media center falls below a full-time professional and a full-time clerical, then the three foundation elements of the program suffer.[2] Professionals tend to take on clerical roles because of the demands of the warehouse; direct services and resource-based teaching suffer. This means that by cutting staff, the services having the greatest impact on education are cut. The same could be said in larger schools where a single professional and a single clerical are insufficient to run a comprehensive program.

Library media specialists who find themselves in understaffed centers would be wise to hone warehousing services rather than resource-based teaching services. Students, teachers, and volunteers would be required to pick up warehousing services to allow the professional to have whatever educational impact is possible under the reduced staffing plan. This is particularly true for part-time library media specialists. Resource-based teaching should always be given more time than less effective tasks.

The job of the library media specialist is a very creative one, full of exciting and varied experiences, but it requires a certain type of person to be successful. Alice Jenkins, Northwood Junior High School Library Media Specialist in Pulaski County, Arkansas, addressed this issue in an in-service program on the taxonomy. To be successful at each level, the library media specialist would have the following requisites of character:

Level 2: The warehouse.   Be organized.

Level 3: Individual assistance.   Be visible.

Level 4: Spur of the moment requests.   Be flexible.

Level 5:	Brief planning.	Be positive.
Level 6:	Planned gathering.	Be knowledgeable.
Level 7:	Evangelistic outreach.	Be zealous.
Level 8:	Formal planning.	Be supportive.
Level 9:	ID level one.	Be active.
Level 10:	ID level two.	Be accountable.
Level 11:	Curriculum design.	Be resourceful.[3]

Several research studies have probed the human qualities that characterize successful library media specialists.[4,5] Herrin, et al. found that the successful school library media specialist is one who:

- Has a positive self-concept

- May be shy/reserved but projects warmth

- Is bright, stable, enthusiastic, experimenting/exploring, trusting

- Is able to be self-sufficient

- Is confident of worth as an individual

- Enjoys people, work, variety/diversity

- Views change as a positive challenge

- Values communication

- Communicates effectively as an individual

- Is caring and especially attentive to others

- Is able and willing to clarify communications

- Is relatively self-disclosing

- Is uncomfortable with conflict

- Is confident of ability to deal with difficult situations in a professional manner

- Is neither critical nor domineering

- Has no great need for achievement, power, or economic advantage

- Views self as leader in curriculum development

- Is willing to take the risks of being a leader[4]

The portrait created is one that is interactive, dynamic, changing, radiating vitality, exuding of a confidence that says: "Even though I may feel reserved or shy, I am capable of leadership because I believe people are important."

This study points out what administrators in schools with good LMC programs already know. It takes a gutsy, creative, organized, and easy-to-get-along-with person to build an exemplary LMC program. It also requires a person willing to become a leader, not only in print media but also in every form of educational technology.

Attracting such people to the profession, particularly capable females, has been increasingly difficult because of the many higher-paying positions in diverse careers which have become available to women in the past ten years. Some principals, having difficulty locating someone, have selected the best teacher in the building and have created some incentives for this person to become certified as a library media specialist.

EVALUATING THE SCHOOL LIBRARY MEDIA SPECIALIST

For a quick gauge to see if the three foundation stones of the library media program are in place, the following evaluative form (figure 3.2, page 18) can be filled out by each of the library media staff members and combined to form a picture of services.

Make one photocopy and one transparency of figure 3.2 for each member of the LMC staff. Have each staff member rate himself or herself on the paper copy of the chart and then, using different colors, transfer these ratings to his or her own transparency. Only the head of the LMC should fill in the percent circles of teacher involvement as an indication of how well the entire staff is reaching the teachers.

Each of the completed transparencies is instructive in and of itself. What role is played by each of the staff members? How do professional and clerical roles compare? Now overlay all of the transparencies. Theoretically, the result should be an entire rectangle of color. Professional and clerical roles should approximate the model shown in figure 2.1 (page 7).

The transparency asks for the percentage of faculty reached at each level of the taxonomy. An alternative would be to chart what percentage of subject departments or grade levels is served on each of the levels.

Appendix A contains a number of other evaluation instruments which are currently being used in states and districts around the country to evaluate the performance of the library media specialist. Some of these ignore the role of the library media specialist in resource-based teaching, but the techniques they use are valuable and could easily be modified.

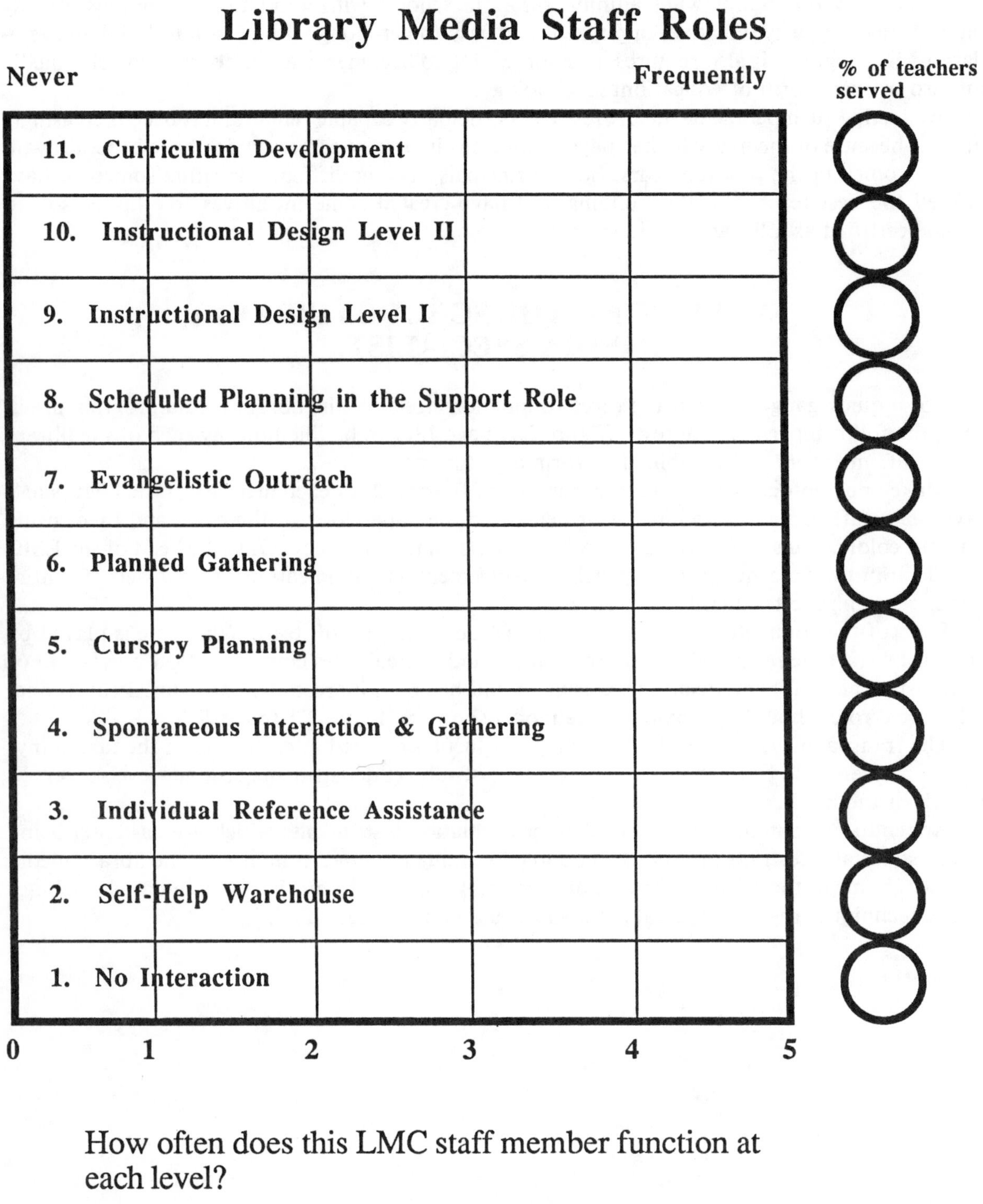

Library Media Staff Roles

Never				Frequently		% of teachers served
11. Curriculum Development						◯
10. Instructional Design Level II						◯
9. Instructional Design Level I						◯
8. Scheduled Planning in the Support Role						◯
7. Evangelistic Outreach						◯
6. Planned Gathering						◯
5. Cursory Planning						◯
4. Spontaneous Interaction & Gathering						◯
3. Individual Reference Assistance						◯
2. Self-Help Warehouse						◯
1. No Interaction						◯
0	1	2	3	4	5	

How often does this LMC staff member function at each level?

Fig. 3.2. Library media staff roles.

NOTES

1. The taxonomy was first published in a slightly different form in David V. Loertscher, "Second Revolution: A Taxonomy for the 1980s," *Wilson Library Bulletin* 56 (February 1982): 417-21. It is reprinted with revisions, along with material from the article, by permission of *Wilson Library Bulletin.*

2. David V. Loertscher, May Lein Ho, and Melvin M. Bowie, "Exemplary Elementary Schools and Their Library Media Centers: A Research Report," *School Library Media Quarterly* 15, no. 3 (Spring 1987): 147-53.

3. Alice Jenkins, Northwood Junior Library Media Specialist, Pulaski County Schools, at a preconference in Dallas, Texas, 1983.

4. Barbara Herrin, Louis R. Pointon, and Sara Russell, "Personality and Communications Behaviors of Model School Library Media Specialists," *Drexel Library Quarterly* 21, no. 2 (Spring 1985): 69-90. Reprinted in David V. Loertscher, ed., *Measures of Excellence for School Library Media Centers* (Englewood, Colo.: Libraries Unlimited, 1988).

5. Jody Beckley Charter, "Case Study Profiles of Six Exemplary Public High School Library Media Programs" (Ph.D. diss., Florida State University, 1982). Charter gave a personality measure to her exemplary library media specialists, with some interesting contrasts to those of the study of Herrin, et al. cited above.

ADDITIONAL READINGS

Personality Studies of the School Library Media Specialist

Bienvenu, Millard J. *Interpersonal Communication Inventory*. Natchitoches, La.: Northwestern State University, 1969.
    An instrument intended for a self-analysis of a library media specialist's own communication process including self-disclosure, awareness, evaluation and acceptance of feedback, self-expression, attention, coping with feelings, clarity, avoidance, dominance, handling differences, and perceived acceptance.

Douglass, Robert R. *The Personality of the Librarian*. Chicago: University of Chicago Press, 1957.
    The classic study of a librarian's personality. Both Herrin, et al. and Charter found the school librarians differed significantly from other types of librarians studied by Douglass.

Leadership

Kulleseid, Eleanor R. *Beyond Survival to Power for School Library Media Professionals.* Hamden, Conn.: Library Professional Publications, 1985.

    A revision of Kulleseid's dissertation. The author extrapolates from actual case histories to offer recommendations on the politics and economics not merely of survival, but also of empowerment for the building library media specialist and school district director.

Kulleseid, Eleanor R., and Carolyn A. Markuson, eds. "Empowering the Professional: Alternative Visions of Leadership." *School Library Media Quarterly* 15, no. 4 (Summer 1987): 195-222.

    This special issue contains articles by the editors, Warren Bennis, Lillian Biermann Wehmeyer, Raymond D. Terrell, Donna Barkman, and Pauline H. Anderson. An excellent collection dealing with the leadership responsibilities and prospects, available as a separate volume from AASL/ALA (50 E. Huron St., Chicago, IL 60611 for $4.00/copy).

Resource-Based Teaching

Craver, Kathleen W. "The Changing Instructional Role of the High School Library Media Specialist: 1950-84." *School Library Media Quarterly* 14, no. 4 (Summer 1986): 183-92.

    Craver provides the best summary of the research literature which documents the change of role for the library media specialist.

Turner, Philip. "Research on Helping Teachers Teach." *School Library Media Quarterly* 15, no. 4 (Summer 1987): 229-31.

    Turner reviews research dealing with the library media specialist's role in resource-based teaching and outlines the direction of future research.

Performance Appraisal

Carroll, S. J., and C. E. Schneier. *Performance Appraisal and Review Systems: The Identification, Measurement, and Development of Performance in Organizations.* Glenview, Ill.: Scott, Foresman and Co., 1982.

Latham, G. P., and K. N. Wexley. *Increasing Productivity through Performance Appraisal.* Reading, Mass.: Addison-Wesley, 1981.

Pfister, Fred C., and Nelson Towle. "A Practical Model for a Developmental Appraisal Program for School Library Media Specialists." *School Library Media Quarterly* 11, no. 2 (Winter 1983): 111-21.

Pfister, Fred C., Joyce P. Vincelette, and Jonnie B. Sprimont. "An Integrated Performance Evaluation and Program Evaluation System: A Case Study of Pasco County, Florida." *School Library Media Quarterly* 14, no. 2 (Winter 1986): 61-66.

The Role of the Teacher

Good teaching meets the needs of every individual student while accomplishing the goals of education. Formerly, a teacher was the conveyor of information. Today, the teacher is as much a manager of learning experiences as the sole source of instruction. Many teachers, for example, have found the management role comfortable in computer education when they find that students know more about the computer than they do.

The demand for excellence in recent years has heaped more and more pressure on teachers to perform. The emphasis on high standardized test scores often leaves teachers frustrated and with a sense of isolation. Examples of mandates to the teacher might include:

1. Improve student learning by matching resources to their learning styles and abilities.

2. Provide opportunities to develop independent learning and problem-solving skills.

3. Provide a variety of methods for classroom teaching and learning activities.

4. Stimulate creativity and experimentation.

Fortunately, there is a wide variety of help for the educational process available in most schools. Counselors, special reading teachers, special education personnel, and library media specialists all work to assist teachers in creating a successful learning climate.

With regard to the library media program, the smart teacher may learn to capitalize on all the resources that the LMC has to offer. The idea is for a teacher to reach out from self-contained teaching to embrace a partnership with the library media specialist in resource-based teaching. This model is presented in figure 4.1, page 22.

The Teacher's Taxonomy of Resource-Based Teaching

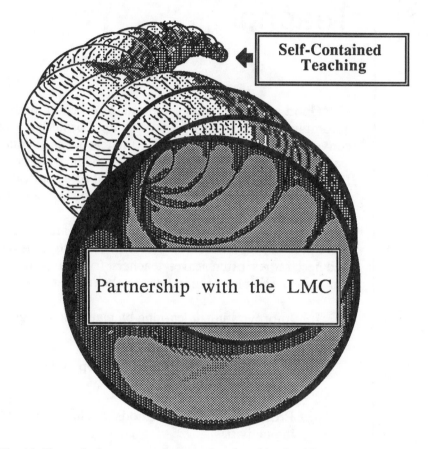

Fig. 4.1. The teacher's taxonomy of resource-based teaching (model).

TEACHING STYLE

Every teacher develops a certain style of teaching as experience grows. Some have a rigid style, others a flexible one. The model shows a more flexible stance—the teacher who is confident of subject matter, but who is willing to incorporate good ideas from many sources. This flexibility is born of a sense that students change, that times change, and that teaching methods will have to adapt to change.

The role of the teacher in an effective library media program is accomplished on a number of levels simultaneously. This means that a teacher may need to reach out for help in teaching a particular lesson or may not need any help at all. The taxonomy in figure 4.2 illustrates various stages of incorporating the LMC into the instructional process. The ideal teacher will operate comfortably at all levels of the taxonomy.

The Teacher's Taxonomy of Resource-Based Teaching

1. **SELF-CONTAINED TEACHING**
   The teacher uses texts and workbooks or instructional packages with no real need for library media center facilities or materials.

2. **TEACHING WITH A PRIVATE COLLECTION**
   The teacher collects/purchases materials of all types to form a permanent room collection. There is little need to interact with the school library media center.

3. **TEACHING WITH A BORROWED COLLECTION**
   The teacher borrows materials from the library media center, the public library, or other sources for use in the classroom during a unit of instruction.

4. **USING THE LIBRARY MEDIA STAFF AS AN IDEA RESOURCE**
   The teacher relies on the library media staff for ideas and suggestions for new materials to use, activities to pursue, training on the use of audiovisual and print media, reference information, what materials are available (when, where, and how), and professional materials and information.

5. **USING THE LIBRARY MEDIA CENTER STAFF AND RESOURCES FOR ENRICHMENT OF A UNIT**
   The teacher uses the library media center facilities, materials, activities, and staff to supplement unit content—to provide the "icing on the cake" for a unit.

6. **USING LIBRARY MEDIA RESOURCES AS A PART OF UNIT CONTENT**
   Library media center materials/activities are integral to unit content, rather than supplementary in nature. Students are required to meet certain objectives while using library media materials.

7. **TEACHER/LIBRARY MEDIA SPECIALIST PARTNERSHIP IN RESOURCE-BASED TEACHING**
   The teacher and library media staff work as teaching partners to construct a unit of instruction that will use the resources of the library media center fully. Joint activities include:
   a. analyzing of students (their needs and abilities),
   b. preparing unit objectives together,
   c. deciding what content will be covered,
   d. planning and preparing the materials that will be used,
   e. creating activities which will meet the unit objectives,
   f. presenting the unit (library media specialist participating whenever possible), and
   g. evaluating the unit together.

8. **CURRICULUM DEVELOPMENT**
   Teachers consult with library media specialists as curriculum changes are being considered. Advance planning for changes and their impact on library media center materials, facilities, and activities are considered.

Fig. 4.2. The teacher's taxonomy of resource-based teaching.

THE TEACHER TAXONOMY EXPLAINED

Level 1—Self-contained teaching: The teacher uses texts and workbooks or instructional packages with no real need for library media center facilities or materials.

For a variety of reasons, many teachers feel compelled to stick strictly to the textbook as a complete guide to their teaching. Some total packages are available which provide an entire curriculum including textbook, workbooks, audiovisual materials, and computer disks. The designers of these packages encourage strict adherence to the objectives designed for the package. While textbook teaching does have merits, many teachers feel the need to reach beyond the content of the text to make learning come alive for a particular group of students. Library media specialists concur with this thinking and spend a good deal of time encouraging teachers to experiment on other levels.

Level 2—Teaching with a private collection: The teacher collects/purchases materials of all types to form a permanent room collection. There is little need to interact with the school library media center.

Often there is a direct relationship between the number of years a teacher has taught and the size of a personal collection of materials. We all like our favorite teaching tools and materials close at hand since there is no wait when we need something (this assumes an efficient filing or piling system). Room collections of materials have always been popular, particularly in the elementary school. For all their advantages—proximity being the greatest—classroom collections usually suffer from lack of organization, size, currency, and a wide enough variety to sustain the interests of students.

Level 3—Teaching with a borrowed collection: The teacher borrows materials from the library media center, the public library, or other sources for use in the classroom during a unit of instruction.

The need to reach beyond the classroom for materials and equipment causes teachers to seek out libraries and media centers which are both convenient and reliable. At this level, the teacher is an independent borrower, knowing exactly what is needed and when. Problems develop when borrowed materials must be scheduled far in advance of the presentation date, such as scheduling a film six months to a year in advance. Such obstacles and other harassment integral to the borrowing process itself may be terribly discouraging, yet the results are often worth the effort.

Level 4—Using the library media staff as an idea resource: The teacher relies on the library media staff for ideas and suggestions for new materials to use, activities to pursue, training on the use of audiovisual and print media, reference information, what materials are available (when, where, and how), and professional materials and information.

Since the library media specialist deals with materials much of the school day, and watches students and teachers use these materials, a bank of good teaching ideas naturally develops. This resource can be tapped by the teacher if a good communications line with the library media specialist can be established. Idea sharing can occur at brief moments during a coffee break, at lunch, or during a brief encounter in the hall. At other times, the teacher is advised to seek out the library media specialist for specific ideas and suggestions. The specialist might have a tendency to flood a client with ideas and materials, so a teacher is advised to describe carefully and on a regular basis the specific areas of interest.

Level 5 – Using the library media center staff and resources for enrichment of a unit: The teacher uses LMC facilities, materials, activities, and staff to supplement unit content – to provide the "icing on the cake" for a unit.

There are numerous library media center activities and projects available that with a little planning will provide richness and extend the activities in the classroom in meaningful ways for students. The activities can be simple or complex, short or of extended length, and can provide an exciting element to a unit of instruction. Activities can range from research in books or magazines to creating computer programs; from oral interpretation for other classes to visiting with a community resource person. Such activities can, however, be counterproductive and turn into baby-sitting sessions if adequate planning is neglected.

Level 6 – Using library media resources as a part of unit content: LMC materials/activities are integral to unit content, rather than supplementary in nature. Students are required to meet certain objectives while using library media materials.

Many students must be motivated through their assignments to use library media materials in order to accomplish a learning task. When library media specialists understand the objectives of the unit of instruction and the type of activity needed to accomplish a task, they can provide the type of activity in the LMC desired by the teacher. At this level, the teacher spends considerable time with the library media specialist explaining unit objectives and planning for LMC activities. Those activities are required rather than considered as supplementary to unit objectives. Advance planning is essential to the success of a level 6 unit, and teacher participation in the LMC activity is vital.

Level 7 – Teacher/library media specialist partnership in resource-based teaching: The teacher and library media staff work as teaching partners to construct a unit of instruction that will use the resources of the library media center fully.

One of the most exciting teaching experiences can occur when teachers and library media specialists join together as teaching colleagues to create, teach, and evaluate a unit of instruction. This process requires extensive advance planning, mutual concern, and the ability to share ideas in a give and take situation. Given a good rapport between these two professional educators, exciting and effective instruction can be developed. The steps to this process are outlined in figure 7.1 (pages 62-63).

Level 8 – Curriculum development: Teachers consult with library media specialists as curriculum changes are being considered. Advance planning for changes and their impact on LMC materials, facilities, and activities are considered.

Too often, the adoption of a new textbook or curriculum comes as a surprise to the library media specialist. It is only an accident if a library media center collection can support a curricular change. Most often, it takes several years to gear up the collection of the LMC to the new text. Just as the support becomes effective, it is time to change the text again. One of the best ways to prevent this roller coaster effect and its subsequent disservice to students is to encourage the library media specialist to report to the curriculum committee how well the present LMC collection can support any of the proposed textbooks or curriculum guides. Bringing the library media specialist into the planning at an early stage allows the committee to make their choice with better information and gives the library media specialist the opportunity to order new materials or request funds to buy new materials before the proposed text is used. In addition to estimating LMC collection support, the library media specialist can serve as a contributing member of the curriculum committee in its dealings, as time permits.

BUILDING PARTNERSHIPS

Teachers pride themselves on having academic freedom, on being an expert in their subject areas, on building a sense of autonomy. Why, then, accept a partnership in the educational process? The answer is that no matter how strong or excellent a teacher is, improvement can be achieved by reaching out to others for ideas of merit.

Incorporating good ideas from others presumes a certain openness, a flexibility of approach. It reflects neither weakness nor uncertainty. Teachers who forge partnerships with library media specialists do so because they perceive that a collegial approach to education is superior to an isolated one. Partnerships presume mutual trust, a sense that both persons have something to contribute.

But what can a library media specialist know about differential equations? The latest theories of nuclear physics? The nuances of good writing? Likewise, what can a teacher be expected to know about the latest materials for teaching differential equations? The latest use of computers which will improve student comprehension? The creation of Boolean searches of online databases? To communicate successfully, the librarian may have to read the textbook or a summary essay in a subject encyclopedia or may even have to attend a teacher's lecture. On the other hand, the teacher might have to participate in an in-service training session for online searching or ask for one-on-one assistance in using a computer simulation to best advantage. Whatever it takes to communicate successfully, both the teacher and the library media specialist make the effort, knowing that the results will be worthwhile.

Library media specialists often complain that teachers will not plan units of study far enough in advance for the LMC program to have any real impact. Likewise, teachers may presume that the library media specialist has no real interest in what is going on in the classroom. Such presumptions are common and lead to empty library media centers, underused resources, misused technology, and feelings of mistrust.

The school administrator who is interested in the instructional leadership role can often create an atmosphere and the policies needed to improve teacher-library media specialist communication. Administrators can begin by providing common planning time and monitoring the success of jointly planned activities. Teachers might demand quality support from the library media center and encourage the administrator to see that a sound program is in place. Teaching need not be an isolated activity. Students deserve to have the best educational program and the best materials that will stimulate their interest.

Teachers who have experienced difficulties incorporating the LMC into instruction often request special planning grants for joint unit development, or take advantage of summer planning workshops with other teachers and library media specialists. Others see that the library media specialist is a functioning member of department planning meetings or cross-disciplinary planning sessions. Neither the teacher nor the library media specialist should assume that good things will happen automatically. Both need to lobby for planning time and for an opportunity to evaluate the success of every joint project. No matter the obstacles, the teacher and the library media specialist vow to cooperate and do it.

Both the teacher and the library media specialist should study chapter 7, which details the steps in creating resource-based teaching units. However, a few suggestions here will illuminate the process:

1. The teacher and the library media specialist cooperate in the creation, the execution, and the evaluation of topical studies and units of instruction.

2. The library media specialist is a part of the teaching team. Likewise, the teacher is an integral part of the library media program.

3. The library media specialist knows *in advance* the precise requirements of and the deadlines for assignments which involve LMC materials.

4. The objectives of topical studies or units of instruction are identified so that new skills can be taught and other skills reinforced.

5. Appropriate materials from a wide variety of sources are available for student and teacher use. Easy access is a must.

6. Resources are available in sufficient quantities to meet student demands.

7. The necessary equipment and appropriate working spaces are available for students when required.

8. Students are taught information skills, technology skills and thinking skills as they interact with the LMC resources to achieve curricular assignments.

9. Evaluation techniques are developed to examine not only the learning outcomes but also the effectiveness of the process.

10. Opportunities are provided for students to use library media center resources for pleasure and enjoyment.[1]

Teachers will want access to the LMC for spontaneous uses and at other times will want individuals or small groups of students to have access to the center at any time during the school day. The important factor is that the center should be available from the beginning of the school day to the end on a flexible schedule.

THE TEACHER AND VERTICAL LMC PROGRAM FEATURES

While the main function of the library media program will be to cooperate with the teacher in resource-based teaching, the library media specialist will also be interested in vertical program features. This means that the specialist will have an agenda in addition to regular curricular support and is likely to ask for teacher assistance and input in that activity.

The library media specialist may be a talented storyteller, a whiz at computer applications, a great booktalker of novels to teenagers, a specialist on Chinese culture, or an excellent amateur photographer. Building on personal strengths and the needs of the school, the library media specialist may spin a program thread which will run through all classes and all grade levels. For these, the library media specialist will ask teacher support, and will request that these programs be integrated into the ongoing classroom curriculum.

Library media center program features might include:

- A schoolwide reading motivational program.
- An information analysis program.
- An interdisciplinary cultural literacy program.
- An audiovisual production skills building program.
- A computer literacy program.
- A thinking skills program.
- A research skills program.

Whatever the agenda, teachers can play an important role in covering their own objectives and the agenda of the library media program as well. For example, a research skills program may be the joint responsibility of the library media center and the English department, but the science department may reinforce those skills.

The library media specialist who has a reading motivational program will encourage teachers to participate with a link into classroom programs. Cooperative LMC and teacher programs might include reading aloud on a daily basis by the teacher, a sustained silent reading program, regular booktalks in the LMC, reading contests, battle of the books competitions, and encouragement for reading in the content areas. Joint teacher/LMC programs are likely to be much more successful than individual ones.

By seeking input into the planning of the LMC vertical program feature, the teacher can shape the program and also build bridges across academic departments and grade levels.

TAKING THE SELF-TEST

As an indication where each teacher is on the continuum of resource-based teaching, the self-check form may be used. The form requires each level of the taxonomy to be rated and all ratings to be collected on the final page (figure 4.3). The form might be used to chart progress by an entire faculty if ratings are taken both before a major program change is made and after. Ratings for individual teachers and collective mean ratings would be of interest.

NOTES

1. *Partners in Action: The Library Resource Centre in the School Curriculum* (Toronto: Ontario Ministry of Education, 1983), 25.

Teacher's Self-Evaluation Checklist

Please check items that apply to your style of teaching and using library media center staff, materials, and services. Then, using those checked items, make a bar graph indicating how often that category of the taxonomy would apply to you. The combined ratings need not add up to 100 percent.

1. *Self-Contained Teaching.* As the main source of information for a unit of instruction (with little need for outside materials), I use:

   _____ textbooks

   _____ workbooks or worksheets

   _____ commercially produced instructional packages (kits that usually come with a textbook series)

How often are textual materials the exclusive source for your teaching?

SELF–CONTAINED TEACHING

20% of time	40% of time	60% of time	80% of time	100% of time
2 units in 10	4 units in 10	6 units in 10	8 units in 10	10 units in 10

2. *Teaching with a Private Collection.* Over the years, I have collected/purchased for the room, materials which students use for a unit that we are studying. This collection contains:

   _____ books and other printed materials

   _____ audiovisual materials

   _____ other types of materials (tactile, charts, globes)

   _____ equipment (audiovisual or laboratory)

How often is the room collection the major source of materials or equipment?

TEACHING WITH A PRIVATE COLLECTION

20% of time	40% of time	60% of time	80% of time	100% of time
2 units in 10	4 units in 10	6 units in 10	8 units in 10	10 units in 10

(Figure 4.3 continues on page 30.)

3. *Teaching with a Borrowed Collection.* For use in a unit of instruction, I use materials/ equipment in my room which are borrowed on a temporary basis from the library media center, the public library, or other libraries in the area. This collection might include:

_____ reference books (encyclopedias, dictionaries, handbooks, indexes)

_____ other books

_____ audiovisual materials

_____ periodicals

_____ audiovisual equipment

How often is a borrowed collection the major source of materials or equipment?

TEACHING WITH A BORROWED COLLECTION

20% of time	40% of time	60% of time	80% of time	100% of time
2 units in 10	4 units in 10	6 units in 10	8 units in 10	10 units in 10

4. *Using the Library Media Center Staff as an Idea Resource.* The library media staff is available to suggest ideas on:

_____ new materials available for use

_____ activities for units of instruction

_____ training and use of audiovisual materials/equipment

_____ use of print materials

_____ reference information I need

_____ when, where, and how to obtain materials

_____ professional materials and information

How often do you use the library media center staff as an idea resource?

USING THE LIBRARY MEDIA CENTER STAFF AS AN IDEA RESOURCE

20% of time	40% of time	60% of time	80% of time	100% of time
2 units in 10	4 units in 10	6 units in 10	8 units in 10	10 units in 10

5. *Use of the Library Media Center for Enrichment.* As a part of a unit, I require students to be involved in library media center activities or the use of library media materials. These activities are for *enrichment*. While use is required, there may be little impact on tests or other student evaluation. Some of these activities might include:

_____ reading or finding information in materials gathered by the library media specialist

_____ finding materials for a temporary classroom collection

_____ students producing audiovisual materials for reports

_____ stories/listening/viewing activities connected to the unit

_____ listening to guest speakers/community persons arranged by the library media specialist

How often are library media center activities used for enrichment?

USE OF THE LIBRARY MEDIA CENTER FOR ENRICHMENT

20% of time	40% of time	60% of time	80% of time	100% of time
2 units in 10	4 units in 10	6 units in 10	8 units in 10	10 units in 10

6. *Use of the Library Media Center for Unit Content.* As part of a unit, I require students to use the library media center, and this use is an integral part of the unit content. Students are expected to achieve certain objectives. Students are evaluated on those objectives. The library media staff will help me provide:

_____ print and audiovisual materials to use in teaching the unit content

_____ materials on the topic that will meet the needs of my students

_____ activities involving library media materials

_____ production activities (making transparencies, slides, etc.)

_____ large and small group work in the library media center

_____ individual student access to materials and equipment

How often is the library media center used for the content of a unit?

USE OF THE LIBRARY MEDIA CENTER FOR UNIT CONTENT

20% of time	40% of time	60% of time	80% of time	100% of time
2 units in 10	4 units in 10	6 units in 10	8 units in 10	10 units in 10

(Figure 4.3 continues on page 32.)

7. *Teacher/Library Media Specialist Partnership in Resource-Based Teaching.* The library media specialist works as a teaching partner with me to construct and teach a unit of instruction which will use the resources of the library media center fully. Work with the library media specialist includes:

_____ analysis of my students' needs and abilities before the unit

_____ preparing objectives of the unit together

_____ deciding what content will be covered

_____ planning/gathering/producing materials that will be needed for the unit

_____ deciding what activities will best meet the unit objectives

_____ presenting the unit (library media specialist helps whenever possible)

_____ using items on tests or other evaluations from library media materials or activities

_____ cooperative evaluation/testing/test correction by teacher and library media staff

_____ evaluating the success of library media center activities and resources (Did we have enough materials? On the correct levels? Were the activities interesting for students? Were the activities worth the effort in terms of learning? How shall we do it differently next time?)

How often do the teacher and the library media specialist plan and carry out resource-based teaching units as a team?

A PARTNERSHIP IN RESOURCE-BASED TEACHING

20% of time	40% of time	60% of time	80% of time	100% of time
2 units in 10	4 units in 10	6 units in 10	8 units in 10	10 units in 10

8. *Curriculum Development.* Whenever curriculum changes are being considered, the library media specialist consults with the teachers in anticipation of those changes. Some considerations might be:

_____ when changes will be made

_____ what library media materials will be needed that we do not now have

_____ what equipment will be needed for the new curriculum

_____ how the new curriculum will affect current activities/services of the LMC

How often does the library media staff assist in curriculum changes?

CURRICULUM DEVELOPMENT

20% of time	40% of time	60% of time	80% of time	100% of time
2 units in 10	4 units in 10	6 units in 10	8 units in 10	10 units in 10

(Figure 4.3 continues on page 34.)

Summary Chart: Teacher's Self-Evaluation Checklist

SELF–CONTAINED TEACHING

20% of time	40% of time	60% of time	80% of time	100% of time
2 units in 10	4 units in 10	6 units in 10	8 units in 10	10 units in 10

TEACHING WITH A PRIVATE COLLECTION

20% of time	40% of time	60% of time	80% of time	100% of time
2 units in 10	4 units in 10	6 units in 10	8 units in 10	10 units in 10

TEACHING WITH A BORROWED COLLECTION

20% of time	40% of time	60% of time	80% of time	100% of time
2 units in 10	4 units in 10	6 units in 10	8 units in 10	10 units in 10

USING THE LIBRARY MEDIA CENTER STAFF AS AN IDEA RESOURCE

20% of time	40% of time	60% of time	80% of time	100% of time
2 units in 10	4 units in 10	6 units in 10	8 units in 10	10 units in 10

USE OF THE LIBRARY MEDIA CENTER FOR ENRICHMENT

20% of time	40% of time	60% of time	80% of time	100% of time
2 units in 10	4 units in 10	6 units in 10	8 units in 10	10 units in 10

USE OF THE LIBRARY MEDIA CENTER FOR UNIT CONTENT

20% of time	40% of time	60% of time	80% of time	100% of time
2 units in 10	4 units in 10	6 units in 10	8 units in 10	10 units in 10

A PARTNERSHIP IN RESOURCE–BASED TEACHING

20% of time	40% of time	60% of time	80% of time	100% of time
2 units in 10	4 units in 10	6 units in 10	8 units in 10	10 units in 10

CURRICULUM DEVELOPMENT

20% of time	40% of time	60% of time	80% of time	100% of time
2 units in 10	4 units in 10	6 units in 10	8 units in 10	10 units in 10

Fig. 4.3. A self-evaluation checklist for the teacher taxonomy for resource-based teaching.

The Role of the Student

The student is the central figure in the program of the school library media center. However, the chief method of affecting the student is vicariously through the teacher. Direct services are extremely important, but lack of influence on the teaching process, on the assignments and activities made by teachers, relegates the LMC to a peripheral role in a student's educational career.

An interesting probe of students' perception of the role of the library media center in their lives is to perform the lunchroom test. In this test, a stranger to the school interviews groups of students eating lunch in the normally crowded, noisy lunchroom. Students are asked about their school library media center and the library media staff. Student responses can range from total lack of interest to a very enthusiastic response, with every shade of opinion in between.

Historically, the school library was a place to find recreational reading. That function has changed radically; it now is a center for personal, educational, and recreational elements as well. Just a few of the expected benefits for students of the modern school library media center include:

1. A place to learn the love of reading.

2. A laboratory to learn the value of information, materials, and technology.

3. A place to learn how to communicate in print, audiovisual, or computerized formats.

4. A central repository of information for personal needs, such as what to do about acne, what college to attend, or how to deal with the death of a friend.

5. A place to enjoy.

6. The best source of materials and information to complete assignments.

7. A place to learn how to locate, evaluate, and use information.

8. The center for the culture of the school and of the world.

9. A place to discover, to probe, to find out what is or is not known.

10. A repository of the best print, audiovisual, and computer media.

Such a place is created by caring library media staffs, interested teachers, the determined support of administrators, and parents who expect and demand quality education for their children. A quality program for students begins with easy access to materials, space, and LMC staff. It improves as young people are involved in active programs which demonstrate the value of the center.

INTERACTION OF STUDENTS WITH THE LIBRARY MEDIA CENTER PROGRAM

A model or picture of what happens as students interact with an exciting LMC program shows consistent growth, from a child with great potential to a mature user of information and technology, as illustrated in figure 5.1.

The model illustrates the need to build, stimulate, motivate, encourage, cultivate, and nurture a young person in an LMC program from the moment schooling begins until it ends. The imperative is not just to create a place where students may find respite from the demands of the school day, but to build, in their minds, a center which is indispensable to their growth and development. Having space, materials, and an adequate staff is no guarantee that the intended result will materialize.

The taxonomy for resource-based learning shows the developmental stages of student growth toward competence in the information society. Through a combination of motivation and design, students are taught to become increasingly knowledgeable and self-sufficient (figure 5.2, page 38).

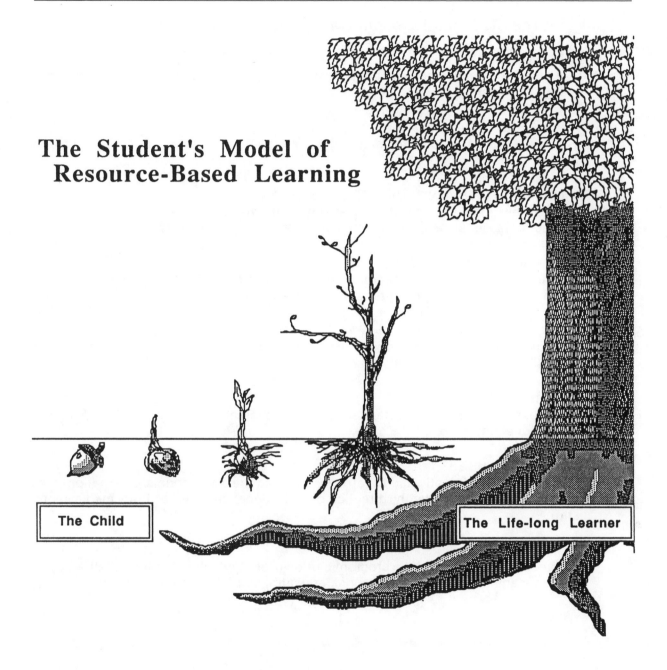

Fig. 5.1. The student's model of resource-based learning.

The Student's Taxonomy of Resource-Based Learning

1. NO INVOLVEMENT
   The student is prevented from using or has no desire to use the library media center materials and program.

2. SPONTANEOUS INVOLVEMENT
   The student unexpectedly finds materials or activities of interest in the library media center.

3. INFORMATION/MATERIALS/PRODUCTION ASSISTANCE
   The student requests and obtains specific information, materials, equipment, and production assistance for personal, recreational, or curricular use.

4. DIRECTED MOTIVATION/PROGRAM
   Students read, view, listen, produce, or perform in response to a motivational campaign of the library media center staff (not necessarily curricular related).

5. UTILIZATION SKILLS
   The student learns basic skills needed to use the resources of the library media center, other libraries, and community resources.

6. STRUCTURED INTERACTION
   The student participates in planned activities designed to carry out a curricular or recreational objective.

7. SELF-MOTIVATED USE
   The student is self-motivated to retrieve, use, and create materials/information in all forms of media both under the direction of and independent of the library media center staff.

8. LIFE-LONG USE
   Reliance on the library media program carries over after schooling into intelligent use of media and information for personal, educational, and recreational needs.

Fig. 5.2. The student's taxonomy of resource-based learning.

THE STUDENT TAXONOMY EXPLAINED

Level 1—No involvement: The student is prevented from using or has no desire to use the LMC materials and program.

Often school rules prevent students from getting to the LMC. Bus schedules, hall pass regulations, teacher restrictions, and library media center rules combine to effectively lock a student out of the LMC. At other times, students show a lack of interest in the materials and activities of the center. It is true that the student does not always need the services of the LMC. It is hoped that the library media staff, teachers, and administrators work together to ensure that maximum access to the center is the rule rather than the exception, and that a concerted effort is made to lift students out of this level if it is a behavior pattern. In many cases, elementary students are assigned forty-five-minute periods in the LMC so that teachers can have a planning period. Many of these programs may be worse than no involvement at all, for the experience can be so negative that the ultimate effect is detrimental to future use.

Level 2—Spontaneous involvement: The student unexpectedly finds materials or activities of interest in the LMC.

Library media specialists often spend a great deal of time and effort to make the LMC both attractive and inviting to the user. Comfortable seating near popular magazines, displays of good books to read, and displays of student work lure the student to probe, examine, enjoy, and discover. Such passive but important features of the LMC may be just the stimulation needed to begin a life-long reading interest, a career, or a hobby. At times, however, students might consider the LMC as a recreational center rather than a center of learning.

Level 3—Information/materials/production assistance: The student requests and obtains specific information, materials, equipment, and production assistance for personal, recreational, or curricular use.

There are three important services in this level for the student. The student has the opportunity to be creative by producing transparencies, audiotape recordings, 35mm slides, or computer programs. The student can request a good book or get an award winning filmstrip. Reference questions can be answered or a database queried for help on a research paper. At this level, the student is given the assistance without question and is not necessarily required to gain independence in any of the skills listed. The focus is on instant retrieval or success—on creativity, analysis, and evaluation—not on retrieval skill.

Level 4—Directed motivation/program: Students read, view, listen, produce, or perform in response to a motivational campaign of the LMC staff (not necessarily curricular related).

Library media specialists create many programs and activities designed to entice students to engage in media consumption and enjoyment. Booktalks, special library week programs, demonstrations, advertising campaigns, reading contests, and other activities have the common goal of presenting great quantities of media to students. The advent of television has made it much more difficult for teachers and library media specialists, who must compete with Madison Avenue professionals for student's attention.

Level 5—Utilization skills: The student learns basic skills needed to use the resources of the LMC, other libraries, and community resources.

Traditionally, this level has been titled "library skills." The trend is now toward a much broader definition involving information retrieval. Emphasis is given to the integration of lifetime use skills into the curricular units of the school rather than teaching them in an isolated curriculum known as "library science." Such skills are broader than those traditionally presented as necessary for the prospective college student. They include information skills for normal life and living and information skills related to fun and relaxation. Retrieval, evaluation, analysis, and synthesis of information are stressed. This level also includes the necessary skills to operate audiovisual and microcomputer equipment.

Level 6—Structured interaction: The student participates in planned activities designed to carry out a curricular or recreational objective.

Recognizing that many students must be purposefully motivated or even required to seek information in the LMC, library media specialists and teachers design units of instruction in which meaningful activities and skills in the LMC lead the student step by step along the path toward higher levels of the taxonomy. This level corresponds to the instructional design levels of the teacher and library media taxonomies.

Level 7—Self-motivated use: The student is self-motivated to retrieve, use, and create materials/ information in all forms of media both under the direction of and independent of the LMC staff.

Some students begin early to exhibit independence in library media centers. They know what they want to do, and require little or no help to find or produce. Other students require much more instruction, motivation, and assistance. All require instruction as the world of media becomes more complex and their needs become more sophisticated. While the number of students in this level may be in the minority, continual and repeated programs are designed to lead to this type of use.

Level 8—Life-long use: Reliance on the library media program carries over after schooling into intelligent use of media for personal, educational, and recreational needs.

School personnel will never observe this level while students are under their direction. They will probably never know how many of their students ever achieve this plateau of self-fulfillment. Many teachers and administrators never achieve this level. Nevertheless, the goal must be the central focus of all activities—the *raison d'être* of the library media program.

THE VERTICAL PROGRAM FEATURE
AND THE STUDENT

One challenge of the library media program is to provide a vertical program feature which students recognize and value. Such a feature might involve a reading motivational program, or a program of computer education, or the stimulation of audiovisual production. Program features will usually stand out in students' minds to such an extent that the interviewer in the "lunchroom evaluation" referred to at the beginning of this chapter would be able to identify the feature even though the interviewer would be unfamiliar with the LMC program. Students might see the LMC as a place where the best work of the school is exhibited, where every award won by a student or group is displayed for a week or month after its presentation.

Building program features across the grade levels which have visibility and an identity is not only challenging but rewarding. Students may never forget the storytelling, the puppet plays, the plush place to relax and enjoy, the experience of making video presentations, or the research skills they learned which helped them win a debate.

A SELF-EVALUATION CHECKLIST
FOR STUDENTS

Students can and should know that the goal of the library media program is to have them become life-long users of materials, information, and technology. Students can measure themselves on some sort of progress chart to help them note their own progress. The self-evaluation checklist (in figure 5.3, pages 42-43) should be modified for the students of a particular school. It could be used for upper elementary grades through high school.

Directions: Revise the questions to meet an individual school situation. Students will answer the questions and then color in their own "My Use of Library Media Centers" thermometer graph (figure 5.4, page 44). For a longitudinal study, file student responses and summary charts and administer the self-evaluation form yearly. Have each student or local researchers evaluate progress over time. Data from many student questionnaires can be compiled on the "Student LMC Taxonomy Summary Chart" (figure 5.5, page 45). This chart will indicate what percentage of the students checked each of the items on the questionnaire. For ease of analysis, a mark-sense answer sheet could be used. *Note:* A student who claimed to be a life-long learner would not color in level one of the thermometer chart.

Figure 5.4 is a thermometer chart. For each question, count the number of check marks you made. Then color in a bar for each check on the thermometer. Example: On question 2, if I check only one item, I color in one block and leave the other four blank.

Student Self-Evaluation Checklist

Put a check on the line in front of those items that would be TRUE about yourself and how you use the library media center in your school.

1. I don't use the library media center because:

    _____a. I don't go there.

    _____b. I can't get there when I need to.

2. When I go to the library media center and walk around, I might find:

    _____a. books I'd like to read.

    _____b. magazines to look at.

    _____c. audiovisual materials (filmstrips, records, kits) to use.

    _____d. displays to look at.

    _____e. activities to participate in (games, contests, discussions, people to watch).

3. When I go to the library media center, the LMC staff helps me by:

    _____a. finding answers to questions I have.

    _____b. finding a book/magazine/filmstrip I'd like to use.

    _____c. showing me or helping me make audiovisual materials (transparencies, slides, videotapes, etc.)

    _____d. finding materials for classroom assignments.

4. When I go to the library media center, the LMC staff may:

    _____a. try to interest me in some books or audiovisual materials.

    _____b. give me book lists to encourage me to read.

    _____c. advertise good books or audiovisual materials.

    _____d. try to involve me in some LMC activities.

5. The library media center staff and/or my teacher try to:

    _____a.   teach me how to find books for classroom use.

    _____b.   teach me how to find books for personal use.

    _____c.   teach me how to do research (how to find information I need).

    _____d.   teach me how to use books/audiovisual materials carefully.

    _____e.   teach me how to use audiovisual equipment carefully.

    _____f.   teach me about other libraries in the community that I can use (the public library, the college library, and other places to get information or materials).

6. When I go to the library, I do assignments such as:

    _____a.   find books or other materials for the classroom.

    _____b.   get information for reports or projects.

    _____c.   participate in activities as part of the assignment.

    _____d.   read/view/listen to materials I have been assigned.

7. When I go to the library media center, I:

    _____a.   can usually find materials or information I need without much help.

    _____b.   like to use the services that are provided.

    _____c.   know how to use the audiovisual materials and equipment by myself.

    _____d.   know how to make audiovisual materials (transparencies, tape recordings, slides, videotapes).

8. When I think about library media centers and my future, I:

    _____a.   think I will always want to use libraries for materials I need.

    _____b.   think I will always use libraries for recreational materials.

    _____c.   will take my children and friends to the library.

Fig. 5.3. A self-evaluation checklist for student use of the library media center.

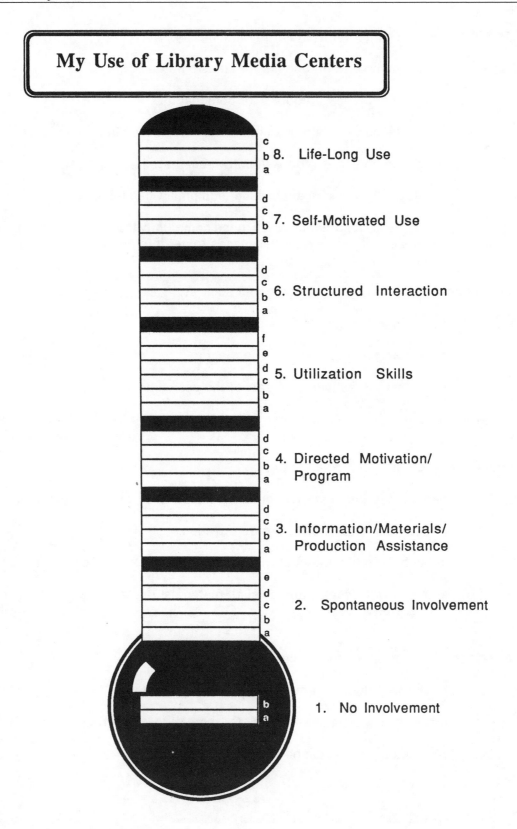

Fig. 5.4. Thermometer graph for student use of the library media center.

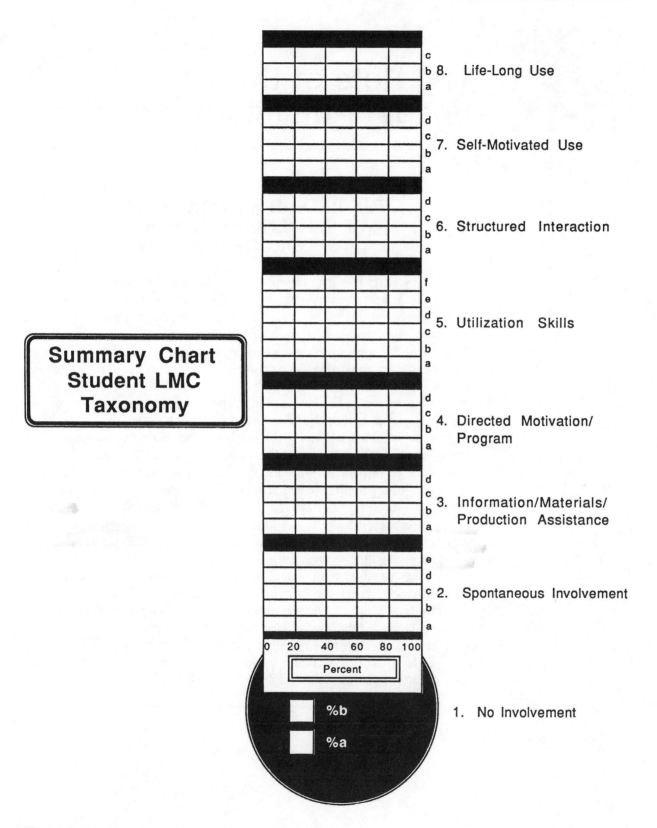

Fig. 5.5. Student library media center taxonomy summary chart.

The Role of the
School Administrator

THE PRINCIPAL'S DIRECTION
OF THE LIBRARY MEDIA
PROGRAM

Thirty years ago, the school library was considered a repository of books for supplementary reading. Today, that role is only one small function of a complete program. Library media centers are expected to be a central component in the instructional program. Since the dollar investment in a complete program is substantial, it should be held accountable for making a major contribution to excellence in the school as a whole.

The principal is the key person in the development, not only of the library media program, but of the environment in which it functions. As instructional leader, the principal first recognizes the potential of a library media program and then uses management skills to see that the center has an impact on the school. Many have assumed that hiring a qualified library media specialist and providing space and a budget for materials and equipment are the major components for success. Excellence, however, doesn't automatically happen. Vision, nurturing support, positive monitoring, and persistence are but a few requisites for building a quality program.

Figure 6.1 shows the principal to be in possession of the keys to four stages of library media center development.

The four stages of library media center development show a progression from a separate and isolated entity within the school to an integrated component in resource-based instruction. These stages are outlined in a taxonomy which prescribes the necessary organizational components (see figure 6.2, pages 48 and 49).

The Principal's Organizational Taxonomy of the Library Media Program

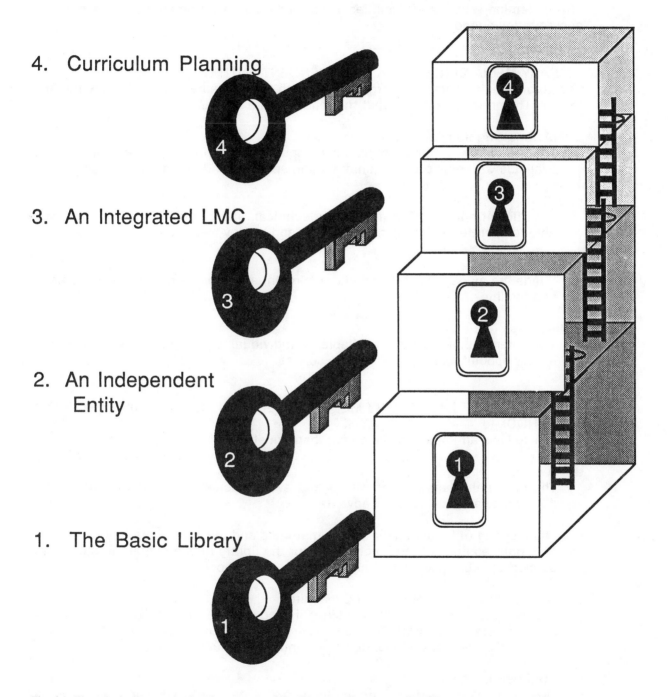

4. Curriculum Planning

3. An Integrated LMC

2. An Independent Entity

1. The Basic Library

Fig. 6.1. The principal's organizational taxonomy of the library media program (model).

The Principal's Organizational Taxonomy of the Library Media Program

1. THE BASIC LIBRARY

    The collection, staff, and facilities meet minimum requirements for the state or accreditation agency.

2. THE LIBRARY MEDIA CENTER AS AN INDEPENDENT ENTITY

    The library media center is an organization with force, vitality, and visibility within the school. The principal ensures that the following are available:

    a. Materials/Equipment/Space

    The best of a wide variety of media, computers, and information technologies are available with supporting equipment and space. Standards are exceeded.

    b. Staff

    A sufficient number of professional, technical, and clerical personnel are available to operate the library media center and its day-to-day services.

    c. Resources

    Funds are made available to build, maintain, and replace materials, equipment, and facilities.

    d. Access

    The library media center is available for individual, small group, and large group use by appointment and for walk-in service.

3. THE INTEGRATION OF THE LIBRARY MEDIA CENTER INTO THE TEACHING PROGRAM OF THE SCHOOL

    In order to have an impact on teaching, there must be:

    a. A climate for use

    The principal creates expectations that every teacher and student will use the library media center to good advantage.

    b. The merging of library media center materials and teaching materials

    Materials, equipment, and technology for the library media center are chosen to support the curricular units being taught in the school.

    c. Joint planning of resource-based teaching

    The principal expects joint planning of resource-based units by teachers and library media center staff. Planning may range from simple gathering of materials to an elaborate instructional design of units of instruction.

    d. Staff development

    Opportunities for teachers and library media center staff to develop skill in working together and making full use of the library media center resources are provided.

e. Staff size
The size of the staff for the library media center is directly proportional to the amount of involvement in instructional units.

f. Monitoring
The principal evaluates student and teacher use of the library media center, the library media center program, and the library media center staff.

4. THE INVOLVEMENT OF THE LIBRARY MEDIA CENTER STAFF IN CURRICULUM PLANNING
The library media center staff participates in:

a. Curriculum change
The library media center is a part of the long-range view of curriculum change. The library media center staff is included in curriculum committees and textbook committees when decisions affecting library media center collections and services are considered.

b. Planning
Plans for curriculum change ensure that materials, equipment, space, and personnel in the library media center will be adequate to support curricular change as it occurs.

Fig. 6.2. The principal's organizational taxonomy of the library media program. Developed by David V. Loertscher and Richard Podemski.

THE PRINCIPAL'S TAXONOMY EXPLAINED

Level 1— The basic library: The collection, staff, and facilities meet minimum requirements for the state or accreditation agency.

Many states have laws dictating minimum support levels for school library media centers. These laws might include minimum expenditures, size of collections, and staff. For example, one state requires an expenditure of $2.00 per student for library books in the elementary school. Accrediting bodies also impose minimum standards. Ten books per student is an example of one common rule.

Minimum laws or standards are set up as the first notch on a continuum toward quality education. They are not and never were intended to indicate quality. Districts that struggle to achieve minimums are advised to consider both the spirit of the rules as well as the letter. For example, having ten books per student is quite different than having ten useful and interesting books per student. It is easy to collect ten books per student from home basements or garage sales. The Library of Congress can supply tubs full of books which are duplicates of their collection, never mind that these books may be in Finnish, Russian, or Chinese. Supplying ten useful books requires careful scrutiny, approved selection policies, and regular weeding of outdated or irrelevant materials. Generous and consistent funding is necessary to provide a quality collection.

Level 2— The library media center as an independent entity: The LMC is an organization with force, vitality, and visibility within the school.

At this level, the principal is concerned with progress beyond minimum standards. Four key areas must be addressed if success is to be achieved: materials/equipment/space, staff, resources, and access.

Materials/equipment/space. The best of a wide variety of media, computers, and information technologies are available with supporting equipment and space. Standards are exceeded.

It is easy to say that a wide variety of materials and equipment and space should be available; it is quite another thing to provide a quality collection. There are hundreds of thousands of books, audiovisual materials, and products of educational technologies available on the market. Sales persons, publishers, and producers constantly bombard school personnel with the latest bells and whistles or the flashiest new materials. Principals should see that time-tested criteria for selection are used. Critical reviews, testimony from current users, and on-site examination or testing are a few reliable methods for selection. As collections grow, space for the library media center must be large enough to handle heavy use. Facilities should be attractive and functional enough to invite use instead of limiting it.

Staff. A sufficient number of professional, technical, and clerical personnel are available to operate the LMC and its day-to-day services.

The term *sufficient* is always troublesome, since one person's sufficient is not usually another's. Research shows that anything less than a full-time professional and a full-time clerical impairs the central function of the library media program: support of resource-based teaching and individualized assistance for students and teachers.[1]

The clerical burden of the principal's office and the warehousing burden of the library media specialist are similar. Without sufficient clerical assistance, the warehouse tends to take precedence. It is difficult to concentrate on instructional leadership when a major report to the school board is due. Likewise, when the LMC is down to one operating 16mm projector and it malfunctions, involvement in resource-based teaching suffers. Occasionally, LMC personnel and administrators may prefer to hide behind warehousing duties. All must struggle to rise above clerical demands to perform professional services. The principal should understand the need for the right mix of professional, technical, and clerical personnel in the LMC to ensure that a program develops beyond a warehouse or baby-sitting facility.

Resources. Funds are made available to build, maintain, and replace materials, equipment, and facilities.

Like school buses, library books, audiovisual materials, and audiovisual equipment require constant maintenance and replacement. Collections of materials deteriorate and die at a steady rate, which may be imperceptible to the eye but is still real. Wear, tear, age, curricular change, and inflation are enemies of library media collections. They are as detrimental as their counterparts in school plant and facilities. Budgets which take into consideration deterioration factors and replacement costs are a must. Occasionally, massive collection renewal efforts from capital outlay funds may be necessary to correct major deficiencies.

Access. The LMC is available for individual, small group, and large group use by appointment and for walk-in service.

Regularly scheduled visits by a class to the LMC each week at the same time and for the same number of minutes is usually not the best way to make a LMC a contributing part of the educational program. Flexible schedules and rules should be set up in such a way that the LMC and its materials can respond whenever a curricular need develops. Principals should also monitor LMC rules which limit access to materials and space. For example, criminal prosecution should be brought against anyone limiting circulation of books to one per student per LMC visit. Seriously, rules must encourage use rather than discourage it.

Level 3—The integration of the LMC program into the teaching program of the school: At this level, the principal requires that the heavy investment in LMC facilities, materials, and staff pay substantial dividends to the instructional program. The principal and the LMC staff negotiate a set of high expectations for the program. Policies needed to meet those expectations are put in place. There are six key factors in building an integrated program as opposed to having a public library housed in a school building: a climate for use, the merging of library and teaching materials, joint planning of resource-based teaching, staff development, staff size, and monitoring.

A climate for use. The principal creates expectations that every teacher and student will use the LMC to good advantage.

Such expectations are discussed in meetings and interviews, and written into policies, memos, and newsletters. Teachers know that use of the LMC will be a part of the teacher evaluation process.

The merging of LMC materials and teaching materials. Materials, equipment, and technology for the library media center are chosen to support the curricular units being taught in the school.

In a number of schools, materials used to teach and materials purchased for the LMC are separate entities. Many years ago, a budgeting distinction was made between textbook materials and library materials. In addition, many academic departments received allocations for teaching materials as a separate budgetary item. Such distinctions seemed necessary because library book money was being used for textbooks or vice versa. Today, budget categories are still a good idea as a way of tracking expenditures, but the distinction should end there.

Instructional materials are instructional materials whether they include textbooks, library reference books, periodical subscriptions, computers, or microscopes. Schoolwide inventories of instructional equipment can be handled by the LMC if sufficient clerical assistance is provided. Department/classroom/LMC "ownership" is a moot point since the support of instruction is the single purpose of acquisition. The objective is, of course, to provide a plentiful supply of materials and equipment that will match teaching and learning styles. Skimpy and limited resources are to no one's advantage.

Joint planning of resource-based teaching. The principal expects joint planning of resource-based units by teachers and LMC staff. Planning may range from simple gathering of materials to an elaborate instructional design of units of instruction.

Joint planning of resource-based teaching units by teachers and library media specialists is the single most important service of the library media program. It is the service which holds the most promise for the LMC having an impact on the instructional program. Building resource-based units, carrying them out, and evaluating the result should take up the majority of a library media specialist's time every day.

Such services may be unfamiliar to a faculty and a library media staff. Principals, teachers, and library media specialists may not have developed any concept of this role in preservice education since it has been advocated widely only in the last ten years. Experimental units using the techniques described in chapter 7, "Resource-Based Teaching in the Library Media Center," can introduce a faculty and LMC staff to the possibilities. Principals need to monitor the success of resource-based teaching by requiring regular reports describing which teachers are involved, what topics are covered, and the impact of those units on learning.

Staff development. Opportunities for teachers and LMC staff to develop skill in working together and making full use of the LMC resources are provided.

Rarely will teachers or students naturally gravitate toward library media centers and services. This is usually true because the LMC and the classroom are separated physically and also because teachers are often unaware of available materials and services. Because LMC collections and equipment are constantly evolving, an effort must be made to inform the staff of those changes and introduce new possibilities for use. This can be done in staff meetings, workshops, scheduled personal conferences, informal encounters, printed notes/brochures, and a hundred other ways. The principal works with the LMC staff to see that every positive means of promotion is explored.

Staff size. The size of the staff for the LMC is directly proportional to the amount of involvement in instructional units.

For a number of years, the recommended staff size for the LMC has been related to the number of students or teaching stations in the school. A library media specialist who has responsibilities for warehousing and direct services (two of the building blocks of a program) can be expected to plan, execute, and evaluate approximately fifteen resource-based teaching units in a 180-day school year. Increased involvement will require an increase in staff size.

The size of the LMC staff is a negotiated matter between administrators, library media specialists, and teachers. It is based on the type of program expected of the LMC staff. Suggestions for planning staff size are given in chapter 9.

Monitoring. The principal evaluates student and teacher use of the library media center, the LMC program, and the LMC staff.

The monitoring function is an essential part of a quality LMC program. Hiring quality personnel and encouraging them to perform is only the first step. Discerning progress, rewarding it, recognizing areas for improvement, and devising programs to make progress are additional steps to take.

Level 4 — The involvement of the LMC staff in curriculum planning: Curriculum change in the American school is an evolutionary process which is accomplished by schools across the country in many different ways. Library media specialists can make a meaningful contribution to the process if the principal includes them in two key ways: curriculum change and planning.

Curriculum change. The LMC is a part of a long-range view of curriculum change. The LMC staff is included in curriculum committees and textbook committees when decisions affecting LMC collections and services are considered.

The library media specialist can analyze the requirements of a new textbook series or curriculum guide in terms of the current resources of the LMC. Collections may already be adequate or may require significant new budgetary allocations. These assessments are important to the committees considering change and to the administration in budgetary planning.

Planning. Plans for curriculum change ensure that materials, equipment, space, and personnel in the LMC will be adequate to support curricular change as it occurs.

Principals must help library media specialists plan for change. The important consideration here is that the LMC can anticipate change rather than react to it. Changes in grade levels in buildings, teaching methods, even remodeling buildings affect LMC programs. New materials take time to select, order, and make available. Special funds may be needed if the LMC is expected to gear up to a change anticipated for the next school year. Often, it takes a LMC several years to meet new curricular requirements if advance planning and budgetary considerations are not adequate. Both students and teachers are negatively affected if they make impossible demands on the LMC because of curricular change.

THE SCHOOL ADMINISTRATOR AND
VERTICAL PROGRAM FEATURES

Over the years, library media specialists have created program components which complement the educational program of the school. The two most familiar programs which span grade levels and curricular areas are reading motivation and library skills. While both have made contributions to student development, in some schools, these programs have become so central to the LMC function that other services have been crowded out. The worst examples come from elementary and middle school LMCs. In some schools, the LMC is perceived as a place where children visit once a week to hear a story and choose a library book. In other schools, the bulk of the library media specialist's time is scheduled to teach classes of library skills. Neither program contributes much to the education of children and young people. Both prevent the central function of the library media center—resource-based teaching and learning—from happening.

The best return on money invested in library media centers comes when the activities, the collection, and the facilities make a direct contribution to instructional units taught in the various classrooms. This means that the agenda of the teachers comes before any agenda created by the library media center. Just because a library exists is no reason to study library science. Library media centers are tools, not ends in themselves. Educators have rediscovered this principle with computers, the newest technology. Just because a school has computers is no reason to conduct massive computer literacy and programming classes. The greatest contribution that computers make to education is in areas such as writing, simulation of science experiments, computer-aided design, and computerized music composition, to name a few.

Many have discovered that computer literacy can be taught as students use computer programs which meet a curricular objective. Likewise, any agenda created by the library media center can be integrated into the larger and more important purposes of the curriculum. Both purposes can be accomplished together in less time with a superior result. Students can learn how to operate a computer and how to care for it as they learn to write science essays. They can also be introduced to the best historical fiction during a Civil War unit.

Administrators should do a time analysis of the library media staff's daily regimen. What activities take up the most time? Warehousing? A vertical program such as library skills? Resource-based teaching? If the latter is not the focus of the program, adjustments in the entire management system of the center are needed.

How can the library media staff teach a program of library skills or conduct a reading motivational program when the bulk of their time is taken up helping teachers plan, execute, and evaluate resource-based teaching units? The answer is that vertical program elements are integrated cleverly into units taught with LMC cooperation. Reading motivation is a part of the reading curriculum in the elementary school. Research skills can be taught to high school sophomores when they have to write a research paper in English. Allowing the LMC program to develop a rigid instructional curriculum of its own locks it out and further isolates it from the curriculum of the school. Mandating that the LMC program be integrated with resource-based teaching promotes cooperation with teachers, a meshing of the classroom with the LMC, and the likelihood of producing a superior product.

Many have assumed that reading motivation and library skills (or research skills) were the only major program components of the library media center. This need not be the case. There are a number of program features worth exploring, depending on the LMC staff's strengths and the needs of the curriculum. Some library media programs may emphasize the use of technology, such as computers or online searching. Others may promote cultural literacy. Still others might go on beyond library skills to teach information analysis and critical thinking.

Administrators should take the lead in planning which vertical program features are offered by the library media staff and how these will be integrated into resource-based teaching activities on a regular basis. Many library media specialists already have K-12 continuums of program features which provide the structure and the method of integration into the curriculum. Administrators should monitor these plans and see that the organizational structure of the school provides the means to carry them out. If the agenda of the LMC begins to take precedence over resource-based teaching, adjustments should be made.

A SELF-EVALUATION CHECKLIST
FOR ADMINISTRATORS

Administrators may wish to rate themselves to judge what type of library media program the organizational structure of the school actually supports. Copies of the self-test can be created, and the results can be rated and transferred to the summary chart for a quick overview of the status of the LMC program (see figure 6.3, pages 56-57, and figure 6.4, page 58).

Directions: For each administrator in the school, make a copy of the self-evaluation check-list. Check each item on the test that is true about the LMC in the school. Transfer the ratings to the summary chart. If more than one administrator completes the self-test, discuss differences of opinion before the summary chart is completed.

NOTES

1.   David V. Loertscher, May Lein Ho, and Melvin M. Bowie, "Exemplary Elementary Schools and Their Library Media Centers: A Research Report," *School Library Media Quarterly* 15, no. 3 (Spring 1987): 147-53.

Principal's Self-Evaluation Checklist

Directions: Check each item on the test that is TRUE about the library media program in the school.

1. The basic library.

    _____a. The library media center meets the requirements of state law for space, materials, and staff.

    _____b. The library media center meets the requirements of an accreditation body in terms of space, materials, and staff.

    _____c. The library media center meets the above standards in both spirit and letter.

2. The library media center as an independent entity.

    _____a. The LMC is a total multimedia center (including computer media)

    _____b. State/accrediting agency standards are exceeded in terms of space, materials, and staff.

    _____c. A selection policy for materials and equipment is written and used as the basis for acquiring quality materials and equipment.

    _____d. Facilities are spacious enough to handle small groups, large groups, and individuals simultaneously.

    _____e. At least one full-time professional and one full-time clerical are available in the LMC (meets or exceeds accreditation standards in large schools).

    _____f. Clerical help in the LMC is sufficient to allow the library media specialist to concentrate on direct services and resource-based teaching.

    _____g. Budgets for the LMC take into consideration the deterioration of materials and equipment.

    _____h. Access to the LMC, its materials, and equipment is exemplary.

3. The integration of the LMC program into the teaching program of the school.

    _____a. The principal's expectation for teacher and student use of the LMC is high and has an impact on the climate for use.

    _____b. Teaching materials, LMC materials, and textbook materials are budgeted separately, but form an integrated bank of instructional materials.

_____c.   Joint teacher/library media specialist planning of resource-based teaching units is common in the school.

_____d.   The principal has taken the lead in ensuring that resource-based teaching is accepted and implemented by the library media staff and the teachers.

_____e.   Staff development opportunities are provided whenever weaknesses in the library media program are discovered.

_____f.   The size of the library media staff is directly proportional to the amount of involvement in instructional units.

_____g.   The principal actively monitors the LMC program as the instructional leader of the school. Monitoring goes beyond warehousing concerns to include an evaluation of the impact of the LMC on the instructional program.

4.   The involvement of the LMC staff in curriculum planning.

_____a.   A member of the LMC staff serves on all curriculum committees.

_____b.   The LMC staff member makes the curriculum committees aware of the impact that curricular change will have on the LMC program.

_____c.   The LMC staff knows about curricular or other changes far enough in advance to be able to meet the change effectively.

Fig. 6.3. Principal's self-evaluation checklist.

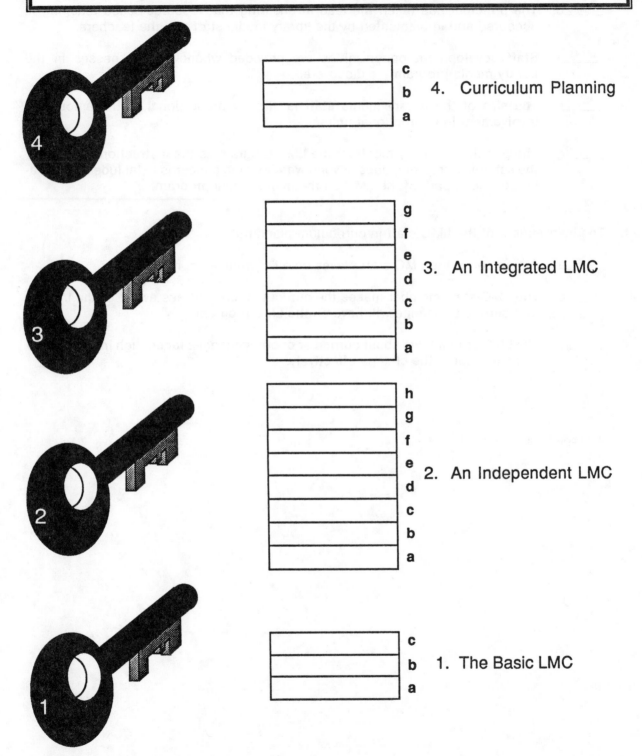

Principal's LMC Taxonomy Summary Chart

4. Curriculum Planning

3. An Integrated LMC

2. An Independent LMC

1. The Basic LMC

Fig. 6.4. Principal's library media center taxonomy summary chart.

Resource-Based Teaching in the Library Media Center

Why would a school board and administrators invest a half a million dollars in a library media center? What is the central purpose of that investment? What is the payoff expected from that investment? Such questions are important in drawing up the mission, goals and objectives, and the evaluation plan for the library media program. The thesis of this book is that resource-based teaching is the central function of the library media program.

A repository rich in materials and technology provides the teachers of today with support that no other teachers have had in the history of education. With a well-stocked LMC, a teacher may design a lesson, a unit, or a project in such a way that every learner can meet the learning objectives. No matter the learning style, the reading level, or the experience of the student, the well-stocked LMC can provide something to assist the learner.

For example, if the objective is that every student will be able to list ten characteristics of the culture in which George Washington served as president, the LMC comes immediately to mind as the perfect resource to tap. There may be filmstrips, films, maps, biographical accounts, historical fiction, large pictures, illustrated periodical articles, musical recordings, books of art reproductions, and treatises in the LMC about that era. Using these materials to good advantage would provide a learning experience superior to reading a descriptive chapter about the era in a textbook.

Resource-based teaching is defined as the use of multiple resources in a variety of media formats and technologies to achieve a curricular objective. It is the opposite concept of the textbook/lecture method of instruction. Theoretically, resource-based teaching could be inferior to the textbook/lecture method; however, the potential for it to far exceed the traditional mode is great. Resource-based teaching is flexible enough that it fits well with many models for teaching. For example, the Madeline Hunter model of effective teaching has been adopted in many parts of the country.[1] Resource-based teaching and the Hunter model mesh easily to achieve the same ends. Thus, any particular teaching strategy popular with educators need not be discarded in favor of the resource-based teaching method.

To be successful, resource-based teaching requires a teacher who is willing to use a wide variety of media, a well-stocked LMC, and a professional library media specialist who is willing to be a partner with the teacher in lesson/unit/research planning. The library media specialist serves as the materials and technology expert, the teacher serves as the content expert, and both draw upon the resources of the center to execute a joint teaching plan.

The research on media and technology indicates that when a wide variety of materials and technologies are used, more can be learned in the same amount of time than when the textbook/ lecture method is employed.[2] Thus, if a maximum of two weeks can be devoted to a unit on insects, a well-planned and well-executed resource-based teaching unit should produce a significant increase in learning compared to a textbook/lecture unit on the same topic. If the research is to be believed, the students who benefit the most from resource-based learning are those on the lower end of the achievement curve.

Two factors probably account for media's impact on learning. The first is the old adage "variety is the spice of life." Working with multiple materials and technologies is much more interesting than a repetitious textbook/lecture experience. The Hawthorne effect will often take over to boost student interest and motivation just long enough to be beneficial.[3] The second factor is media attributes. Each technology has a certain characteristic that is unique and serves the learner better than any other medium. Films provide motion, slides show realism and color, pictures show detail, words provide facts, charts and graphs provide instant analysis of data. Each of these characteristics assists learners better than any other medium could do. When the teacher and library media specialist capitalize on both variety and media characteristics, student interest increases, learning styles are served, and the possibilities for thinking, creativity, and inquiry grow.

There are, however, some disadvantages to the use of media and resource-based teaching methods. Media can be misused. Friday afternoon at the movies is a classic example of the misuse of film. Here, media may be used to take up time or are used as pure entertainment and probably contributes little to education.

Resource-based teaching requires planning time by teachers and library media specialists, a commodity in short supply in most schools. In many elementary schools, the LMC is used as a baby-sitting facility while teachers have a planning period. Such a practice prevents teacher/ library media specialist interaction and is counterproductive.

Resource-based teaching also is more demanding. It requires creativity, imagination, flexibility, and cooperative strategies. Some teachers prefer the security of the structured textbook/ lecture method since it is usually easier to organize and provides a mechanism for control of students and content. The textbook/lecture is often viewed as "safe." Resource-based teaching may be viewed as more work and "risky."

The advantages of resource-based teaching are numerous. Increased learning is the most important advantage, but there are many others. Increased variety in the techer's school day, an opportunity to share the teaching responsibilities with another professional, a chance to reach students who are having trouble with regular classroom procedures, and an opportunity to be creative are all important reasons to consider resource-based methods. While no research poll has been taken of teachers, an administrator can expect very positive results as teachers reach out to the library media program.

THE RESOURCE-BASED TEACHING METHOD

As stated previously, resource-based teaching has three prerequisites:

1. A teacher who is willing to use a wide variety of media.

2. A well-stocked LMC.

3. A professional library media specialist who is willing to be a partner with the teacher in lesson/unit/research planning.

Given the above, the library media specialist and the teacher go through a four-step process to jointly plan a resource-based teaching unit.

1. Begin

2. Prepare

3. Teach

4. Evaluate

The process is illustrated in figure 7.1, pages 62-63, "Teachers + librarians = co-designers of instruction." Photocopy the two pages of this double-fold brochure, place the photocopies back to back, cut off the part of the page with the page number on it, and fold twice to make the brochure, as illustrated in figure 7.2, page 64.

The brochure can be used as a step-by-step guide for teachers and library media specialists the first few times resource-based teaching units are planned. A briefer planning sheet might also be created to be used after the process has become second nature. The process might also be very different for various teams in the same school. Different personalities, communicaiton patterns, and content of instruction will affect the type of planning which is done.

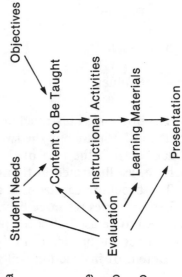

☆☆☆☆☆
☆
Teachers

+

Librarians

=

Co-Designers
of
Instruction

☆☆☆☆☆

Originally designed by
Marilyn Goodrich Peterson and
Beverly J. White
Revised by David V. Loertscher

LMC Taxonomy of Involvement in Instruction

Levels 8-10

8. Scheduled Planning in the Support Role

Formal planning is done with a teacher or group of students to supply materials or activities for a previously planned resource-based teaching unit or project.

9. Instructional Design, Level I

The library media specialist participates in every step of the development, execution, and evaluation of a resource-based teaching unit. LMC involvement is considered as enrichment or as supplementary.

10. Instructional Design, Level II

The library media center staff participates in resource-based teaching units where the entire unit content depends on the resources and activities of the LMC program.

Student Needs → Content to Be Taught → Objectives → Instructional Activities → Learning Materials → Presentation

Evaluation

---

4. Evaluate

Provide Opportunities for Feedback

A. Teacher and LMS evaluate:
    1. Unit objectives and content.
    2. Materials:
        a. Enough materials?
        b. Interest and difficulty okay?
        c. Variety of media okay?
    3. Activities:
        a. Did they motivate?
        b. Lead to unit objectives?
        c. Worth the effort and cost?
        d. Provide for student skill levels?

B. Seek input from students on any of the above topics.

C. Test learning (cognitive, affective, and psychomotor):
    1. Paper and pencil tests.
    2. Other types of tests.
    3. Tests should include learning from LMC materials—not just lectures and textual materials.
    4. Tests of any library or media skills presented.

D. Postlude:
    1. Plan to teach the unit again?
    2. Materials need replacing?
    3. New materials need to be ordered?
    4. Any issues for administrators to handle?
    5. Report successes and failures to administrator as appropriate.
    6. Any other plans to make?

Teachers + Librarians = Co-Designers of Instruction

1. Begin

Teacher/Library Media Specialist Meet

A. Identify what unit of instruction is to be planned and approximate dates to be taught.

B. Briefly discuss the abilities and interests of the students if necessary.

C. Determine the objectives of the unit:
1. Clarify and simplify.
2. Are objectives manageable in view of the resources of the LMC?
3. Bloom's taxonomy considerations:
   a. Knowledge (memory).
   b. Comprehension (understanding).
   c. Application.
   d. Analysis.
   e. Synthesis.
   f. Evaluation.

D. Decide what each person is expected to do prior to the next meeting.

2. Prepare

Getting Ready

A. Library media specialist locates instructional materials remembering:
1. Levels of difficulty.
2. Interest levels.
3. A variety of media.
4. Materials for special students.
5. Materials from other sources outside the LMC.
6. People resources.

B. Both get creative ideas ready:
1. Ideas for activities using commercial and locally produced materials.
2. Ideas for effective use of print, audiovisual, and computer media.
3. Ideas for appropriate library, media, and information skills.
4. Ideas for building critical reading, viewing, and listening skills.

C. Second meeting of the team:
1. Discuss unit content changes if necessary.
2. Discuss materials available and preview if necessary.
3. Discuss creative ideas.
4. Decide exactly who will be responsible for presenting each activity in the unit.

D. Prepare and pilot, if necessary, the materials and activities.

3. Teach

Present the Unit to Students

A. Jointly introduce the unit and its objectives and activities.

B. Carry out planned activities. Be open to change as the activities develop.

C. Some activities will be carried out by the teacher alone, some by the library media specialist alone, and some jointly. The teacher will generally team on activities based in the LMC, particularly when students are locating and analyzing information and materials.

D. Share enthusiasm for the unit with students.

E. Expect students to achieve the objectives.

Fig. 7.1. Teachers + librarians = co-designers of instruction. Used with permission of Marilyn Goodrich Peterson and Beverly J. White.

Fig. 7.2. Teachers + librarians = co-designers
of instruction (model).

There are some important characteristics at each stage of the process which can affect the success of the entire experience.

Step One: Begin. Step one asks the teacher and the library media specialist to plan together. This requires a minimum of twenty minutes well in advance of the time to teach the unit. Step one also asks the teacher to share unit objectives with the library media specialist and be willing to revise those objectives. Both requirements may be very difficult to achieve the first few times.

If administrators find that either element is missing, a number of experimental situations should be created to force an effective first step to occur. For example, teachers and library media specialists might attend a workshop where they and the principal are forced to plan a unit of instruction jointly. Summer joint planning sessions might help. In-service day activities might include several joint planning sessions.

Step Two: Prepare. Step two is the most creative and the most challenging part of the entire process. Three things must be done at this stage to ensure that the objectives for learning are achieved:

- select the materials to be used

- prepare the activities to use those materials

- decide on the product to be created by the students as a result of the activities

To assist in generation of ideas at this stage, three checklists have been created (see figures 7.3-7.5, pages 66-68). Used together, these lists contain literally millions of ideas for resource-based teaching.

As a quick exercise to understand the usefulness of the three checklists, do the following:

1. Think of a topical teaching objective (example: Describe why a screw will work itself into a piece of wood when turned.).

2. Choose an item from the media list at random (example: film).

3. Choose an activity from the second list at random (example: peer tutoring).

4. Choose an end product at random from the third list (example: videotapes).

5. Combine the three and ask how they could be used to meet the teaching objective. (How can a film be used with peer tutoring, the product being a videotape, to teach students to describe why a screw will work itself into a piece of wood when turned?)

In the example, one might envision a learning station where groups of four students see a three-minute segment of a film which describes an inclined plane and shows how a screw is an example of that simple tool. Together, the four must discover from the film and from their mutual discussion what actually happens when a screw is turned in wood, and then as a team they would have to produce a two-minute video segment which demonstrates for the class the principle at work. All the videos produced would be shown and critiqued for accuracy by the entire class.

Since time is a critical factor and the basic objective of resource-based teaching is to teach more in the same amount of time, the teacher and the library media specialist would have to consider whether the entire activity proposed would not only meet the learning objective but do it within the time constraints imposed. A major temptation with resource-based teaching is to expand the unit/lesson/research project beyond the normal time allowed for that topic. Sometimes, extended study will be desirable since it will provide students with a chance to specialize in a topical study and gain depth as well as breadth of knowledge. At other times, time constraints will dictate that activities be compressed.

Meeting the time constraints of the unit and ensuring that every student meets the learning objective is the creative and the most satisfying aspect of resource-based teaching. The teacher and library media specialist can almost create a game or challenge out of the process to see just how successful they can be.

(Text continues on page 69.)

Checklist of Types of Media to Use in Instruction

Printed Media
Books
- Picture books
- Fact books
- Encyclopedias
- Reference books
- Literature
- Textbooks
- Paperbacks
- Workbooks

Ephemera
- Pamphlets
- Clippings
- Documents

Graphic
- Pictures
- Charts
- Graphs
- Maps
- Globes
- Paintings

Periodicals
- Magazines
- Newspapers

Miscellaneous Media
- Games
- Laboratories
- Field trips
- Puppets
- Learning centers
- Kits
- Equipment and supplies
- Bulletin boards
- Puzzles
- Dolls
- Models
- Dioramas

Audiovisual Media
Visual
- Transparencies
- Slides
- Filmstrips (sound and silent)
- Film
- Microfilm
- Microfiche

Audio
- Tape recordings
- Records
- Radio programs

Video
- ETV
- Videotapes
- Videodiscs

Computer Media
- Drills
- Simulations
- Tutorials (CAI and CMI)
- Computer-assisted teaching
- Interactive CAI
- Databases
- CD-ROM

Human Resources
- Resource persons
- The voice (for storytelling, dramatic reading)
- Body language

Realia
- Plants
- Animals
- Rocks and minerals
- Built or manufactured things
- Artifacts

Keep in Mind

Media characteristics such as color, black and white, graphic vs. realistic, sight, still, motion, sound, interaction, and potential for immediate feedback. Also plan for varying learning styles.

Fig. 7.3. Checklist of types of media to use in instruction.

Checklist of Types of Teaching Activities

Browsing	Demonstrating	Doing
Searching	Experimenting	Making
Silent reading	Discovering	Collecting
Analyzing	Simulating	Drawing
Brainstorming	Experiencing	Painting
Thinking	Traveling	
Taking notes		
Working		
Explaining	Individualizing	Viewing
Showing	Peer tutoring	Listening
Discussing	Grouping	Storytelling
Debating	Tutoring	Puppetry
Lecturing	Contracting	Oral reading
Writing		Book or media talking
Dramatizing		Webbing
		Photographing
		Cooking

Keep in Mind

The teacher's and library media specialist's agenda for student learning:

Bloom's Taxonomy

Cognitive:	Affective:
1. Knowledge	1. Receiving (Attending)
2. Comprehension	2. Responding
3. Application	3. Valuing
4. Analysis	4. Organization
5. Synthesis	5. Characterization by a value or value complex

The library media specialist's agenda which may include:

Thinking skills
Library skills
Information analysis
Literary skills
Listening and viewing skills
Production skills

Fig. 7.4. Checklist of types of teaching activities.

Checklist of End Products

Work sheets	Oral reports	Creative writing
Report	Showing	Written music
Research paper	Demonstration	Written poetry
Database	Dramatization	Newspaper
Enjoyment	Art product	Realia or models
	Fairs	Food to eat
	Contests	
	Displays	
	Collections	
Books	Charts	Transparencies
Picture books	Graphs	Slides
Sound books	Maps	Filmstrips
Pamphlets	Pictures	Films
Tape recordings	Videotapes	Games
Computer programs	Learning centers	Puppets/Puppet shows
Products of living things (plants, animals)		Community service project School service project

Keep in Mind

Improved learning
Improved thinking skills
Personal development
Preparation for the future
Maintained or improved attitudes

Fig. 7.5. Checklist of end products.

During step two, the library media specialist will want to add something to the unit which the teacher may not have originally intended. Library media specialists have their own agendas, known as program features, which they are trying to accomplish as a part of resource-based teaching across the entire school. These agendas were illustrated in the model presented in chapter 2, and could include library skills, thinking skills, motivational reading, etc. Thus, during the planning stage of the unit, the library media specialist will suggest as one activity the furthering of that agenda.

For example, if the library media specialist has an audiovisual production program feature and has the goal of having every student become literate in the creation of audiovisual products in graphic, film, video, and audio formats while in the school, that agenda can be combined with the resource-based teaching units. In the example discussed on page 65, the teams of four might have to take a short mini-lesson in the production of videotapes before being allowed to create their own videotape about the screw as an inclined plane.

By combining the learning objective of the classroom and the program feature of the LMC, both objectives are accomplished at the same time. If the activities are well designed and executed, then an improved learning situation will result. More will be learned in the same or less time.

As both the teacher and the library media specialist approach step two of the planning process, the three checklists might be kept handy for generation of ideas. Sometimes particular media and activities will be chosen for convenience or because the activity can be done easily in a limited amount of time. At other times, the teacher and the library media specialist might experiment not only for variety's sake, but also to see if they can reach an unreached or uninterested class or individual student.

It is important as each checklist is used to consider the items listed at the bottom of each. For example, a type of media should be used for the particular thing it does best. A film is used because of its motion characteristic and its ability to carry the learner to places and to experience things impossible to do within the confines of the school. If the medium is not used properly, then great teaching and learning opportunities are missed.

Theoretically, media and materials to teach any objective should be available. Such is not usually the case. The LMC collection may contain materials on the topic which do not match what the teacher and the library media specialist want to accomplish. Compromise is in order. Sometimes, the team must start with the available resources and decide what can be accomplished with those resources. At other times, resources will be plentiful enough to accomplish almost any learning objective. In the example discussed on page 65, the library media specialist might discover that the only film available on simple tools is not available on the day that it is needed. What then? Students might have to work from a set of pictures which are available on the topic. Lacking a set of pictures, the students may have to discover on their own how the phenomenon works by being given a screwdriver, a piece of soft wood, and a screw.

If time after time the teacher and the library media specialist must make compromises in their plans because of the lack of resources or inappropriate resources, these facts should be noted and reported to the administration. Budgets may have to be increased, the collection might have to be built in certain curricular areas, or types of materials that would suit special student needs might have to be purchased.

An experience of the author might clarify the importance of a well-stocked library media center. I was once asked to substitute for a fellow professor in a basic audiovisual production class. Members of the class were practicing classroom teachers who taught in small rural schools. The objective was to teach them a number of simple production ideas for use with students in the three hours allotted. I demonstrated the use of a camera to take slides. The teachers replied that they had no camera or film. So I showed them some lettering techniques. They had no pens or ink. I demonstrated handmade transparencies with "Sharpie" pens. They had no transparency film or pens. No matter what I demonstrated, they couldn't do it—or if they could, they would be required to purchase the materials out of their own pockets for the students. In desperation, I demonstrated using trash as instructional aids. They were uninspired. Here was a group so demoralized by the lack of resources and encouragement from parents and administration that they had given up. Teaching was the only job in town for people who had no mobility. The objective was to control the students, spend no money, and see that the basketball team got to play in the state tournament.

It is quite possible to kill creativity and the incentive to teach effectively when a lack of resources and supplies is a consistent problem. On the other hand, having ample resources is no guarantee that those resources will be used to good advantage.

One thing which might help in teacher/library media specialist planning is to use a planning sheet in addition to, or instead of, the brochure and the idea sheets printed earlier in this chapter. Several planning sheets are included in figures 7.6-7.12, below and pages 71-74, and they vary in completeness from great detail to almost none. A more detailed planning sheet might be used for the first several times, and as both partners become used to the process, a simpler one might be employed.

(Text continues on page 75.)

Planning Guide for a Library-Based Research Assignment

Subject:_____   Topic:_____

Grade: _____   Number of
                            students: _____

Starting   Completion
date: _____   date: _____

1. How are topics to be chosen by students?

2. What resources will students need?

3. What library/learning skills will students need?

4. How are students to record information?

5. How will students present information?

6. How will students be evaluated?

7. a) Teacher responsibilities:

   b) Library media specialist responsibilities:

Fig. 7.6. Planning guide for a library-based research assignment. Revised from *Partners in Action: The Library Resource Centre in the School Curriculum* (Toronto: Ontario Ministry of Education, 1982), 27.

Teacher/Library Media Specialist Planning Guide

WHO? Subject: _____   Teacher: _____

Grade: _____   Number of students: _____

Special student learning needs: _____

WHAT? Unit of study:
Aim(s):
Objectives:
Performance criteria:

HOW? Teaching strategies:
Resources:

WHERE? Facilities:

WHEN? Period(s):
Dates:

WHO? Student grouping or organization:

HOW? Learning activities:
Program evaluation:
Specific responsibilities:
Teacher:
Library media center:

Fig. 7.7. Teacher/library media specialist planning guide. Revised from *Partners in Action: The Library Resource Centre in the School Curriculum* (Toronto: Ontario Ministry of Education, 1982), 26.

Teacher LMC Request

Teacher: _____ Date: _____

Topic: _____

Service required: _____

Date required: _____

Fig. 7.8. Teacher/library media center request. Revised from *Partners in Action: The Library Resource Centre in the School Curriculum* (Toronto: Ontario Ministry of Education, 1982), 27.

Steps in Unit Planning: A Teamwork Approach

Subject:_____

Unit: _____ _____

Grade: _____

1. Goals:

2. Aims:

3. Objectives:

   a) Attitudes:

   b) Concepts:

   c) Skills:

4. Unit development:

   a) Persons involved:

   b) Time allotment:

   c) Unit content:

   d) Resources:

   e) Teaching strategies:

   f) Learning activities:

5. Evaluation techniques:

   a) of the student:

   b) of the process:

   c) of the teacher and library media specialist (self-evaluation):

Fig. 7.9. Steps in unit planning: a teamwork approach. Revised from *Partners in Action: The Library Resource Centre in the School Curriculum* (Toronto: Ontario Ministry of Education, 1982), 27.

Planning Guide

Teacher: _____ Date: _____

Grade: _____ Number of students: _____

1. Topic:

2. Desired learning outcomes:

3. Resources required:

   Location:

   Date(s):

4. New library/learning skills required by students:

   When to be taught:

   By whom?:

5. Method of introducing unit:

   Location:

6. Learning activities for students:

   Location of activities:

7. Criteria for evaluation:

   a) of the students:

   b) of the process:

8. Special needs or requests:

Fig. 7.10. Planning guide. Revised from *Partners in Action: The Library Resource Centre in the School Curriculum* (Toronto: Ontario Ministry of Education, 1982), 37b.

Cooperative Planning: Materials Needed

Teacher/Grade level: _____   Class size: _____

Content area: _____   Unit of study: _____

Estimated time: _____   When: _____

Print resources	Nonprint resources	Audiovisual equipment
		Circle needed equipment carousel projector cassette player/recorder filmstrip projector filmstrip viewer microcomputer opaque projector overhead projector record player 16mm projector sound filmstrip projector sound system VCR other

Fig. 7.11. Cooperative planning: materials needed.

Cooperative Planning Sheet

Teacher/Grade level: _____   Class size: _____

Content area: _____   Unit of study: _____

Estimated time: _____   When: _____

Skills or process to be developed:

Classroom teacher's responsibility:	Media specialist's responsibility:

Abilities, interests, and special needs of students	Media, research and/or study skills	Evaluation of student learning

Fig. 7.12. Cooperative planning sheet.

Step Three: Teach. As a team, the actual teaching of a resource-based teaching unit is shared between the teacher and the library media specialist. This means that some unit activities will be taught jointly, some individually. It does not mean that the library media specialist spends an equal amount of time as does the teacher, neither does it mean that the library media specialist takes over or is in charge of the teaching. While the teacher is firmly in control, the students recognize that a team approach is being used.

Step Four: Evaluate. The evaluation component is a combination of measuring student learning, the process itself, and the response of the library media program. Evaluation of student learning may proceed like any other test of learning, with one caution. Both the teacher and the library media specialist should test concepts and skills in such a way as to evaluate the impact of the multimedia activities. This means that if a textbook chapter and a film have been used for the lesson, questions for a test would come from both sources.

In addition to the normal things that can be tested, the evaluation may cover concepts which were the result of certain media characteristics. For example, if a film was used, then a concept which was taught effectively in the film through motion should be tested. If a computer program was used, that program might track the number of times it took a student to achieve mastery of a certain concept. Progress and problems should be noted.

The library media specialist should remember to evaluate the LMC program feature integrated into the unit. For example, what was the production quality of the videos made by students to illustrate the screw as an inclined plane? What video skills will have to be retaught? What skills should be practiced in another unit another time? If a library skill was taught, did the students learn it?

The teacher and the library media specialist should spend a few minutes evaluating the success of the unit. This includes whether the students achieved the objectives, whether the activities were effective, and whether the collection of the LMC was adequate. Students can be invited to participate in this process in various ways to determine whether the collection responded well, whether the activities helped them to learn the material, and whether they enjoyed the experience.

The results of the evaluation should be systematically reported to department heads and the administration. Problems which are encountered should be registered so that administrative decisions can be based on concrete evidence rather than subjective feelings.

The library media specialist will need to know if the lesson or unit will be taught again in a similar fashion. If so, the evaluation at the conclusion of the unit is essential in planning for collection building, or planning to acquire materials from neighboring schools or networks for the next time. Much grief can be saved the second time around if the evaluation has been thorough and plans made in advance for a repetition.

A recent research study showed that only 10 percent of library media specialists spend any time with teachers in reviewing the outcome of a joint unit of instruction.[4] How can resource-based teaching improve if no evaluation is made? How can the impact of the library media program be assessed if evaluation is neglected? Evaluation of the effect of joint projects should be more important than collecting LMC circulation data and attendance data or doing inventory.

Three samples for the joint evaluation of a resource-based teaching project appear in figures 7.13-7.15, pages 76-79. Library media specialists are encouraged to create their own form, one which is fast and simple, yet evaluates the collection, the process, and most important, the learning which resulted from the unit.

(Text continues on page 79.)

Cooperative Evaluation of Resource-Based Teaching

Teacher/Grade level: _____   Class size: _____

Content area: _____   Unit of study: _____

What worked well in the unit?

_____

Suggestions for improvement:

_____

What media center materials were most helpful?

_____

What materials were not available?

_____

How well did the media center collection respond to the unit objectives?

Scale: 5 = excellent
           4 = above average
           3 = average
           2 = below average
           1 = poor

_____ diversity of formats (books, audiovisual)

_____ recency (books, audiovisuals up-to-date?)

_____ relevance of collection to unit needs

_____ duplication (enough materials for number of students taught?)

_____ reading/viewing/listening levels meet students' needs

Time Allotment:
    Cooperative Planning _____
    Actual Teaching Time _____ (Library media specialist)

Fig. 7.13. Cooperative evaluation of resource-based teaching.

Curriculum Involvement of the Library Media Center

Curricular area: _____   Unit title: _____   Grade level: _____

Teaching techniques used:

How well did the LMC collection respond to unit objectives?

Scale: 5 = excellent
4 = above average
3 = average
2 = below average
1 = poor

MEDIA ACTIVITIES

Research and study skills taught (if needed):

_____ diversity of formats (books, audiovisuals)

_____ recency (book, audiovisuals up-to-date?)

_____ relevance of collection to unit needs.

_____ duplication (enough materials for number of students taught?)

_____ reading/viewing/listening level ok for all students?

What do we need that we don't have? (books, audiovisuals, periodicals, etc.)

Other activities (brief description)

How well did the LMC staff, facilities, and equipment function?

How well did the activities contribute to the unit?

How well did students respond to the LMC activities and materials?

Compliments and notes for improvement:

_____ taxonomy level(s) of LMC staff.

_____ taxonomy level(s) of teachers.

_____ taxonomy level(s) of students.
(See DVL's taxonomies for rating.)

Fig. 7.14. Curriculum involvement of the library media center.

Library-Based Teaching Units 1987-88

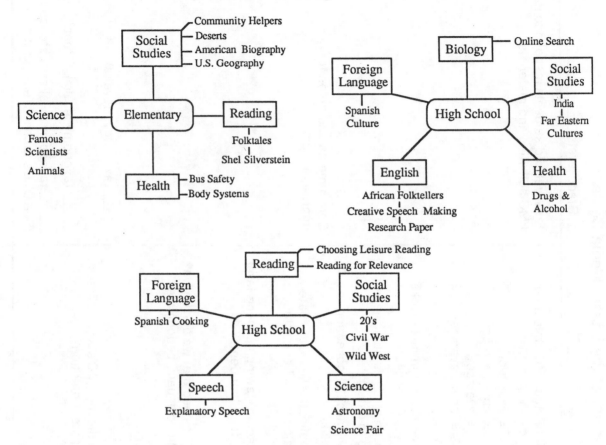

Overlay of Units To Be Planned During the Next School Year:

Elementary:

Social Studies: Immigration, Elections
Science: Energy, Magnets
Health: Home Safety, Drugs, Smoking
Reading: Nonsense Rhymes

Junior High:

Social Studies: Pennsylvania History
Foreign Language: Spanish Holidays
Speech: Techniques of Debating
Science: Space, AIDS
Reading: Making a Database of Favorite Fiction

High School:

Biology: Formulating a Biology Database
Foreign Language: Spanish Cooking, Other Cultures' Lifestyles
English: Folklore
Health: AIDS
Social Studies: Vietnam, Terrorism

Audience: The local school board and administration

Time: Annual library media center presentation

Objective: To present a picture of the school library media program's integration with the school district's classroom curriculum in 1987-88 along with the additional units planned for 1988-89. The library media staff have asked for another professional on the elementary level to help with development and want to show the school board what difference additional staff will make. One additional professional has been requested for the elementary schools and additional clerical staff has been requested for the secondary LMCs.

Format: A web transparency which clearly shows the 1987-88 schedule with an overlay adding the 1988-89 units.

Directions: Prepare a visual which would graphically show the school board the impact on instruction of the district's library media program. The web transparency would illustrate the actual library-based teaching units by subject area over a school year. An overlay would give the contrast between the current year and the next year's additional units which the staff plan to develop. Both library media specialists and teachers have a goal to expand the number of units and have asked the school board to fund additional LMC staff.

Fig. 7.15. Library-based teaching units 1987-88. Developed by Julie Tallman, Nancy L. Nahi, and D'Nis Lynch. Reproduced by permission.

EVALUATING STUDENT RESPONSES TO RESOURCE-BASED TEACHING UNITS

Following is a generic guide to creating an effective measure to test the students' response to resource-based teaching units versus textbook/lecture units. An actual sample evaluation will then be given.

Each measure includes five different types of responses:

1. Activities of the unit.

2. Attitude toward the learning environment (the LMC or the classroom).

3. The collection of materials used (either the classroom or the LMC collection).

4. Attitude toward learning.

5. Open-ended questions.

Every questionnaire will be constructed on the same pattern, but the questions will be tailored to meet the specifics of the unit. Thus, the questions in figures 7.16-7.17 are models to follow rather than exact questions to ask.

To control for the quality of teaching and subject matter taught, select three teachers who have differing styles of teaching or differing abilities as perceived by students but who teach the same subject matter or, in the elementary school, the same grade level. Each teacher will have two units of instruction measured: a resource-based teaching unit done cooperatively with the library media staff, and a textbook/lecture unit taught in the classroom.

Two questionnaires must be prepared for each teacher. These questionnaires will include parallel questions and will cover the five topical areas listed above. For example, if the resource-based questionnaire has the question:

When I found out we were going to work in the LMC for this assignment, my reaction was ...

The parallel questions for a textbook/lecture unit would be:

When I found out we were going to work in the classroom for this assignment, my reaction was....

The sample questionnaires were constructed to test a foreign-language unit at the high school level.* Students had been divided into four groups by the teacher to spend several days in the LMC researching an aspect of French culture. Students went back to the classroom and reported their findings to their peers. Then they evaluated the unit (see figure 7.16). The second questionnaire was constructed for a parallel classroom-based unit on French government (see figure 7.17, page 82).

GETTING STARTED: A CASE STUDY

Many library media specialists have asked how to get started on a program of resource-based teaching in their schools. There are a number of ways. One effective method is to start with a friend. Create some reason to experiment. After a success, move to another friend and let success speak for itself. Other teachers will be attracted by a good idea.

Another technique is to hold a planning session in the summer or on an in-service day at which teachers and library media specialists are forced (encouraged) to work together on unit planning as the activity for the day. Such "excuses" to plan together, unfettered by the pressures of everyday work, often provide the catalyst to get started.

A third technique is to be ever wary of golden opportunities to cooperate and evolve gradually into the program. A good example of this technique was tried by Nancy Minnich, the library media specialist at the Tower Hill School in Wilmington, Delaware. Nancy is in a school of very fine teachers and above average students, but she found that the library media center was an appendage to the curriculum rather than a central teaching facility. Teachers would schedule what research was needed a day or so in advance and bring the students in at the appointed hour. Nancy found herself, like most library media specialists reacting to instruction, not participating actively in the planning or the evaluation of what was going on.

In 1984, she was asked to participate in a pilot program to introduce database searching to students as a part of a research study being conducted by Jacqueline Mancall and Carl Drott at Drexel University. That research was written up and became the basis of a major advance in the study of bibliometrics with high school students.[5]

---

*Appreciation is expressed to three library media specialists and one interested parent who attended the author's workshop at the University of Pittsburgh and helped develop the questionnaires: Peggy Mott, Yardley, Pennsylvania; Laurie Dell, Warren, Pennsylvania; Chrissolula Torlidas, Pittsburgh, Pennsylvania; and Jane Wilson, Pittsburgh, Pennsylvania.

Student Questionnaire
French Culture LMC-Based Unit

Activities

1. How much did you enjoy the following activities?
    a. Researching the culture in the LMC   Disliked 1 2 3 4 5 Enjoyed
    b. Presenting your findings to the class   Disliked 1 2 3 4 5 Enjoyed
    c. Listening/watching the presentations of
        your classmates   Disliked 1 2 3 4 5 Enjoyed

Attitude toward the LMC

2. When I found out we were going to work in the
    LMC, my reaction was   Negative 1 2 3 4 5 Positive

3. The LMC was a pleasant place to work for this
    assignment   Disagree 1 2 3 4 5 Agree

4. The LMC staff was helpful for this assignment   Disagree 1 2 3 4 5 Agree

Collection

5. The LMC had enough materials for this
    assignment   Disagree 1 2 3 4 5 Agree

6. Most of the materials I used were   Too easy 1 2 OK 4 5 Too hard

Learning

7. Compared to other assignments, this one was

Less enjoyable	About the same	More enjoyable
1	2 3	4 5

8. Compared to other assignments, I learned

Less enjoyable	About the same	More enjoyable
1	2 3	4 5

Open-ended questions:

9. What materials or equipment would you suggest that the LMC buy for this assignment?

10. Is there anything that the LMC staff and classroom teachers could have done to help you
    complete your assignment?

11. If you used other libraries/places/or people for materials, what did you find and where?

Fig. 7.16. Student questionnaire: French culture library media center-based unit.

Student Questionnaire
French Government Classroom-Based Unit

Activities

1. How much did you enjoy the following activities?
   a. Reading the textbook chapter   Disliked 1 2 3 4 5 Enjoyed
   b. Seeing the film   Disliked 1 2 3 4 5 Enjoyed
   c. Classroom discussion   Disliked 1 2 3 4 5 Enjoyed
   d. The lecture   Disliked 1 2 3 4 5 Enjoyed

Attitude toward the classroom

2. When I found out we were going to work in the classroom for this unit, my reaction was   Negative 1 2 3 4 5 Positive

3. The classroom was a pleasant place to work for this assignment   Disagree 1 2 3 4 5 Agree

4. The teacher was helpful for this assignment   Disagree 1 2 3 4 5 Agree

Collection

5. The classroom had enough materials for this assignment   Disagree 1 2 3 4 5 Agree

6. Most of the materials (texts and other materials) I used were   Too easy 1 2 OK 4 5 Too hard

Learning

7. Compared to other assignments, this one was

Less enjoyable		About the same		More enjoyable
1	2	3	4	5

8. Compared to other assignments, I learned

Less enjoyable		About the same		More enjoyable
1	2	3	4	5

Open-ended questions:

9. What materials or equipment would you suggest that the school buy for this assignment?

10. Is there anything that the classroom teacher could have done to help you complete your assignment?

11. If you used libraries/places/or people for materials, what did you find and where?

Fig. 7.17. Student questionnaire: French government classroom-based unit.

Nancy says of that experience: "While the database project successfully taught students how to access large amounts of information from online searches, students lacked the skills of critical thinking necessary to help them evaluate the accuracy and worth of the mass of information located." What Nancy realized was that teaching online database searching when it is not integrated into a meaningful instructional experience is less than satisfactory.

Nancy then worked with the history department to modify the approach. They called their experience the "Clipping Thesis." As Nancy described the plan:

> The history department and I decided to see if we could modify the Clipping Thesis so it could be used as part of the ninth grade curriculum where there already was an emphasis on doing outside reading of current events.
>
> The history department wanted the readings to be done outside of regular class time. One class period was to be made available for the library media specialist and teacher to give instructions to the students. While, at first, the library staff felt this to be a problem, it turned out to be beneficial in that it made it necessary for the students and library media specialists to work on a one to one basis the rest of the year. Students came from study halls, or whenever it was convenient, and proved they could success-fully carry out independent work on the library media center.
>
> The students had a different assignment for each cycle. The timetable in each cycle was three weeks to clip articles and write summaries; one week to write a one page initial summary complete with a bibliography; one week to write a final summary complete with bibliography.
>
> The students in the first class were provided with their own copies of the daily *New York Times*. They read and clipped as many articles as they could find on their chosen topics and then pasted these on notebook paper on the left side in a looseleaf notebook. On the sheet of paper opposite the clipping(s) on the right side, the students wrote the proper bibliographic entry and a brief summary. At the end of three weeks, the students had 15 pages of brief summaries which they synthesized into a one page initial summary with a properly annotated bibliography. This was marked and returned by the teacher. The students had one more week to make corrections and turn in final summaries.

A second class read the current *New York Times* on microfiche for their articles. A third class used current periodicals as their source.

The fourth class went online with DIALOG which meant their directions were slightly different. They saw a slide/tape presentation entitled "Graffiti on a Database: A Light-hearted Look at Database Searching" which provided an interesting and informative introduction to database searching. They had to learn to set up their "arguments" on a form we developed as preparation for going online. The procedure was carefully explained in a handout similar to that given the other classes.

Students located articles in Magazine Index and Newsearch.

Students were allowed a mix of newspaper and periodical articles with a required minimum of three articles to be read each week. The printout from the online search was attached to their papers.

The four cycles during the year with the four classes allowed each class to go through all four types of clipping assignments. The students' enthusiasm for online searching greatly contributed to the success of the project. The basic skills of reading and summarizing in writing were reinforced through repetition while the different forms in which information was provided added variety and held the students' interest. The quality of the bibliographies improved with each cycle as did the writing. The fact that the students were forced to deal with current events in a thoughtful manner caused a subtle change in their critical awareness. As one student wrote in his evaluation, "I can never go back to reading newspaper articles in the thoughtless way I once did."

As positive as this history/LMC project was, Nancy did not give up. As she said: "Three of the teachers at Tower Hill and I met with the headmaster in January, 1987 to recommend a pilot project that would build upon a modified and expanded Clipping Thesis." Their idea was to incorporate thinking skills and writing skills across the departments of history, English, computer science, and biology. The headmaster (the principal) approved the project and three teachers and Nancy met in the summer for a week to plan together.

A few statements from their summer plans are illuminating:

Biology and history are the disciplines in which the research will take place. English and the library are subsets and will plug in where needed [the computer coordinator was to assist with word processing skills]. The library will do most of the work of coordination. All of us agreed that we want students to realize that science, history, English, and the library are all tied together. Having said that, students also need to realize that, although the physical process and purpose in pursuing evidence are the same, the methods vary according to the discipline. Science deals with data in a different way than history. Historians draw conclusions and make points from library research. Science may just ask why or how a thing happened, and apply the library research to experimental design. Abstracts of articles and the bibliographies are often done differently in science and history. The similarities and differences should become clear as we work through this project.

Beginning with an experiment, Nancy finds that after four years, she is a part of instructional planning. The teachers have found new ways to communicate and coordinate their teaching across disciplines. The students will reap the benefits.[6]

MAKING THE GREATEST IMPACT

It is important that the library media specialist build experience with resource-based teaching founded on a program of unit plans with individual teachers. Concentration on one-to-one planning efforts will help in building planning skills, creating sound professional relationships, testing ideas, and gaining a solid reputation of effectiveness. A repertoire of successful units and approaches often develop over time. A unit on dinosaurs might require major planning once and only fine-tuning in succeeding years. This would allow the specialist and the teacher to attack one unit a year, using their limited planning time together more effectively.

As these skills with individual teachers are built, the library media specialists can seek to make a broader impact in resource-based teaching by planning with groups of teachers. A single well-prepared unit can be carried out in many classrooms rather than in one, saving time and energy for teachers and library media staffs.

Group planning will depend on the organizational structure of the school and the willingness of the faculty, but there are a number of possibilities. The most logical groupings are subject departments in the secondary school or a grade level team in an elementary school. Many schools already use teaching teams; these teams are natural groups for planning. For example, library media specialists in the Aurora, Colorado, middle schools are members of grade level subject teams, which, organized by the principals, meet on a regular basis for curricular and unit planning. In these schools, the library media staff have become natural and respected members of the teams and resource-based units are the rule, not the exception.

Some of the most effective library-based teaching units can be planned with multidisciplinary teams of teachers. Art, music, and social studies teachers can form solid partnerships with the library media specialists and produce magnificent in-depth studies of a culture. The same could be true if the foreign language teacher and the science teacher joined to help students grasp a culture from the perspectives of the teachers' subject areas. But multidisciplinary planning need not stop with the academic departments. Teachers of physical education, home economics, auto repair, and business can combine with many other disciplines in the school to create effective units of study. The possibilities are fascinating and will produce many additional opportunities for motivating students. One of the most satisfying leadership roles a library media specialist can play is to serve as a catalyst for multidisciplinary planning and watch exciting things happen. In the elementary school, the library media specialists might experiment with cross-grade-level planning groups where some magnificent peer tutoring units might be developed.

The perfect mix, as the library media specialist becomes proficient at resource-based teaching, is to have subject-oriented units, multidisciplinary units, and individual units of instruction happening simultaneously.

THE DAILY SCHEDULE

In order to orchestrate a program of resource-based teaching and vertical programs, the library media specialist must be a master juggler of schedules and people. With the support of the principal, key teachers, and department heads, three major logistical plans will be needed.

First, individual students must be able to flow in and out of the library media center throughout the school day. Students who can use the center independently should be able to come any time. Many libraries have some sort of pass system for students which encourages rather than discourages visits. Individual students who need intense personal attention by the LMC staff are scheduled in advance so that precious time is not wasted. LMC facilities should allow for individual student study space and leisure activities which will not disturb other people or groups working in the center.

Second, small groups should flow in and out of the center during the day. These groups are of two types. Those who can work independently may come at any time as space permits. Other groups needing assistance by a member of the LMC staff should be scheduled in advance. Facilities should be arranged so that small groups can study together, produce audiovisual media, or do research without disturbing others.

Third, large groups should have the opportunity to use the center. Schedules and facilities permitting, some large groups can come at any time if they can work independently. But, for the most part, large groups will need to be scheduled in advance and arrangements made for activities and supervision in the LMC.

It is possible that as all of these groups use the center simultaneously, total chaos might erupt. Generally, however, a skillful arrangement of facilities, good cooperation from teachers, plus some firm expectations for students will create a purposeful and busy atmosphere. A library media specialist who can calendar well and can handle ten different activities going on simultaneously in the center will be the most successful.

NOTES

1. Madeline Hunter, *Mastery Teaching* (El Segundo, Calif.: TIP Publications, 1982).

2. See Gene L. Wilkinson, *Media in Instruction: 60 Years of Research* (Washington, D.C.: Association for Educational Communications and Technology, 1980). See also the report of the National Task Force on Educational Technology, reprinted as "Transforming American Education: Reducing the Risk to the Nation," *Tech Trends* 31, no. 4 (May/June 1986): 10-24. See also David V. Loertscher, "Review of Research on Computer-assisted Instruction," in *The Microcomputer Facility and the School Library Media Specialist*, ed. Blanche Woolls and David V. Loertscher (Chicago: American Library Association, 1986), 145-51. Additional discussion is available in Robert E. Holloway, *Educational Technology: A Critical Perspective* (Syracuse, N.Y.: ERIC Clearinghouse on Information Resources, 1984).

3. For one of many explanations of the Hawthorne effect, see Robert D. Stueart and Barbara Moran, *Library Management*, 3rd ed. (Littleton, Colo., Libraries Unlimited, 1987), 154-55.

4. David V. Loertscher, May Lein Ho, and Melvin M. Bowie, "Exemplary Elementary Schools and Their Library Media Centers: A Research Report," *School Library Media Quarterly* 15, no. 3 (Spring 1987): 147-53.

5. Jacqueline C. Mancall and M. Carl Drott, *Measuring Student Information Use: A Guide for School Library Media Specialists* (Littleton, Colo.: Libraries Unlimited, 1983).

6. Nancy P. Minnich and Carrol B. McCarthy, "The Clipping Thesis: An Exercise in Developing Critical Thinking and Online Database Searching Skills," *School Libraries Activities Monthly* 2, no. 8 (April 1986): 45-50; Nancy P. Minnich, "The 'Clipping Thesis': A Year Later," *School Library Media Activities Monthly* 3, no. 10 (June 1987): 43-45. Reprinted by permission of LMS Associates, School Library Media Activities Monthly, © 1986, 1987. Followup comments and reports of the faculty supplied by Nancy P. Minnich.

Note: For "Additional Readings," see appendix C.

Direct Services of the Library Media Center

Building the second foundation stone of the LMC program is a very satisfying experience for a library media specialist who enjoys communication and who enjoys serving others. There are so many occasions during the school day when positive and productive individual assistance can be given. Many people choose librarianship as a career based totally on their perception that a service-oriented profession is a very attractive job. Like other levels of the model, however, it is easy to spend an inordinate amount of time on direct services and ignore the warehouse and resource-based teaching. In schools with large LMC staffs, some persons can be assigned for certain periods of the day to staff the reference desk and concentrate on direct services. Where the library media specialist is alone, direct services must be juggled as one of many daily tasks.

Direct services concentrates on the individual or the small group. A student may have a reference question, a teacher may need some ideas on discipline, twenty students may need to perform online searches for science research papers, other students may be clamoring for a good book to read, and a teacher may send a request to the LMC to pull all the Civil War biographies. A myriad of requests come hourly, providing variety and challenge to the service-oriented library media specialist. If the success ratio is high, a great deal of satisfaction is felt. If resources are meager, dismay sets in and requests for assistance can diminish to almost nothing. If the library media specialist is not service-oriented or does not enjoy working with teachers and students, barriers are often erected to discourage requests for service. Administrators are wise to hire a library media specialist who is an effective communicator and who enjoys working with people.

The purpose of this chapter is to explore various direct services and to provide some suggested methods of evaluating the success of those services.

REFERENCE AND ONLINE SERVICES

Reference services involve the provision of information to students and teachers. Library media specialists assemble a collection of encyclopedias, handbooks, atlases, guidebooks, statistical sources, and dictionaries so that a wide variety of questions can be answered in a short period of time. Answering reference questions is very satisfying, particularly when seemingly impossible answers can be located almost instantly. Longer research-oriented questions may take several hours or even a few days to research. The library media specialist may need to go far beyond the local collection for the answer to a query. In this case, a telephone and a good link to other schools and libraries are essential elements of success.

In order to have a high degree of success, every library media center must have a well-stocked reference section which is updated on a regular basis. Outdated encyclopedias and other reference books should be discarded or cut up for their pictures and valuable historical articles.

Much has been written in the literature about the evaluation of reference services as they occur in academic and public libraries where these services are carried out as the major portion of a person's job. In school library media centers, students rarely have the luxury of having a full-time reference person available on the reference desk at all times. Thus, any evaluation that is carried out is usually of a part-time service and is often governed by a limited reference collection. There are three main factors in the quality of a reference search:

1.   The ability of the searcher.

2.   The size and quality of the reference collection.

3.   The accuracy of the information obtained in the search.

Library media specialists pressed for time should keep track of reference search failures and classify them. For example, a list might be kept handy in the reference area for students, teachers, or the library media specialists to record failed searches. A form such as that in figure 8.1 might be used.

Reference Success/Failure

Topic of Reference Search	Cause of Failure			Comments
	No Source	Could Not Find	Out of Date	

Fig. 8.1. Reference success/failure.

Online services have emerged in the last ten years as an extension of the reference process. These services, usually accessed through giant telecommunications networks, provide access to databases of all types, and in some cases provide the full text of articles and statistical sources. Many school library media specialists have found that a whole new world opens up to their services when they provide access to online databases for students and teachers. While many of the databases available online are of a very sophisticated nature, a great number of useful citations to periodical articles can be retrieved online.

Carol Tenopir, at the University of Hawaii, lists the advantages of doing online searching with children and young adults. She points out that:

1. Students learn research and problem-solving skills during online searching.

2. Students use logical thinking processes to develop search strategies.

3. Students will work to refine their questions for a computer search much harder than for a verbal search.

4. Online searching opens up new worlds of information for the students, even when they can't retrieve the actual text of the documents retrieved from the search.

5. Students will go far beyond the use of the popular literature for information.

6. Students enjoy the online search experience.[1]

One of the major problems enountered in providing online services is that a bibliography of useful periodical articles can be retrieved in a short time, but access to the actual articles is limited. In the state of Iowa, regional centers now provide access for any student to any article on Magazine Index within forty-eight hours. This means that a whole new world of research possibilities is open to the school-aged student.

CD-ROM is a new technology which is rapidly changing the concept of online searching. This technology has the potential to store vast quantities of information in such a small space that every library might be able to have access to hundreds of thousands of sources without increasing floor space. The dream for CD-ROM is that online searching would be almost eliminated, since the local library could have complete backfiles of large numbers of periodicals, statistical sources, and other databases. Should this technology prove to be affordable to the mass of schools in the country, the entire picture of research possibilities, the need for information skills training, and a rethinking of collection development will occur.

The evaluation of online searching and searching via CD-ROM has been explored in academic and special libraries where online searching is a main service the library provides. Generally, a quality search is one that provides the exact information in the quantity desired by the patron. The term *recall* is often used to judge whether a system can systematically provide every article of interest within the system. The term *precision* is used to judge whether the system returns only articles of interest rather than superfluous ones.

For any search, the following questions might be asked to judge precision:

1. Documents: Were the documents retrieved relevant to the desired topic?

2. Questions: Were the search terms used to query the database good ones?

3. Judges: Are the persons making the relevance judgment knowledgeable enough to do so?

4. Method: Is a proper method being used to judge the result?

Judging the recall of the database requires a different set of criteria, some of which are very difficult for the end user to apply. These criteria include:

1. Quality: Was the person(s) indexing the material accurate? (Everything that should have been indexed was, and the correct subject headings were used.)

2. System: Does the system include everything that the indexer intended and handle it properly?

3. Retrieval: Will the system retrieve every document using a given subject heading? (That is, given the subject heading "cats," will every document in the system having that subject heading appear on a search?)

As both students and library media specialists gain experience with online searching, they tend to make a number of the judgments listed above. For example, a person might know that a certain magazine article is in a database and that the article has been indexed under a certain subject heading. The person knows that fact because the document has been retrieved before. If on another search, the document is not retrieved when the same subject heading is used, the person suspects that something in the system is not working properly.

READERS', VIEWERS', AND LISTENERS' ADVISORY SERVICES

Readers' advisory services are some of the oldest services performed by libraries. In their most simple form, a library media specialist helps a patron find "a good book to read." In a more sophisticated sense, the library media specialist analyzes a reader's preferences and reading habits and then prescribes a reading program which will broaden taste, build awareness of quality materials, and make the person aware of the best of what is published annually.

The 1960 *Standards for School Library Programs* contained an entire section devoted to reading guidance. A few of the principles outlined follow:

1. Reading guidance starts in kindergarten and continues through grade 12.

2. A warm and friendly atmosphere is needed if students are to feel comfortable in asking for individual help.

3. Teachers and library media specialists must work together to build knowledge of individual needs and to satisfy requests.

4. A wide range of reading materials must be made available.

5. A wide variety of approaches to individual students is needed to encourage student reading.

6. Reading guidance goes beyond just books to encompass listening and viewing guidance.[2]

Knowing whether a readers' advisory service is effective is an imprecise measure at best. However, one unmistakable sign for the library media specialist is the number of repeat customers who say, "I just finished the book you recommended last week, how about another one."

Just as library media specialists suggest the best books, their recommendations should extend to other media. The best motion pictures currently playing and on video, the best books to listen to on tape, recorded music from pop to jazz to classical, the best short films, the best of the best no matter the format.

Reading motivation is covered as a vertical program feature of the library media program in chapter 10. Why then are readers' advisory services covered here in the direct services chapter? Every library media specialist should develop the talent of knowing what media to recommend to individual patrons. Some will not have the time or energy to build an entire program based on reading, listening, or viewing, as desirable as that may be. To neglect the area of materials specialist, critic, and personal advisor, however, would be missing one of the great and most satisfying direct services of the LMC program.

GATHERING MATERIALS

Given enough lead time, library media specialists generally can gather sufficient materials on any topic requested by a student or teacher. These materials may come from the local collection or be supplied through networks. Since no library can hope to contain everything patrons need or request, the emphasis for the past ten years has been upon networking to provide materials not held locally.

A number of states have led the way with exemplary statewide efforts to network schools as just one note in a network of all types of libraries. New York, through its BOCES and multitype networks, has created a method by which schools within a network have specialized collections and then share those collections with other members. Pennsylvania has converted many school library catalogs to machine-readable form in their program Access Pennsylvania so that high school students will have access to the rich collections of schools all over the state. Indiana has been one of the pioneers in networking public libraries and has many school library members. Likewise, in Illinois, many school libraries belong to cooperatives which share cataloging, interlibrary loan, and other services.

Evaluating whether gathering services are effective requires that a simple log be kept of requests, the lead time given, the results, and a judgment of whether relevant and sufficient materials were supplied.

IN-SERVICE

When the library media specialist observes that some teachers either are unaware of a particular service or are having difficulty with a part of the LMC program, an in-service program is instituted. In-service can range from very formal classes offering credit from local institutions of higher education to district in-service credit. It can be a part of faculty meetings, in-service days, or districtwide in-service programs. The format can be relaxed or formal, but should always be informative and interesting. The topics may also vary from production of audiovisual media, online searching, computer training, resource-based teaching, or cross-disciplinary unit planning to a myriad of other topics.

Library media specialists should spare no effort to make certain that when they get the faculty's attention, the experience is positive, helpful, and informative. The best teaching strategies should be employed, and the most creative and clever ideas used. A mark of success of an in-service program, be it five minutes or five hours long, is the attitude of the teachers who attend and the change in their behavior as a result of the session.

PUBLIC RELATIONS

It may seem out of place to put public relations in the category of a direct service; however, advertising what a library can do for the patron and what its function is are basic components of serving individuals. Few will take advantage of direct services if they are unaware of what is possible and how to take advantage of those services.

Much has been done over the years to teach library media specialists how to "toot their own horn," and increase the awareness of LMC services. Numerous excellent books and articles have been written on the topic. A selected list of the best has been provided in the additional readings section at the end of this chapter.

Evaluating the success of a public relations campaign has two facets. There are immediate effects such as increased usage of a service which has been advertised. However, a long-term impact is much more difficult to document.

Mildred Nichol, the author of *Steps to Service*, a popular LMC manual, once told a story which illustrates the long-term effects of public relations. She had built a library media program in her school district over a period of twenty years. When a severe censorship case came before parents and the school board, the public sided with Mildred because of the long history of trust and confidence in her and her program. Such a story is repeated hundreds of times around the country each year. The issue may be a discipline problem, a fund-raising campaign, financial pressures to cut staffing, or a crisis in public respect for education in general. Individualized service and public relations campaigns conducted years before may have a major payoff as an unexpected crisis arises. Public relations require a constant and extended effort over many years.

NOTES

1. Carol Tenopir, "Online Searching in Schools," *Library Journal* 111, no. 2 (February 1, 1986): 60-61.

2. *Standards for School Library Programs* (Chicago: American Library Association, 1960), 15-17.

ADDITIONAL READINGS

Barber, Peggy, ed. *68 Great Ideas: The Library Awareness Handbook*. Chicago: American Library Association, 1982.

A lively potpourri of ideas for PR, fund raising, publicity, cooperative programming, special events, advertising, etc.

Edsall, Marian S. *Practical PR for School Library Media Centers*. New York: Neal-Schuman, 1984.

A basic source for information on how to create a PR program and keep it running. Ideas include working with faculty, administrators, boards of education, parents, and the media.

Franklin, Linda Campbell. *Publicity and Display Ideas for Libraries*. Jefferson, N.C.: McFarland, 1985.

Hundreds of ideas for displays, bulletin boards, newsletters, and events to promote the LMC are presented.

Garvey, Mona. *Library Public Relations. A Practical Handbook*. New York: H. W. Wilson, 1980.

A beautifully illustrated guide to marketing approaches, programs, and displays.

Great Library Promotion Ideas: JCD Library Public Relations Award Winners and Notables. Chicago: American Library Association, 1985- . Annual.

This annual pamphlet reviews all of the winning applications for the John Cotton Dana Public Relations Award. The pamphlet is packed full of ideas, mostly from public libraries, but includes very useful tidbits for any library.

Keefe, Betty, Joie Taylor, and Marian Karpisek. "High Touch: PR." *School Library Media Quarterly* 14, no. 3 (Spring 1986): 128-30.

These three authors provide a range of ideas for communicating with the school staff, administrators, parents, and the community.

Tuggle, Ann Montgomery, and Dawn Hansen Heller. *Grand Schemes and Nitty Gritty Details: Library PR That Works*. Littleton, Colo.: Libraries Unlimited, 1987.

An analysis of libraries that have won the John Cotton Dana Award (*see Great Library Promotion Ideas* above). Tuggle and Heller provide not only ideas for PR but the principles which underlie the winning programs they analyzed.

The Warehouse

The warehouse of the library media center encompasses a myriad of operations and duties. For many years, the image of the librarian has been one of a warehouser, a guardian of space, materials, and equipment. That image is counterproductive when the more important aspects of the library media program are presented to both patrons and decision makers. Warehousing is one of the three foundation stones of a library media program. It is not the most important part of the program, but if it fails, little else of importance can happen.

To achieve a smooth running warehouse, the library media specialist must set in motion what may seem like a million procedures for handling operational details. The patron's image of the LMC is often affected by the most trivial functions. A student may have been overcharged on an overdue book by five cents and holds a grudge. The book the teacher needed was not on the shelf—it was either misfiled or on a cart awaiting shelving. The teacher stomps out complaining about the service. Just when the teacher has fifteen minutes of class time left to show a fifteen-minute film, the projector bulb fails. Everyone seems to want services instantly, and they are less forgiving and less tolerant than they should be. No wonder the topics of conversation at many gatherings of library media specialists are numerous operational matters.

Operations can easily dominate a day, a week, or a school year. No matter how well a day is planned, operational problems will intrude upon the scene. It is tempting to require that each library media specialist be an expert in systems analysis, operations research, and time management. Since that is not possible, the profession generally assumes that persons who enter the field are organization-minded. Beginners who don't have these abilities often burn out when the press of operational problems mounts.

The warehouse consists of a number of important functions. This chapter treats each of the major categories briefly. The categories include staffing, the collection, technology, facilities, the budget, technical services, access, and evaluating operations.

STAFFING

Staffing the library media center is the single most important factor in the success of the warehouse and of the program in general. Three types of people are needed in a center to provide a complete array of services: professional, technical, and clerical.

The professional is a person who has full teacher certification in addition to the required professional education in library science and educational technology. The head of the library media program is selected for leadership potential, a broad view of print and nonprint technologies, and a willingness to make resource-based teaching the focal point of the LMC program.

Technical staff member(s) are persons who have special talents or training, not necessarily from an academic institution, which contribute to the technical part of the LMC program. A technician may repair the audiovisual and computer equipment, operate and maintain a television studio or computer lab, or be a graphic artist. There are many other possibilities.

Clerical staff provide warehouse support for the library media program. These persons, who should have pleasant personalities and organizational ability, provide efficient access to the materials and equipment of the center. Circulation, storage and retrieval, support of acquisition and technical processing, and typing/word processing are just a few of the duties.

Staff Size

There are five major considerations in determining the size of the staff needed in a library media center.

1. The minimum staff size.

2. The commitment to resource-based teaching.

3. The commitment to programmatic themes.

4. The commitment to instructional technology.

5. The financial well-being of the school/district.

The size of the staff is negotiated by the library media specialist, the teachers, and the school administration and will vary depending on the expectations for the program. Figure 9.1, page 96, may be helpful in determining the size of the LMC staff for a particular building.

Many schools in the country have difficulty achieving the minimum staffing size listed. This difficulty occurs not just because of financial constraints but also because of the expectations of the library media program. The form assumes that the size of the library media staff is directly proportional to the involvement of the center in the instructional program. Some school districts have been able to increase the library media staff by hiring a minimum of staff for the center and then creating a position known as a teacher on special assignment or an instructional supervisor. This person cooperates with the library media professional to concentrate on resource-based teaching in the school.

In some districts, financial constraints have dictated that a single professional library media specialist must serve multiple schools. Generally, such a pattern is ineffective and relegates the

Staff Size Negotiation Form

	# Professional	# Clerical	# Technical
1. Minimum staff size. Except for the smallest schools, research indicates that staffing below one full-time professional and one full-time clerical is self-defeating of the investment made in a center.	1	1	
2. Commitment to resource-based teaching. Above the fifteen in-depth resource-based teaching units that the minimum-sized staff can be expected to perform, what additional staff is needed to provide teachers needed support?			
3. Commitment to programmatic themes. Considering programs such as reading motivation, information analysis, research and thinking skills, or other vertical program features, what is a reasonable size staff needed beyond the basic?			
4. Commitment to instructional technology. Considering features such as computer or television laboratories, what is a reasonable size staff to operate special technologies for teachers and students?			
5. Financial well-being of the school/district. Are there financial problems to consider which would decrease the size of the staff planned above?			

If a negative number is entered in #5, which of the above programs will suffer as a result?

_____

Total negotiated staff size   _____   _____   _____

Fig. 9.1. Staff size negotiation form. Appreciation for assistance in developing this staffing chart is expressed to **William Murray**, District Library Media Supervisor, Aurora, Colorado; **Barbara Dobbs**, Assistant District Library Media Specialist, Aurora, Colorado; **Charlie Willsea**, Principal, Aurora, Colorado; **Ed Brainard**, Assistant Superintendent, Aurora, Colorado; **Betty Bankhead**, High School Library Media Specialist, Cherry Creek Schools, Colorado; **June Level**, Kansas State Department of Education; **Jean Donham**, District Library Media Supervisor, Iowa City, Iowa; **Retta Patrick**, Consultant, Little Rock, Arkansas; and **Barbara Stripling** and **Judy Pitts**, High School Library Media Specialists, Fayetteville, Arkansas.

professional to a clerical role. Research has shown these professionals to be the most frustrated of the profession.[1] Some experimentation has been done to allow a part-time professional to be almost full-time in a single building, but on a rotational basis. This person is able to establish a program of resource-based teaching in one school with a minimum of supervisory responsibilities in other schools.

Administrators are advised to ascertain the type of program which is being provided to teachers and students. Are only warehousing services being provided? How much resource-based teaching is actually being performed? If the staff size is increased, will the amount of resource-based teaching increase? Experimental staffing patterns might be created to test the impact on the instructional program.

THE COLLECTION

It is a simple matter to spend money using publishers' catalogs or responding to a commercial audiovisual equipment or computer representative. It is quite another matter to build a collection of materials and equipment which are useful to students and teachers. The inflationary pressures of the past fifteen years require that a concerted effort be made to match the needs of the curriculum with the efforts to build the collection within the constraints of available funds. To do so, six main principles should be taken into account.

Principle 1: The collection of a library media center must support the curriculum of the school. This means that the collection is focused on a particular school's curriculum rather than buying the best of what is published in diverse topical areas.

Principle 2: A plan to build a curricular-oriented collection with the accompanying policies, staff expertise, and realistic budgeting practices is in place. Principals, teachers, and library media specialists should plan what areas of the collection need to be strong, who will select the materials, and how the best materials will be selected to meet collection targets, and how collection building will be financed. This group generally begins the task by creating a collection map and a selection policy which guides the growth of the collection.

Principle 3: An acquisition system which matches curricular priorities is in place. Library media specialists should be able to show that the selection system for new materials is accountable to the collection building plan as opposed to spending money from catalogs. Several questions should be readily answered by the LMC staff including: How do you select materials? How do you prioritize your purchases? How do you keep track of spending in terms of curricular support?

Principle 4: Each type of media included in the library media center is considered a system consisting of the materials, the accompanying equipment, the support staff, and facilities, among other concerns. In the past, a school may have acquired a computer but no software; a computer with no one who knew how to operate it; 16mm projectors, but no classrooms with darkening drapes. Such practices show lack of planning and management skills. Experimentation with new technologies is a must, but it should be done with forethought and with a determination to test the value of that technology properly.

Principle 5: Collections in single schools are constantly changing to meet current needs. Collections are supplemented from local, regional, and national networks. The curriculum of the school, the needs of teachers, and the needs of students are moving targets, not stationary ones. This means that a school cannot invest once in a group of materials and expect them to last indefinitely. No school can own everything it needs. One school in New Hampshire has a library of 170,000 volumes housed in a nine-story library. That collection still does not satisfy every request. Schools can supplement their collections by reaching out to others in their area to mutually share materials and equipment.

Principle 6: Collections reflect democratic ideals, intellectual freedom, and cultural diversity. In spite of pressures from certain individuals and groups, the library media specialist recognizes the principles upon which a democratic society is built and purposely builds diversity into the collection.[2]

Building a focused collection as called for in the stated principles requires a carefully constructed plan and an organized procedure of acquisition and evaluation. One technique to accomplish this task is to map the collection: ascertain its strengths and weaknesses, create targets for growth, and track the impact of expenditures. Such careful tracking is now possible since microcomputer systems have been made available to libraries.

One such system, created by the author, is known as computerized collection development. This system begins with the mapping of the collection. The sample map in figure 9.2 shows the strengths and weaknesses of a collection in terms of size and quality.

A collection map is a visual supplement to the card catalog which graphically displays the breadth and depth of a library media collection. Such a map may be displayed as a large poster in the library media center. Each school's library media collection map might be completely different from the collection map of a neighboring school.

The collection map is divided into three major segments:

1. A basic collection designed to serve a wide variety of interests and needs. This collection provides breadth. In figure 9.2, this is graphed as the "total collection" from left to right.

2. General emphasis collections, which contain materials that support a whole course of instruction such as United States history or beginning reading. These collections provide intermediate depth in a collection. In figure 9.2, "Folklore & fairytales" and the animal collections are graphed as general emphasis collections.

3. Specific emphasis collections, which contain materials that support units of instruction such as "Civil War" or "Dinosaurs." These collections provide full depth and support to topical studies. In figure 9.2 the specific emphasis collections include "Indians of North America," "Frontier & pioneer life," and "Dinosaurs."

Building a curricular-oriented collection can be accomplished by concentrating on building parts of the collection rather than the collection as a whole. The planning sheet in figure 9.3, pages 100-101, forces planners to subdivide the collection into segments which consider the needs of courses, individual topics of instruction, the needs of particular technologies, and what is available through networking.

Sample Elementary School
Current Collection Map

Date:	Sept. 5, 1986
School Name:	Washington
No. of Students:	597
Total Collection Size:	8289
Items / Student:	13.88

General Emphasis Area Names	# of Items	Items / Student
Folklore & fairytales	305	.51
Animals	263	.44
Specific Emphasis Area Names		
Indians of North America	150	.25
Frontier & pioneer life	79	.13
Dinosaurs	53	.09

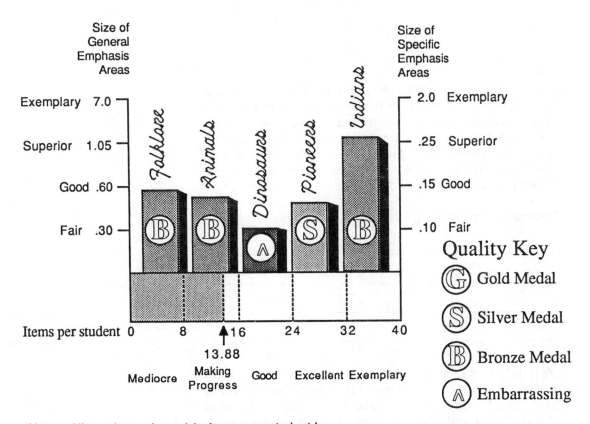

(Note: All numbers charted in Items per student.)

Fig. 9.2. Sample elementary school current collection map.

Collection Size Planning Form

	# of items	
	held	needed

1. The base collection should be ten books and audio-visual items per student or 3,000 items, whichever is greater. This provides breadth to the collection.

   _____ _____

2. A block of materials for courses. For each course of instruction where resource-based teaching will be an important factor, add two items (print and audiovisual) for each student enrolled in the course, or 500 items, whichever is greater.

   Courses requiring resource-based teaching collections:

   _____ _____ _____

   _____ _____ _____

   _____ _____ _____

   _____ _____ _____

3. A block of materials for resource-based teaching units. Some units of instruction require in-depth collections because of research requirements or because multiple copies of materials on many levels are needed. For each resource-based teaching unit, add one item per student (print and audiovisual) for each student enrolled in the topical study, or 250 items, whichever is greater.

   Topical units requiring in-depth collections:

   _____ _____ _____

   _____ _____ _____

   _____ _____ _____

   _____ _____ _____

4. Materials to support a particular technology. Acquiring any new technology requires a block of materials just to experiment adequately across the curriculum. After initial experimentation, the size of collections supporting a technology should be increased and merged into the curricular areas under numbers 2 and 3.

# of items

held   needed

Technologies to be supported by in-depth collections:

_____   _____   _____

_____   _____   _____

_____   _____   _____

_____   _____   _____

5. Special collections. List here any special collections which do not fit into any other category. Examples are the periodical collection, professional collections, textbook collections, and reference collections. Each will have a collection size to match its particular objective.

Special collections to be supported:

_____   _____   _____

_____   _____   _____

_____   _____   _____

_____   _____   _____

Total in-house collection size: _____   _____

6. Materials available through networks. List the major collections available by topical area to the school via interlibrary loan or from the district or regional collections:

Topics supported through networking:

_____   _____   _____

_____   _____   _____

_____   _____   _____

_____   _____   _____

Fig. 9.3. Collection size planning form.

Sample Collections

Three sample collections are shown here for illustration.* An elementary collection is pictured in figure 9.4, a middle school collection in figure 9.5, page 104, a high school collection in figure 9.6, page 105, and access through networks in figure 9.7, page 106.

The Canadian document *Partners in Action* shows an effective alternative collection building chart. Specific needs are identified and costed out for budgetary planning. Figure 9.8, page 107, shows a prediction of what a high school will need to build for a school year and the cost of these additions to the collection.

The preceding collection maps and the Canadian chart have concentrated on collection size. While size is a major factor, collection quality must be a part of total collection analysis. Collection quality has always been a rather nebulous concept for librarians. Some have recommended matching titles held to a standardized list, such as *High School Catalog* or *Elementary School Library Collection*. That approach has been rejected generally because it makes no reference to the curricular needs of a specific school.

Two ways of measuring quality are recommended here. The first measure is a recency analysis and the second is a systematic usage evaluation.

Recency Analysis

The push to spend money for library collections in the 1960s and the inflation coupled with lower spending in the 1970s has made many library media collections sorely out-of-date and in need of collection renewal. Gloria Mattson, Mentor Librarian in the Long Beach Unified School District, developed the following dating analysis with a corresponding graph which shows the problem plainly.

Gloria recommends that the librarian isolate a number of topical areas which match the curriculum or narrow ranges of the Dewey Decimal System such as 520-529 (Astronomy) and using the shelflist to fill in a tally sheet. The tally sheet lists the topic and has spaces for each decade (1940s, 1950s, etc.). Choosing random cards (one in five or one in ten, depending on collection size) or every card, Gloria matches each book's copyright date with the proper decade. She then graphs the result as an overlay on a meaningful drawing. Figure 9.9, page 108, shows the tally sheet and the resulting graph, which can be used with the collection map, for effective presentations to principals and school boards.

(Text continues on page 109.)

---

*The author wishes to thank Barbara Dobbs, Assistant District Library Media Specialist, Aurora, Colorado, for supplying the data upon which these examples are based.

Elementary Collection

1. Basic collection (for 622 students)...................................6,703 items

2. Materials for courses
   a. U.S. geography and history (5th grade, 111 students)......................418 items
   b. Easy readers (K-3rd grade, 320 students)............................855 items
   c. Animals (K-5th grade science, 622 students)..........................465 items
   d. Folklore and fairy tales (1st-5th grade, 517 students)....................447 items

3. Materials supporting topical units
   a. Human body (5th grade, 111 students)..................................96 items
   b. Mythology (3rd grade, 95 students)..................................44 items
   c. Dinosaurs (2nd grade, 110 students)................................53 items

4. Materials supporting a particular technology
   a. Computer software...150 titles
   b. Videotapes (in-house collection)...................................75 titles

5. Special collections
   a. Periodicals..40 titles
   b. Teacher idea books...100 titles

Total in-house collection...9,446 items

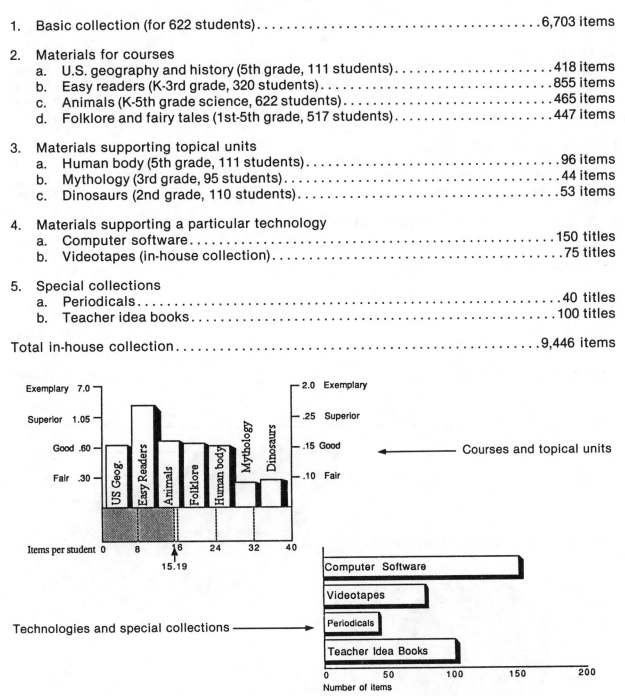

Courses and topical units

Technologies and special collections

Comments: The basic collection for this school is about on target. Materials for courses on animals, fairy tales, and U.S. geography are limited. If all teachers use these materials at the same time, there will be severe shortages. The number of items for use in the dinosaur and mythology topical unit is limited. More titles and duplicates should be purchased.

Fig. 9.4. Sample elementary school collection (K-5) for 622 students.

Middle School Collection

1. Basic collection (620 students)......................................8,600 items

2. Materials for courses
   a. American history (8th grade, 209 students)..............................739 items
   b. Eastern Hemisphere (7th grade, 216 students).........................1,055 items
   c. Environment (6th grade, 195 students)..................................872 items
   d. Biology (7th grade, 216 students)......................................856 items

3. Materials for topical units
   a. Human body (7th grade, 216 students)..................................160 items
   b. Plants (7th grade, 216 students).......................................79 items
   c. Mythology (7th grade, 120 students—elective)..........................72 items

4. Materials supporting a particular technology
   a. Computer software..200 titles
   b. Videotapes...90 titles
   c. Online databases available..2

5. Special collections
   a. Periodical collection..70 titles
   b. Professional collection..200 titles
   c. Reference collection...300 titles

Total in-house collection...13,295 items

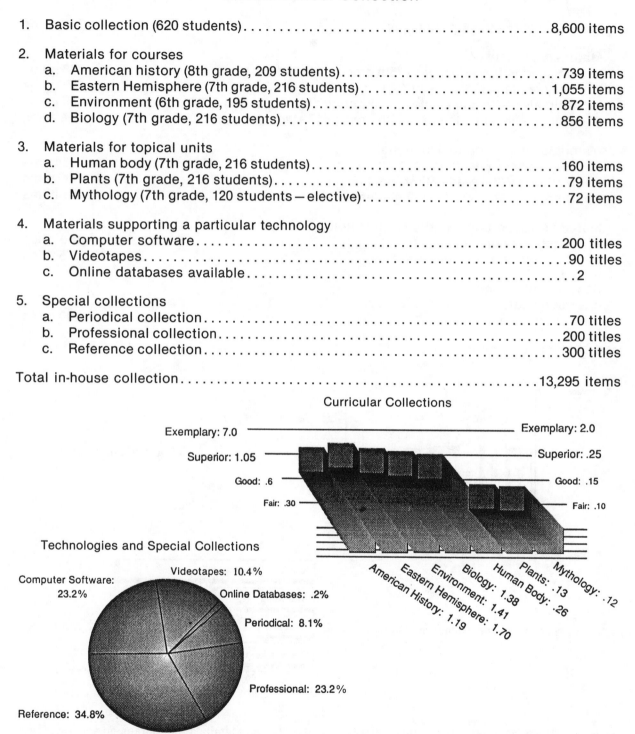

Comments: The materials to support courses are very strong, but the number of materials to support topical units is generally weak. A few collection goals in these areas would be helpful.

Fig. 9.5. Sample middle school collection (6-8) for 620 students.

High School Collection

1. Basic collection for 1,570 students......................................8,202 items

2. Materials for courses
   a. U.S. history (grade 11, 320 students)..................................773 items
   b. World cultures (grade 10, 302 students)..............................1,439 items
   c. Biology (grade 10, 302 students)......................................802 items
   d. American literature (grades 11-12, elective, 190 students)..................273 items
   e. Children's literature (grades 11-12, elective, 95 students)..................278 items

3. Materials for topical units
   a. Civil War (grade 11, 320 students)....................................400 items
   b. Hemingway (grades 11-12, elective, 190 students)........................90 items
   c. The human body (grade 10, 302 students).............................350 items
   d. Energy conservation (grade 11, 150 students)..........................125 items

4. Materials supporting a particular technology
   a. Computer software..320 items
   b. Videotapes...175 items
   c. Online databases available...3

5. Special collections
   a. Periodical collection..150 titles
   b. Professional collection..500 titles
   c. Reference collection..900 titles

Total in-house collection..14,780 items

Comments: This high school collection is quite strong in materials for certain courses, low in items for topical collections, and very low in the basic collection size. The result would be excellent service to a few academic departments, but limited support for most others.

Fig. 9.6. Sample high school collection (10-12) for 1,570 students.

Access through Networks

1. District collection
   a. Professional books. . . . . .3,500 items
   b. 16mm film and video. . . . . .4,300 items
   c. Computer software. . . . . .250 items

2. Regional collection
   a. Professional periodicals/ERIC. . . . . .125 titles
   b. Supplemental small media. . . . . .2,350 titles
   c. 16mm film and video. . . . . .6,000 items

3. Other networks
   a. Computer access to regional public/academic libraries. . . . . .1,250,000 items
   b. Access to computer databases. . . . . .125 databases

Total access above the local collections. . . . . .1,266,650 items

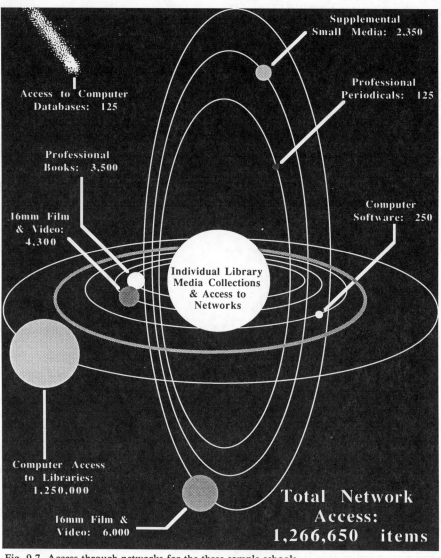

Fig. 9.7. Access through networks for the three sample schools.

Resource Centre Program Objectives	Requirements of Program	Number of Resources		Approximate Unit Cost	Total
		Have	Need		
1. **Grade 12** Family studies students will read a Canadian novel written by a woman or having a woman as the central character.	•Canadian novels and novels about Canada [reinforced paperbacks]	25	25	$ 4.00	$100.00
2. **Grade 9** Students will locate information for assignments related to an environmental studies unit on pond life using a variety of learning materials.	•multimedia kits	2	1	$120.00	$120.00
	•transparency kits	7	1	$ 18.00	$ 18.00
	•books on pond life	20	10	$ 15.00	$150.00
	•fiction on related themes	17	3	$ 12.00	$ 36.00

Fig. 9.8. Needed resources. From *Partners in Action: The Library Resource Centre in the School Curriculum* (Toronto, Ontario Ministry of Education, 1982), 37.

CHINA

1940s	1950s	1960s	1970s	1980s
THL III	THL THL THL THL THL THL THL I	THL THL THL THL THL THL THL THL THL THL THL THL THL THL THL THL THL THL THL THL THL THL	THL THL THL THL THL THL THL THL THL I	THL THL I

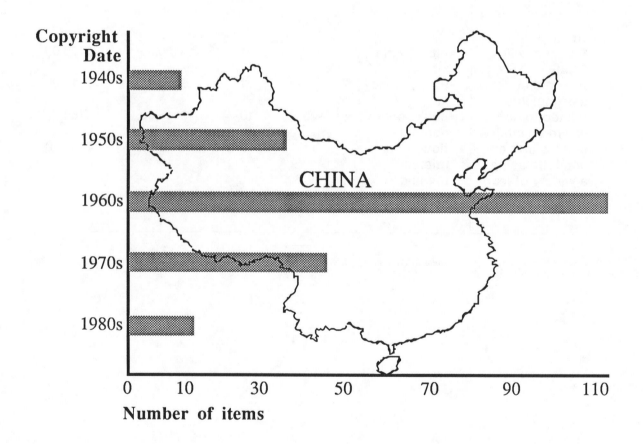

Fig. 9.9. Tally sheet and graph for recency analysis. Reprinted with permission of Gloria Mattson.

An alternative method and a more statistically precise measure is to use Gloria Mattson's shelflist analysis, but calculate the mean age of the collection and its standard deviation. The formula for calculating the mean age of the collection is demonstrated in table 9.1.

Table 9.1

Computation of Variance and Standard Deviation
for the Copyright Dates of Ten Books

General formula

$$\sigma = \left[\frac{\Sigma X^2 - n\mu^2}{n} \right]^{1/2}$$

Sample computation for ten book copyright dates

	X	X²
Copyright date of the first book	75	5625
	76	5776
	77	5929
	78	6084
	79	6241
	80	6400
	81	6561
	82	6724
	83	6889
	84	7056
Add other book copyrights as needed	—	
	$\Sigma X = 795$	$\Sigma X^2 = 63285$

$$\mu = (\Sigma X)/10 = 795/10 = 79.5$$

$$\sigma^2 = \frac{\Sigma X^2 - n\mu^2}{n}$$

$$= \frac{63285 - (10) \cdot (79.5)^2}{10}$$

$$= \frac{63285 - 63202.5}{10}$$

$$= 8.3 \text{ and } \sigma = \sqrt{8.3} = 2.85$$

If you have the AppleWorks Spreadsheet and are somewhat familiar with it, the following template can be constructed. Do the following:

1. Create the template with the accompanying formulas as follows. Column B can be widened, if desired, as shown. The example shown is with the Apple-Z command toggled on.

```
==========A===========================B==============
 4|year of
 5|copyright              year squared
 6|first line, don't delete
 7|75                     +A7*A7
 8|76                     +A8*A8
 9|77                     +A9*A9
10|78                     +A10*A10
11|79                     +A11*A11
12|80                     +A12*A12
13|81                     +A13*A13
14|82                     +A14*A14
15|83                     +A15*A15
16|84                     +A16*A16
17|last line, don't delete
18|@SUM(A6...A17)         @SUM(B6...B17)
19|                       +A18/@COUNT(A6...A17)
20|mean coll. date        +B18-(@COUNT(A6...A17)*B19*B19)/@COUNT(A6...A17)
21|+A18/@COUNT(A6...@SQRT(B20)
22|mean coll. date                    Standard deviation
```

2. Toggling the Apple-Z command, the computed results would be:

```
==========A===========================B===============================
 4|year of
 5|copyright                                            year squared
 6|first line, don't delete
 7|              75                                             5625
 8|              76                                             5776
 9|              77                                             5929
10|              78                                             6084
11|              79                                             6241
12|              80                                             6400
13|              81                                             6561
14|              82                                             6724
15|              83                                             6889
16|              84                                             7056
17|last line, don't delete
18|             795                                            63285
19|                                                             79.5
20|                                                             8.25
21|            79.5                                        2.8722813
22|mean coll. date                              Standard deviation
```

3. If the numbers and formulas match the above examples, you are ready to use the spreadsheet. Replace the numbers in column A just below the words "first line, don't delete" with copyright data from the shelflist. When additional lines are needed, use the Apple-I command anywhere *between* the first and last lines. When you add lines, you will have to reconstruct the squaring formula in column B. Use the copy command to do so or type in by hand.

4. Interpret the statistic. In the example above, the mean of the collection is 1979.5 with a standard deviation of 2.87. This means that the average book was copyrighted in June of 1979. Eighty-three percent of the collection is older than April 1982 (1979.5 + 2.87 = 1982.37) if you want to interpret the statistic negatively; or, 83 percent of the collection is newer than July 1976 (1979.5 − 2.87 = 1976.63) if you want to interpret the statistic positively.

If the statistical method is used on portions of the collection particularly vulnerable to age, such as science and the reference, impressive statistics can be used to show the precise age of the collection.

Recency analysis has been very successful in a number of school districts around the country. Bill Murray, the supervisor of the Aurora, Colorado, schools, used a combination of the collection map and a recency analysis to build with the school board a long-range collection renewal program for the district, infusing many thousands of dollars into the project over a five-year period of time.

Systematic Usage Evaluation

The second recommended collection quality measure must be taken over a long period of time and presumes that true collection quality can be judged only as demands are made upon the collection. If a teacher or student is attempting to locate information or materials and the collection cannot or does not respond, then the collection is poor no matter how large it is. On the other hand, if a collection provides everything a person requests at a particular time, then for that person, the collection is excellent.

This author, May Lein Ho, and Melvin Bowie have developed a method for a national study which asks library media specialists and teachers to jointly fill in an evaluation form *after* a major draw on the collection has been attempted. This evaluation is done *after a topical study or instructional unit* which tried to rely on the library media collection. Figure 9.10, page 112, is the evaluation form used for this effort.

The data collected on such a form are immediately valuable to the library media specialist who is seeking teacher input for the needs of the collection in a specific area. They are also extremely valuable over time if some analysis is done. By hand tallying or using a computerized spreadsheet, the library media specialist can analyze how well the collection responds to certain characteristics and across curricular areas.

For example, data from numerous sheets can be combined to see how the collection generally responds to each of the rated concerns such as recency, enough materials, relevance, etc. If averaged responses are low or high, this fact is reported to administrators. The data can also be analyzed by curricular area. For example, just topical studies in science can be isolated and analyzed. When science teachers attempt to draw materials from the collection, what is the result? Enough materials? Current materials? The answers are very valuable in collection building and budgeting.

Collection Quality Evaluation Form

Directions: Together, library media specialists and teachers should fill in the following items:

1. Curricular area: _____ Unit title: _____
   Grade level: _____ Date evaluated: _____
   Library media specialist's name: _____
   Teacher's name: _____

2. How heavily was the collection used for this unit?

   _____ SCALE: 5 = Very heavy use
                       4 = Heavy use
                       3 = Moderate use
                       2 = Some use
                       1 = Not used

   _____ Actual circulation or use figures (optional)

3. Please rate the collection in the following eleven aspects:
   SCALE: 5 = Excellent
            4 = Above average
            3 = Average
            2 = Below average
            1 = Poor
            X = Doesn't apply

   _____ Variety of media: Were there books, audiovisuals, periodicals, etc.?
   _____ Currency of materials: Were the materials up-to-date considering the topic needs?
   _____ Relevance of materials: Did materials match requests and needs?
   _____ Durability of materials: What was the condition of the materials?
   _____ Enough?: Were there enough materials for the number of students studying the unit?
   _____ Span read/view/listen: Were there materials which span the reading/viewing/listening/comprehension levels of the students?
   _____ Interesting?: Were the materials interesting to students?
   _____ Span opinion: Were there materials which span opinion/cultural/political issues if appropriate?
   _____ Accessibility: Did the users have easy access to materials, equipment, and facilities, if reasonable time was given for planning?
   _____ Unit objective: Were the materials of help to the students in accomplishing the objective(s) of the unit?
   _____ New items: Rate the new items added since last request for the unit.

   _____ AVERAGE RATING (Calculate this figure if you want to analyze the data locally. Don't average in "X" items.)

4. Comments on the ratings and needs:

Fig. 9.10. Collection quality evaluation form. This form is currently being used in a national collection evaluation study being conducted by David V. Loertscher, May Lein Ho, and Melvin Bowie. Further information can be obtained by writing the author at Libraries Unlimited.

Linda Hardy of the Gardnerville Elementary School in Gardnerville, Nevada, used the collection evaluation form during three spring months of 1987. She rates her school as average in wealth, having a generous book budget and a large collection. Table 9.2 lists her results.

Table 9.2

Systematic Collection Evaluation

Teacher's Name	Curricular Area	Unit Title	Use	Variety	Currency	Relevant	Durable	Enough?	Span rvlc
Jones	History	Explorers	5	4	3	4	3	4	4
Fischer	Reading	Fairy Tales	5	4	4	4	4	5	5
Fischer	Reading/Social Studies	Historical Events	3	4	5	4	3	4	4
Reynolds	Science	Planets	4	3	4	3	3	4	4
Morgan	Science	Experiments	4	3	3	4	4	2	4
Reynolds	Science	Magnetism	4	3	3	4	3	2	4
Fischer	Science	Air	3	2	2	4	3	1	3
Reynolds	Science	Animals	5	5	4	5	4	5	5
Rajs	Science	Eagles	3	2	2	3	3	3	2
Reynolds	Science	Whales	5	4	4	4	4	4	4
Miller	Science	Weather	5	5	5	4	4	5	5
Fischer	Science	Birds	3	3	5	5	5	5	4
Rajs	Science	Light	4	2	3	3	3	3	4
Fischer	Science	Plants	3	3	4	4	3	4	3
Reynolds	Science	Trees (Arbor Day)	4	4	4	5	4	3	4
Dinsmore	Social Studies	Cinco de Mayo	5	3	3	3	3	2	3
Davey	Social Studies	Europe	3	3	2	3	3	4	3
Dressler	Social Studies	Hong Kong	3	3	2	3	3	3	3
Analysis by item			3.87	3.27	3.53	3.87	3.47	3.40	3.73

Teacher's Name	Curricular Area	Unit Title	Interest	Span ocp	Access	New Mats.	Average
Jones	History	Explorers	4	na	3	2	3.60
Fischer	Reading	Fairy Tales	5	na	4	4	4.40
Fischer	Reading/Social Studies	Historical Events	4	na	4	3	3.80
Reynolds	Science	Planets	4	na	5	3	3.70
Morgan	Science	Experiments	4	na	4	2	3.40
Reynolds	Science	Magnetism	4	na	4	2	3.30
Fischer	Science	Air	3	na	4	1	2.60
Reynolds	Science	Animals	5	na	5	4	4.70
Rajs	Science	Eagles	4	na	3	1	2.60
Reynolds	Science	Whales	4	na	4	4	4.10
Miller	Science	Weather	5	na	5	2	4.50
Fischer	Science	Birds	5	na	5	4	4.40
Rajs	Science	Light	4	na	3	2	3.10
Fischer	Science	Plants	4	na	4	3	3.50
Reynolds	Science	Trees (Arbor Day)	4	na	4	3	3.90
Dinsmore	Social Studies	Cinco de Mayo	5	na	5	1	3.30
Davey	Social Studies	Europe	4	na	3	3	3.10
Dressler	Social Studies	Hong Kong	3	na	4	2	2.90
Analysis by item			4.20		4.13	2.53	3.60

Used with permission of Linda Hardy, Gardnerville, Nevada.

The data from Linda Hardy's school show that the science teachers dominated the usage of the library media center during the spring months. One teacher, Mrs. Reynolds, was a particularly heavy user. The data indicate the following needs:

1. More materials are needed on the topics of experiments, magnetism, air, and Cinco de Mayo.

2. A wider variety of media is needed on the topics of air, eagles, and light.

3. The collection needs weeding and purchase of current materials for air, eagles, Europe, and Hong Kong.

4. Materials on various reading levels are needed for eagles.

5. New materials purchased for air, eagles, and Cinco de Mayo were either unsatisfactory or nonexistent.

Overall, the collection rates just above average. It would appear that the lack of new items is contributing to collection problems. Linda could concentrate more funds in the science areas of the collection for the next year to try to improve the response of the collection in commonly researched subjects.

TECHNOLOGY

In the past thirty years, library media centers and schools have experimented with a number of new educational technologies. Some of these technologies have been very successful, others have not. Many times, failure has not been based on what the technology can offer to education, but on the lack of support for the technology as a system.

Computers as instructional tools is one of the latest of a long line of technologies to attract educators. In the early experimentation with this technology, it was common for a school to acquire a computer without any software and with no training or plans for its use. With no purpose for the technology, no support, and no followup, many found that computers did not really make any contribution. Other educators such as Jean Donham, Library Media Supervisor for the Iowa City Schools, could see the vision of what computers could do and led her district in a thorough planning and adoption program for this technology.[3]

If any technology is to make a contribution to education, a systematic program of adoption must be followed. Generally, there are seven steps to be made in any systematic test:

1. Probe the philosophical foundation for a technology. What characteristics of the technology have the potential to make a contribution to education? How is this contribution supposed to be realized?

2. Investigate fully the equipment needed for the technology. To experiment right, what will really be needed? How much will it cost? If corners are cut in acquiring a full complement of equipment, will there be a fair test of the technology?

3. Decide how much software the technology will require for a fair test of its potential. Is there enough quality software on the market for a fair test? How much will it cost? What areas of the curriculum can be supported by software developers?

4. Determine the needed facilities for proper use of the technology. Will the technology require major or minor adjustments? How much will it cost to convert the present facilities in order to have a fair test of the technology?

5. Decide what personnel will be needed to operate the technology. Who will be responsible for the technology? How will they be trained?

6. Determine what maintenance will be needed for the hardware and software of the technology. Are repair sources available in-house or nearby? How much will normal repairs cost?

7. Prepare a plan to promote the use of the technology. Will everyone in the school be encouraged to experiment? Only a few?

Such questions will need to be asked at the experimentation phase and also periodically after that. The checklist in figure 9.11, pages 116-20, probes the support an educational technology is receiving in a school by first looking at the goals, then the resources available, and finally the processes used by the school to support the chosen technology. If a technology cannot be supported properly, it ought not to be advertised as a part of the library media program.

Directions for using the checklist:

1. Decide on one or more technologies to be evaluated. Examples could be computer-assisted instruction, 16mm film, online database searching, audiotape recording, 35mm slides, overhead projectors and transparencies, filmstrips, etc.

2. Duplicate two copies of the evaluation form for each type of media to be evaluated.

3. Have both the administrator and the library media specialist rate the items on the form independently. Items considered inappropriate or not applicable need not be rated.

4. Chart the ratings of both raters on a single form.

5. In conference, discuss any differences in ratings and all ratings below a 4.

6. In conference, ask and answer the following questions:

    a. Is our support for this technology sufficient to make it a success in this school?

    b. Is our level of involvement in this technology appropriate for our school?

    c. Should we abandon this technology in favor of other technologies we could support better? In other words, should we support a few technologies well or a number on a cursory level?

    d. What steps should we take to improve our support for this technology?

7. Prepare plans and implement them.

(Text continues on page 121.)

Technology Evaluation Form

Type of technology being rated: _____

Raters: Administrator:_____

Library media specialist: _____

Directions: Duplicate a copy of the questionnaire for each rater. For the technology mentioned above, rate each of the following items in each section. Combine the administrator's ratings and the library media specialist's ratings and compute the average rating for each section and for the questionnaire as a whole.

A. *The Philosophical Foundation for a Technology*

According to the research and theory for _____
(name the technology) the benefits to accrue to the education of the students of this school
are: _____
_____
_____
_____

1. The theoretical contributions of this equipment have been considered:

   Very little   1 2 3 4 5   Systematically

2. The results of research have been analyzed before this technology was adopted:

   Not researched   1 2 3 4 5   Researched

3. Input from teachers, library media specialists, administrators was considered before adopting the technology.

   Disagree   1 2 3 4 5   Agree

4. The level of involvement in this technology was planned in advance.

   Disagree   1 2 3 4 5   Agree

5. We know where we are going with this technology.

   Disagree   1 2 3 4 5   Agree

B. *The Purchase Process for the Technology*

Briefly stated, our purchase procedure for _____
(name the technology) is: _____
_____
_____
_____

1. We know what hardware is available on the commercial market.

   Disagree   1 2 3 4 5   Agree

2. We have drawn up specifications for purchase to allow competitive bidding within our quality criteria.

        Disagree 1 2 3 4 5 Agree

3. We have sought reputable dealers to bid on the equipment.

        Disagree 1 2 3 4 5 Agree

4. We have investigated warranties and repair services before we purchased.

        Disagree 1 2 3 4 5 Agree

5. Quality and sturdiness are as important as lowest price.

        Disagree 1 2 3 4 5 Agree

6. Some effort to standardize purchases of this equipment is made.

        Disagree 1 2 3 4 5 Agree

C. *The Equipment Used in the Technology*

Name the type of equipment used in this technology _____

How much equipment for this technology is owned and is in operating condition? _____

1. How often can patron requests to use this equipment be filled?

        Rarely 1 2 3 4 5 Always

2. The sophistication of our equipment meets our level of involvement for this technology.

        Rarely 1 2 3 4 5 Always

3. The cost of this equipment is reasonable considering its contribution.

        Rarely 1 2 3 4 5 Always

4. The life expectancy of this equipment is:

        Unacceptable 1 2 3 4 5 Acceptable

D. *The Accompanying Software*

The type of software used with this technology is: _____

_____

Approximately how many software items are available:

                    locally? _____

          at the district center? _____

     at a regional media center? _____

        at a state media center? _____

at any other center _____? _____
                        (name)

(Figure 9.11 continues on page 118.)

1. Access to this software is: Limited 1 2 3 4 5 Extensive

2. Access to software across subject areas is: Narrow 1 2 3 4 5 Broad

3. Access by teachers to this software is: Inconvenient 1 2 3 4 5 Convenient

4. Students have access to this software on a free choice basis. Disagree 1 2 3 4 5 Agree

5. The software is: Outdated 1 2 3 4 5 Current

6. Money budgeted for this software on a regular basis is: Inadequate 1 2 3 4 5 Adequate

7. The condition of the software is: Poor 1 2 3 4 5 Excellent

8. The academic level of the software is: Inappropriate 1 2 3 4 5 Appropriate

E. *Facilities for Proper Use*

What special needs are there for use of this equipment (screens? darkening? special sound system? large screen? etc.) _____

_____

1. Considering optimum facilities for this equipment, ours are: Inappropriate 1 2 3 4 5 Exemplary

2. Facilities are available for special needs. Rarely 1 2 3 4 5 Always

3. Considering the risk of theft and mutilation, our facilities are: Insecure 1 2 3 4 5 Safe

4. Storage for this equipment and its special needs is: Inadequate 1 2 3 4 5 Adequate

5. Carts for moving and/or desks or special furniture are: Inadequate 1 2 3 4 5 Adequate

6. Electrical needs for this equipment are: Inadequate 1 2 3 4 5 Adequate

7. Seating for appropriate audience size is: Inadequate 1 2 3 4 5 Adequate

Facilities for use of this equipment can accommodate:

8. Individuals: Disagree 1 2 3 4 5 Agree

9. Small groups: Disagree 1 2 3 4 5 Agree

10. Large groups: Disagree 1 2 3 4 5 Agree

11. Facilities for this equipment provide privacy
     and control distraction to others.   Disagree 1 2 3 4 5 Agree

F. *Personnel to Operate the Technology*

What special training or personnel is needed to operate this technology? _____
_____
_____

1. LMC staff who operate this equipment are: Untrained 1 2 3 4 5 Trained

2. Teachers who need to use this equipment
    are: Untrained 1 2 3 4 5 Trained

3. Student operators (for teachers) are: Untrained 1 2 3 4 5 Trained

4. Students who use this equipment are: Untrained 1 2 3 4 5 Trained

5. Training and renewal of skills are conducted: Never 1 2 3 4 5 Regularly

6. Observers of our equipment operators would
    rate them as: Careless 1 2 3 4 5 Careful

G. *Maintenance of Hardware and Software*

Maintenance for this equipment is carried out by _____
_____

Maintenance of the software is carried out by _____
_____

1. Preventative maintenance for this equip-
    ment is: Inadequate 1 2 3 4 5 Adequate

2. Preventative maintenance for this software
    is: Inadequate 1 2 3 4 5 Adequate

3. Repair services for this equipment are: Inadequate 1 2 3 4 5 Adequate

4. Repair services are: Distant 1 2 3 4 5 Nearby

5. Time needed to repair this equipment is: Unreasonable 1 2 3 4 5 Reasonable

6. The cost of repair for this equipment is: Unreasonable 1 2 3 4 5 Reasonable

(Figure 9.11 continues on page 120.)

7. Time for software repair or replacement is: Unreasonable 1 2 3 4 5 Reasonable

8. Cords and other hanging items are not a hazard to users. Disagree 1 2 3 4 5 Agree

9. Upon equipment malfunctions, users can expect immediate help/replacement. Disagree 1 2 3 4 5 Agree

H. *Promotion of Use*

Promotion of use for this technology is done by_____.

1. Users understand the potential contribution of this technology. Disagree 1 2 3 4 5 Agree

2. Users understand the limitations of this type of media. Disagree 1 2 3 4 5 Agree

3. Promotional efforts for this equipment are: Nonexistent 1 2 3 4 5 Active

4. Directions for operating machines are available on the equipment or are in close proximity. Disagree 1 2 3 4 5 Agree

5. Individual users can expect one-to-one instruction in operating this equipment. Disagree 1 2 3 4 5 Agree

Fig. 9.11. Technology evaluation form. Developed by David V. Loertscher and Blanche Woolls.

THE BUDGET

Many attempts have been made over the last fifty years to assist planners in constructing realistic budgets for school library media programs. Many attempts have failed because of unexpected inflationary pressures and the development of so many new technologies which have had potential for education. From the perspective of 1988 materials prices, technologies available, and national research measuring what is actually spent on school library programs, it appears that a simple guideline can be constructed to guide spending.

Three levels of budgetary support are recommended. This money would be spent on materials, including books, audiovisual materials, computer software, and periodicals. It does not include funds for salaries, equipment, facilities, or supplies. This formula presumes that the cost of a book can be used as a good inflationary standard for all forms of materials. Each year, the materials budget would be equivalent to:

Minimum level: one book per year per student

Standard level: two books per year per student

Excellence: three books per year per student

What does a book cost? Compute the average from local records of spending. Elementary books cost less than do books at the secondary level. A sample materials cost sheet and accompanying graphs are presented in figure 9.12, page 122.

How Should the Money Budgeted Be Spent?

Historically, library media specialists have received funds categorized by type of media. There have been funds for books, audiovisual materials, periodicals, supplies, and equipment. Library media specialists would be wise to follow whatever budgeting procedures are in place in a particular school, but allocate available money by its function. A number of categories should be constructed. These might include money for:

1. Curriculum changes or new textbooks.

2. Building-specific parts of the collection which will support courses taught and resource-based topical units.

3. Maintaining the present collection (replacing worn or missing materials, buying the best of newly published materials to keep the collection current).

Figure 9.13, page 123, shows how a traditional budget may be divided into the categories listed above, complete with a justification for decision makers.

Materials Cost Analysis

Books (hardcover, not reference)							_Lee Elementary School_		
Type of media / equipment or summary							School name		

	83	84	85	86	87	88	89	90
Total Expenditures	2680	2618	2022	2765	3042			
# Items Purchased	341	321	253	378	394			
Average Cost per Item	7.86	8.16	7.99	7.31	7.72			
% increase / decrease of cost per item	X	+4%	-2%	-9%	+6%			

Graphs of Local Purchases

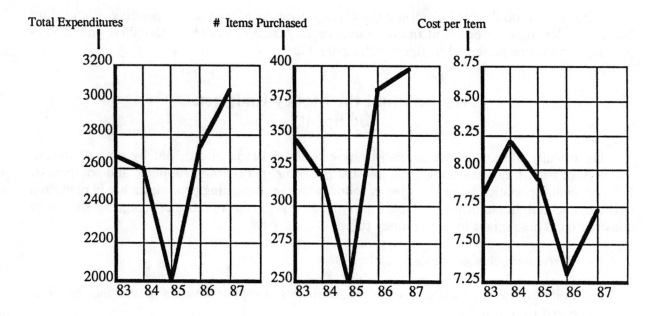

Fig. 9.12. Materials cost analysis and graphs of local purchases.

Library Media Budget Allocation Form

Amount available _____

Curriculum Changes or New Textbooks	Teacher/Library Media Specialist Course and Unit Targets (the team identifies one or several areas which need significant expenditure)	Support for Present Collection (build-up or maintain current collection strengths: periodicals, reference, other basic items)
Curricular area(s):	General/specific emphasis collections:	Collection segment(s):
Justification:	Justification:	Justification:
Proposed amount: _____	Proposed amount: _____	Proposed amount: _____

Fig. 9.13. Library media budget allocation form.

The collection map and the collection size planning form (figures 9.2-9.3) can be of great use in prioritizing budget needs and planning expenditures. A friendly competitive bidding for spending priorities among the faculty might be encouraged. Those grade levels or departments that propose sufficient use of resources might be funded. Those departments and teachers who follow through by making good use of materials could continue to be funded. Those who make little or no use of LMC resources would not be funded or would be encouraged to change their teaching styles. Money might be set aside from the LMC budget as competitive grants (bribe money). Teachers willing to engage in cooperative resource-based teaching units with the library media specialist might be funded on a project-by-project basis. The objective would be to provide incentives for cooperative planning and heavy use of the materials purchased for the LMC.

A final aspect, the actual administration of the budget, needs to be considered. The person(s) who control the money and the process of spending it in schools and districts vary widely. In some cases, principals maintain very tight control, with total secrecy surrounding the budgeting process not only for the LMC but for every other department of the school. Other principals are very open about the budgeting process and include department heads as needed in the dispersal of funds. Still other schools have little say in the budgeting process, since it is a district function.

Library media specialists need some independence in the budgeting process, not because they demand power, but because they need the flexibility to provide materials and equipment as needs arise. They can also exercise cost-saving procedures, since they come in contact with the business world directly. The budgetary report card in figure 9.14, pages 125-27, assumes that the budget making process is lodged at the building level, with the school principal in charge. In districts where that practice is not the case, the report card would have to be modified so that the functions reflect district as well as building level concerns.

FACILITIES

There have been numerous designs of facilities over the years for library media centers. No design has proven to be long lasting because of changing technologies and the increasing role that the LMC has played in the educational program. In planning for new or remodeled facilities, or in rearranging present facilities, four principles should be considered carefully:

1. Facilities should be spacious enough and arranged in such a way that they can accommodate large groups, small groups, and individuals simultaneously without undue confusion.

2. Facilities should accommodate all forms of materials and technologies in a single complex of spaces easily supervised by the LMC staff. Spaces to consider include: audiovisual production areas for students and teachers, technical services, reference and indexes, circulation, reading/viewing/listening, materials and equipment storage, entrance, displays, individual study, small group study, storytelling, administration, media production laboratories (television, photography, computer), and professional library.

3. Facilities should be located with easy access from every part of the school in mind.

4. The facility should be designed to be inviting and attractive, and to serve as the cultural center for the entire school.

Budgetary Report Card

Both the administrator and the library media specialist should rate each of the following statements concerning the budgetary process on a report card-like scale (A-F). Take into consideration the total budgetary situation for the district and the community when rating. In difficult times, for example, holding budget levels to those of the previous year might be a positive step and thus might receive an A rating. Local, federal, and grant funds can be combined or separated as mutually agreed upon for this rating.

A = excellent
B = above average
C = average
D = below average
F = failing
X = doesn't apply

administrator's rating library media specialist's rating

_____ _____ 1. The library media specialist is involved in the budgetary process (planning, expending, evaluating).

_____ _____ 2. Funds are allocated to meet short- and long-range goals of the library media center.

_____ _____ 3. Funds are allocated to meet textbook or other curriculum cycles so that LMC resources are available as curricular changes are made.

_____ _____ 4. Funds are allocated to meet the needs of special units of instruction planned between the library media specialist and teachers.

_____ _____ 5. Inflationary factors are built into budget proposals for materials and equipment.

_____ _____ 6. Expenditures are made at regular intervals throughout the school year rather than all at one time.

_____ _____ 7. Ample planning time is available before purchasing deadlines so that pressure purchasing is avoided and careful selection of materials is possible.

_____ _____ 8. Purchasing practices are kept within legal procedures.

_____ _____ 9. The library media specialist knows the status of budget accounts (balance of account, actual P.O. charges vs. estimated amounts, etc.).

_____ _____ 10. The library media specialist is given an actual amount to spend for materials and equipment, i.e., budget figures are not withheld for the specialist.

(Figure 9.14 continues on page 126.)

For the following items, grade yourself on your efforts to make every dollar go further.

administrator's rating   _library media specialist's rating_

Book purchasing and acquisition:

_____ _____ 11. We receive good discounts on purchases.

_____ _____ 12. We make an effort to select titles carefully.

_____ _____ 13. We make a concerted effort to maintain existing materials.

_____ _____ 14. We coordinate purchases with other schools or libraries to have access to more titles.

_____ _____ 15. We have increased our borrowing from other schools or libraries.

Audiovisual materials purchasing and acquisition:

_____ _____ 16. We make an effort to select titles carefully.

_____ _____ 17. We make a concerted effort to maintain existing materials.

_____ _____ 18. We coordinate purchases with other schools or libraries to have access to more titles.

_____ _____ 19. We have increased our borrowing from other schools or libraries.

Periodical purchases and acquisition:

_____ _____ 20. We make an effort to select titles carefully.

_____ _____ 21. We solicit donations of desired titles from the community.

_____ _____ 22. We coordinate purchases with other schools or libraries to have access to more titles.

_____ _____ 23. We have increased our borrowing/photocopying service with other schools or libraries.

Audiovisual equipment purchases and acquisition:

_____ _____ 24. We have a maintenance program for existing equipment.

_____ _____ 25. We purchase with durability in mind.

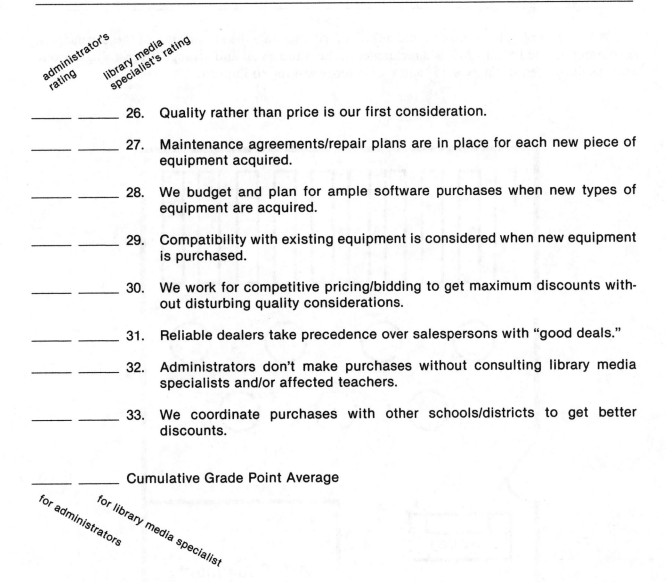

administrator's rating   library media specialist's rating

_____ _____ 26. Quality rather than price is our first consideration.

_____ _____ 27. Maintenance agreements/repair plans are in place for each new piece of equipment acquired.

_____ _____ 28. We budget and plan for ample software purchases when new types of equipment are acquired.

_____ _____ 29. Compatibility with existing equipment is considered when new equipment is purchased.

_____ _____ 30. We work for competitive pricing/bidding to get maximum discounts without disturbing quality considerations.

_____ _____ 31. Reliable dealers take precedence over salespersons with "good deals."

_____ _____ 32. Administrators don't make purchases without consulting library media specialists and/or affected teachers.

_____ _____ 33. We coordinate purchases with other schools/districts to get better discounts.

_____ _____ Cumulative Grade Point Average

for administrators   for library media specialist

Plans for improvement:

Fig. 9.14. Budgetary report card.

A few examples, both positive and negative, will illustrate the importance of these principles. A common shape for an LMC is a rectangle. Make it too small and arrange it for a single group area, as illustrated in figure 9.15, and a disaster is waiting to happen.

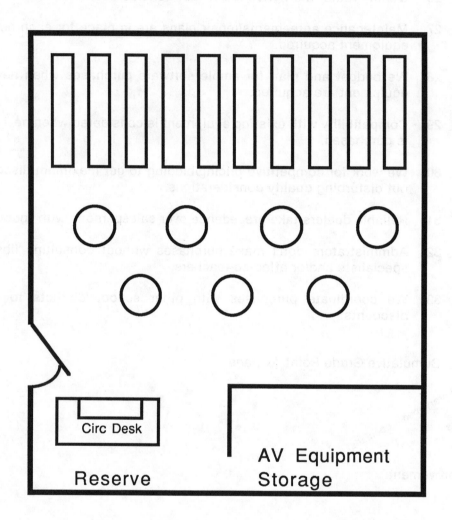

Fig. 9.15. Example of an overcrowded facility.

Here, a single space for people guarantees confusion if more than one group tries to use the center. Traffic patterns encourage conflict and simultaneous activities are almost impossible. In this case, the facility needs to be enlarged and the furniture rearranged to facilitate more groups (large and small).

One library media center visited by the author was a sunken circle surrounded by a moat. Figure 9.16 shows access to the center via four arching step bridges.

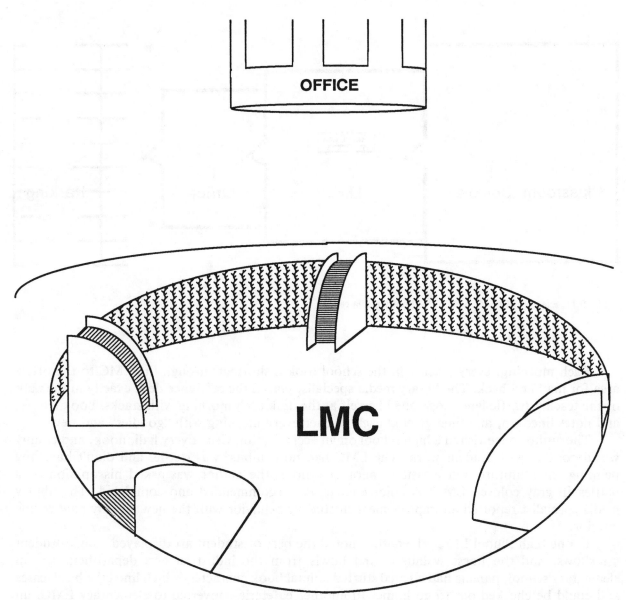

Fig. 9.16. Example of a sunken circle library media center.

Provision had been made to have small seating areas separated by low bookshelves. Book trucks could not navigate the four access stairways so all materials had to be hand carried to and from classes. No audiovisual materials or equipment storage was designed. Audiovisual equipment, if stored, would have had to be hand-carried over the bridges. The center could not be expanded. The "moat" consisted of a steep bank planted with tropical greenery. The main office for the school was suspended directly above the LMC. The result was breathtakingly beautiful, but totally unfunctional.

One of the best designed LMCs in terms of access for teachers happened to be located between the office area and the classroom complex, as shown in figure 9.17.

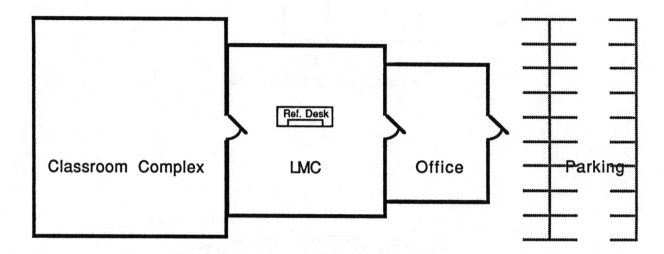

Fig. 9.17. Example of good access to the library media center.

Each morning, every teacher in the school took a shortcut through the LMC to the office area for mail and back. The library media specialist placed the reference desk exactly in the path of the teacher traffic lane, positioned herself at the desk each morning with stacks, book trucks, and notes lined up, and then greeted each teacher every morning with "goodies" and news.

The author once visited a high school on an accreditation visit. Every hall, nook, and cranny was decorated with student work. The LMC had no exhibits, was sterile, and didn't have any paintings or sculpture. On a visit to another school, the author was asked his opinion of a battleship gray colored LMC. A color change was recommended and completed. The library media specialist reported an improvement in student behavior with the new creamy pale yellow interior.

In one high school LMC, the author noted the best of student art displayed, single-student art shows, and the finest walnut carved bowls from the industrial arts department. In an elementary school, parents had created stuffed animal book characters which lined the book cases and could be checked out to go home. In another cafeteria-converted-to-elementary-LMC, an entire twelve-foot-high wall was used by one class a month to share a topical study with the rest of the school. Life in the sea was the topic of the month when the author visited. The wall was a giant collage of realia and student-created materials. That same LMC was a veritable treasure trove of things to do, displays to observe, projects to listen to, and experiments to interact with. Students viewed the center as the most exciting place in the school. One student swore the author to secrecy about his three-mile bicycle ride to attend the school each morning. He lived outside the school's boundaries but was determined to spend his sixth year in the school.

Such experiences, good and bad, lead one to conclude that much can be done to create a LMC which is the cultural center of the school. Suppose every award won, every notable project, belonged to the LMC for one week immediately following its reception? Student-run and coordinated displays of notable items could create a feeling that the best of what's happening and what's going on can be discovered through a visit to the LMC. The best projects from every subject area, including displays from extracurricular activities, the best products from every student cultural group, from every level of student achievement, would be displayed as a way of building pride, understanding, and a sense of accomplishment.

TECHNICAL SERVICES

Technical services is the behind-the-scenes operation which consists of selecting and acquiring materials, cataloging and indexing, inventory control, circulating, and retrieving overdue materials. It is quite possible for these operations to require the complete time of a library media specialist, particularly when there is no clerical help available. Some hope has been forthcoming in the past several years with the rise of microcomputer-based automated systems designed to handle one or more of the functions listed above. Nancy Everhart collected some impressive data comparing an automated system to a manual system of doing a number of technical service-type operations. The comparative chart is shown in figure 9.18, page 132.

As of 1988, no microcomputer system has demonstrated excellence in handling the complicated and huge tasks of technical services well. There are a number of systems available. Some handle a single function such as circulation; others integrate an online catalog with an acquisitions and circulation system. Much development and experimentation is taking place. Administrators and library media specialists are cautioned to evaluate every system offered very carefully before purchase.

In an article describing administrative uses of computers for library media centers, the author noted that

When the task of automation is complete, the computerized method should meet the following criteria:

1. The computerized method should save time. This means that it does the job in less time than a comparable task done by hand or by another machine.

2. The computerized method should be more accurate. When a human does a repetitive task, we make allowances for error. When the computer (and humans operating it) performs a task, the error rate should be at least as low (or lower) than the manual operation.

3. The computerized method should be more efficient. Do not think only of saving time, but also of doing more work in the same amount of time. Oftentimes a task can be done by microcomputer that cannot be done manually because the manual task is much too much work. For example, the school library media specialist may be able to take inventory several times a year using a microcomputer and a light pen, where the same task is done annually (if that often) when individuals must do the task.

TIME SAVED WITH COMPUTERIZATION

Number of hours:		1	2	3	4	5	6	7	8	9	10	11	12	13	14	15	16	17	18
Catalog Card Production (50 books with complete cards, pockets and labels)	BEFORE																		18 HOURS
	AFTER	2 HOURS																	
Check in 50 books (accuracy is increased tremendously with computer)	BEFORE	30 MINUTES																	
	AFTER	5 MINUTES																	
Check out 50 books	BEFORE	1 HOUR																	
	AFTER	1 HOUR																	
Compose overdues and fines (for one week's circulation)	BEFORE	4 HOURS																	
	AFTER	15 MINUTES																	
Reports to patrons when they come in library as to books out, fines, etc.	BEFORE	10 MINUTES																	
	AFTER	5 SECONDS																	
Monthly circulation report	BEFORE	1 HOUR																	
	AFTER	10 SECONDS																	
New book newsletter (typed listings with graphics, borders, etc.)	BEFORE	3 HOURS																	
	AFTER	30 MINUTES																	
Bibliography updates (4-page bibliography)	BEFORE	2 HOURS																	
	AFTER	15 MINUTES																	
Letters (25 individual)	BEFORE	4 HOURS																	
	AFTER	30 MINUTES																	
Lists (update memorials, patrons benefactors)	BEFORE	1 HOUR																	
	AFTER	5 MINUTES																	
Searching for periodical articles	BEFORE	VARIES — COULD BE HOURS																	
	AFTER	15 MINUTES																	
Inventory	BEFORE	2 WEEKS																	
	AFTER	2 DAYS																	

Programs used Circulation Plus, Quick Card, Bibliography Writer, The Print Shop, AppleWorks, The Newsroom, Pennsylvania's Lintel system for on-line data base searching, Create with Garfield, Bank Street Writer, and Bank Street Filer

Based on: MMI MODEL LIBRARY BY NANCY EVERHART.

Fig. 9.18. Time saved with computerization. Reprinted with permission of Nancy Everhart.

4. The computerized method must be easy. Sometimes, it will be so complicated that untrained workers or clerical personnel cannot do it. This returns the responsibility for the activity to the professional library media specialist and defeats the purpose of the original design.

5. The computerized method must be adaptable. School library media specialists must be able to integrate the method into ongoing administrative operations. If primary consideration must be given to the microcomputer in terms of where a task must be done, when it can be done, and precisely what must be done, then the microcomputer uses more time—time needed to plan how to meet its specifications rather than meeting management needs. If school library media specialists find that their days are planned around the micro-computer and what it can do, it is time to reconsider. Microcomputers are tools, not masters.

6. The computerized method must be cost effective. The microcomputer must do as much (or more) work for less money than a manual system. At times, it will be necessary to compute the time of professionals and clericals when costing out computerized methods vs. manual methods. Microcomputer hardware is just one cost to take into account. There are also supplies, maintenance, and software costs to be totaled when thinking of using the microcomputer for management statistics.[4]

ACCESS

Access to facilities, materials, and equipment is a vital component of an efficient LMC program. The temptation in most organizations is to build rules of access for the benefit of the organization and its workers rather than of the patron. Doctors may see patients only between the hours of 10:00 A.M. and 4:00 P.M. Banks may close at 2:30 P.M. State and federal governmental offices may never be open when the normal worker has time to go to them. On the other hand, most consumer-oriented institutions generally cater to the needs of the majority of patrons. Extended hours of business during the weekdays and weekend hours are just a few of the amenities provided.

Library media specialists are advised to arrange their operational procedures, hours of service, and staffing to benefit patrons, particularly at times when traffic is likely to be heavy. Several basic principles of access are observed:

1. Open hours of the LMC respond to the needs of 99.9 percent of the patrons.

2. All materials and equipment circulate. Exceptions are extremely rare. It is better for equipment and materials to wear out than rust out.

3. Circulation restrictions are based on individual responsibility rather than on assumed group morality. The higher usage figures are, the better.

4. Penalties for noncompliance with LMC rules are administered on an individual basis in preference to group-oriented punishment.

5. Large groups and small groups have access to the LMC by appointment. Individuals have access to the LMC at all times of the school day.

6. Flexible schedules take precedence over rigid schedules.

7. Patrons take their share of responsibility for maintaining collections, circulation details, and warehouse operations. The goal of such responsibilities is to encourage a sense of group pride, ownership, and care of publicly owned property.

8. The LMC is not closed while school is in session. Meetings, workshops, absence of the LMC staff, and LMC operations are no excuse for depriving students of access to the center.

9. Arrangements are made for teachers and students to have access to materials and equipment during vacation periods. This is done cooperatively with public libraries in the community.

10. Teachers and students can expect to have an operating piece of audiovisual equipment where and when it is needed.

Principals should monitor the operational rules of the LMC for access. Each restriction should be viewed from the patron's point of view. The fewer the rules, the better. Punishments assigned to infractions should be applied swiftly, but with a positive outcome.

EVALUATING OPERATIONS

There are many ways of evaluating the operations of a library media center. Only one measure is suggested here, with others included in chapter 12. Since there are so many routines in the LMC, a simple success/failure measure can often be set up to probe whether the routine is accomplishing its objective. Since success/failure measures are easy to construct, tally, and analyze, many different ones can be instituted, all done on a random basis. For example, if only five minutes of the day are available to think about evaluating the success or failure of the warehouse, the same measure could be taken every day for the school year, or, better yet, ten measures could be taken alternatively for one day out of every ten. Ten measures could be taken the first semester and ten others the second. Multiple measures would present a much broader picture of operations than a single one or even several would.

A success/failure measure is essentially a tally sheet which records the number of times a certain operation or service succeeds or fails. Since success rates for LMC operations are generally over 90 percent, so an analysis of why a failure occurred is essential. The following steps outline the creation of a success/failure measure.

1. Decide what operation/routine should be measured.

2. Construct a definition of what constitutes a success and what would be considered a failure. This is a very important step, since a great deal of latitude can be taken in a definition, or very little. For example, a successful circulation of a 16mm projector may be defined as one in which the projector was available when requested, and was used and returned without a malfunction. Or, a successful circulation of a 16mm projector could be tallied only on the basis that it was taken in and out of the LMC door. Failure, in the latter case, would include any requests that could not be filled.

3. Construct a tally sheet with columns for tally marks: Successes, Failures, and Reason for Failure.

4. Decide by whom, when, and how the measure will be taken. To improve accuracy, the person directly connected with the operation or routine should mark the tally sheet as each success or failure occurs or at the same time each day when memory is fresh.

5. Collect the data.

6. Analyze the rate of success as a percentage of the total. Analyze the reasons for failure.

7. Take appropriate action to redesign the operation if the failure rate is unacceptable.

Figure 9.19, page 136, is a sample tally sheet which shows the number of times requests for periodical articles are actually filled.

An analysis of the failures could result in making provision for a larger periodical collection, duplication of popular periodicals on microfiche, better storage and retrieval systems for periodicals, or better ways of distributing student topics so that everyone isn't after the same few articles.[5]

Examples of other possible measures:

1. How often a certain type of equipment or a certain piece of equipment works or malfunctions.

2. How often a trained operator is available/is not available to use a complex piece of equipment.

3. How often requests for equipment were turned down because equipment was undergoing repair.

4. How often certain materials are available/unavailable.

5. How often collections of materials respond/don't respond with the requested item.

6. How often the LMC facility responds/can't respond to group requests in terms of space.

7. How often materials processing for new items took more than five working days.

8. How often student/teacher successes were/were not displayed in the LMC.

9. How often the LMC is open/closed to regular patron business.

10. How many hours students did/did not have professional guidance when using the LMC.

11. How often students were given/denied access to home circulation of audiovisual equipment.

Periodical Success Rate Form

Dates taken: _____

Criteria: The patron receives the correct magazine and the article needed is actually in that magazine (assuming that the patron has the citation correct).

# of Successes	# of Failures Tallied by Reason
	Periodical in use:
	Periodical missing:
	Periodical there but article missing:
	Periodical not in the collection:

Fig. 9.19. Periodical success rate form.

NOTES

1. The frustration of the part-time library media specialist has been demonstrated in a number of research studies, for example, David V. Loertscher and Phyllis Land, "An Empirical Study of Media Services in Indiana Elementary Schools," *School Media Quarterly* 4, no. 1 (Fall 1975): 8-18.

2. See David V. Loertscher and May Lein Ho, *Computerized Collection Development for School Library Media Centers* (Fayetteville, Ark.: Hi Willow Research and Publishing, 1986).

3. Jean Donham, "Developing a District Plan for a Middle-sized School District," in *The Microcomputer Facility and the School Library Media Specialist*, E. Blanche Woolls and David V. Loertscher, eds. (Chicago: American Library Association, 1986), 165-70.

4. David V. Loertscher, "Administrative Uses," in *The Microcomputer Facility and the School Library Media Specialist*, E. Blanche Woolls and David V. Loertscher, eds. (Chicago: American Library Association, 1986), 63-64.

5. For an example of using the suggested periodical measure, see Tom Olson, "Periodicals on Microfiche," in *Measures of Excellence for School Library Media Centers*, David V. Loertscher, ed. (Englewood, Colo.: Libraries Unlimited, 1988), 126-36.

ADDITIONAL READINGS

Manuals

Adams, Helen R. *School Media Policy Development: A Practical Process for Small Districts*. Littleton, Colo.: Libraries Unlimited, 1986.
　　Contains many sample policies on a wide range of topics and how to put them in force.

Nickel, Mildred L. *Steps to Service: A Handbook of Procedures for the School Library Media Center*. Chicago: American Library Association, 1975.
　　The most well known library media manual on the market.

Procedures Manual for School Library Media Centers. Oklahoma City, Okla.: Oklahoma State Department of Education, 1982.
　　One of the best procedures manuals available. It is an amalgamation of many available manuals from all parts of the country.

Collections

Van Orden, Phyllis. *The Collection Program in Schools: Concepts, Practices, and Information Sources*. Englewood, Colo.: Libraries Unlimited, 1988.
　　Van Orden has combined her two previous volumes into a single one and covers most of the theories of collection which have been popular in the last quarter of a century.

White, Brenda H., ed. *Collection Management for School Library Media Centers*. New York: Haworth Press, 1986. Also published as *Collection Management 7*, no. 3/4 (Fall 1985/ Winter 1985-1986).

A collection of theoretical and practical articles written by many well-known library media specialists and library educators.

Technology

Casiero, Albert J., and Raymond G. Roney. *Audiovisual Technology Primer*. Englewood, Colo.: Libraries Unlimited, 1988.

A basic text which covers most of the forms of technology that a library media specialist will have to know. It provides an excellent review for those who think they are familiar with technology but who desire a somewhat more technical approach.

Costa, Betty, and Marie Costa. *A Micro Handbook for Small Libraries and Media Centers*. 2nd ed. Littleton, Colo.: Libraries Unlimited, 1986.

The most popular introductory work for computers in the school library media program.

Murray, William, ed. *A Guide to Basic Media Materials and Equipment Operations Training*. Aurora, Colo.: Aurora Public Schools, 1985. Order address: 875 Peoria St., Aurora, CO 80011, $8.53.

An excellent handbook and training guide for simple repair and maintenance of audiovisual equipment.

Vertical Program Features of the Library Media Program

Library media specialists come to their jobs with a whole array of individual interests and talents. Whatever these are, a very fine program can be built which crosses the curriculum and the grade levels of the school where the librarian practices. There can be one or many of these programs depending on the size and talents of the LMC staff and the needs of a school or district. Many districts set program emphases as district goals. There are also state, regional, and national programs from time to time which can and should affect the LMC program.

As with every program of the library media center, success is more likely if the program is integrated with classroom agendas. In fact, the library media specialist may only promote and assist in a program rather than take the total responsibility for its success. There is only so much room on anyone's back for monkeys.

This chapter provides samples of just a few of the wide array of programs which might be promoted by the LMC staff. Library skills, research skills, information analysis, reading motivation, technology skills, cultural literacy, gifted and talented, and enjoyment are those that are fleshed out. Others are suggested at the end of the chapter.

One of the dangers of installing a vertical program feature is that it can begin to dominate the entire program of the library media center. It can be so overwhelming that there is no time for the basics. In the past ten years, the national trend to teach every child a course in library skills is an example of an overwhelming program which often crushes out other legitimate programs. One library media specialist from Iowa counted the number of hours she was required to teach students in grades four through six library skills. She determined that every student spent more time learning library skills in just three years, than she had spent in getting a master's degree in library science! Library skills are not bad, but if they crowd out other concerns, then their role should be reassessed.

The author wrote a very controversial article for *School Library Activities Monthly* in which library skills were severely criticized. That article could have been about any of the vertical program features covered in this chapter. It describes a situation in which a program becomes a behemoth, a giant juggernaut pushing every other program of the LMC out to make room for itself. The article follows.

GOLDEN LIBRARY CHILLS AWARD*

The following is a true report to the author. Only the names and locations have been changed to protect the guilty.

Rhonda Harvey was hired as an elementary school library media specialist in Goldmine, Kansas. She had learned one role for school library media specialist in her library education but in the interview for the job with the principal, she learned that he had something else in mind. Needing the job badly, Rhonda agreed.

"In this school," the principal said, "Our teachers need a 45 minute break each day for their planning period. To accomplish this, we have hired music, physical education and now library teachers. We would like you to teach library skills to each of the classes in the school for 45 minutes twice a week. We certainly hope that by doing this, the scores on the reference section of our basic skills tests will improve. Here is your schedule."

Rhonda noted that 90% of her day was taken up with library skills classes so that there was little time to be devoted to the myriad of other duties that she knew needed done.

The first two weeks of her schedule were difficult for Rhonda because she was preparing her

curriculum. She wondered why her professors at the local university had been so little help for this practical challenge. One of the biggest problems was the constant interruption of her library skills classes by students from other classes coming into the library. Since the library was small, any student coming in distracted her class and teachers had a bad habit of sending notes with students requesting materials. Rhonda decided that something had to give.

Rhonda scheduled an appointment with the principal. "You have hired me to teach library skills classes, but students from other classes keep coming in and disturbing us. I feel that I need uninterrupted time to teach. Therefore, I'd like to ask that we set a policy that no one may come to the library when skills classes are in session."

The principal agreed.

The policy statement was distributed to the faculty. Some grumbling was heard in the teacher's lounge, but since planning periods were sacred, no solution was suggested openly. Thus, 90% of the time, no one except scheduled groups may go to the Goldmine Elementary School Library—neither teachers nor students.

The GOLDEN LIBRARY CHILLS AWARD is presented to Rhonda for completely missing the point of the function of a library and to her principal who was gullible enough to write an extraordinarily foolish policy on library usage.

---

*From David V. Loertscher, "Golden Library Chills Award," *School Library Media Activities Monthly* 2, no. 10 (June 1986): 46. Reprinted by permission of LMS Associates, *School Library Media Activities Monthly*, © 1986.

P.S. If you find yourself as a library media specialist in a similar situation, do the children of America a favor. Quit. If you are a principal and your library media specialist favors the closing of the library to use, fire that person.

In a similar article, the author made the case why too much stock should not be placed in library skills as the central component of any library media program. That article follows.

THE CHALICE

On a lovely fall evening in the Ozarks in the year of our Lord 1998, the 12 disciples of library skills led a small procession of high school seniors and television camera technicians through the blazing red and orange foliage into a small protected clearing. Since 1986, the disciples had retreated annually to this sacred spot, but tonight was the first occasion for outside visitors.

In the center of the clearing, a stone altar had been built and the group seated themselves, cross-legged, in a semi-circle before the shrine. When the TV cameras were readied, the chief disciple rose to address the group and the world.

"Twelve years ago, in 1986, a famous encyclopedia company gave a very large grant for the creation of a multi-type library skills continuum. The publication was heralded throughout the land as *the* definitive guide and standard for the nation. Using the seed money generated by the grant, other funds were sought. A national campaign was conducted to herald the arrival of the guide and to promote its use. State departments of education mandated use of the guide. K-12 scope and sequence charts were constructed. Library media specialists implemented a massive effort to teach the lessons beginning in Kindergarten and continuing through grade twelve.

Thirty-seven million students were taught for 45 minutes a week for 20 weeks each year to complete the instruction. Five hundred fifty-five million (555,000,000) hours were invested each year in the project for a total of 6,660,000,000,000 hours or 760,273,973 person years."

"For twelve years, this august body has conducted a massive longitudinal study of the results through strict standardized testing and re-teaching programs for those students who feel below the minimally accepted score. The senior class of 1998 is the first generation of students to complete the entire program. During this year, a national library skills competition has taken place and six finalists have been selected to be here this evening."

The television camera technicians were just about to zoom in on the faces of the six high school seniors when a dazzling vision burst over the altar. Descending out of heaven in a shaft of light were an elaborately decorated silver flask and six crystal goblets of exquisite design. As the flask came to rest just above the altar, a golden mesh fence appeared surrounding the flask. A small gate studded with diamonds gave entrance to the flask but was locked with a small platinum lock. A sign on the gate read: Insert the right library skill key into the lock and you may enjoy the elixir of lifelong learning.

The chief disciple invited the first student to the altar. "What key do you bring, young man?" "I bring the key of the Dewey Decimal System which I have studied for 12 years," replied the lad. "I know the 10 main classes, 37 subject numbers, 10 of my favorite subject classification numbers, and regularly volunteer in the library at school to classify all the new materials." "Insert the Dewey key into the lock," commanded the disciple. The boy slipped the key into the lock and turned. Nothing happened. The disciples groaned. The boy was dejected and crumpled in his seat.

The second student brought her key, "Catalog Card Skills," to the gate, bragging of a perfect memorization of every item of information and its location on the card including indentation, punctuation (AACR2), and capitalization. The key would not unlock the gate. Another groan pierced the night air.

One by one, the other four students brought their keys forward. The key of the *Reader's Guide*, the key of the Printed Encyclopedia, the key of the Hand-Written and Typed Research Report, and the key of Sears Subject Headings. Each key failed.

The students were horrified; the disciples, appalled. The camera technicians kept recording. Before anyone could recover from the devastation, a voice came from heaven.

"In the world of 1998, students who use large libraries must navigate their way through the Library of Congress Classification, card catalogs have been replaced by computer catalogs, printed encyclopedias are now on compact discs, periodical indexes are online, typed and hand-written papers are word processed, technical thesauri—not Sears are used. The generic information skills needed by this generation are missing."

The leading disciple rushed toward the cameras to pull the plug. It was too late. The next day, a class action suit was filed against the school librarians of the United States for malpractice.

The point of the article, of course, is that we must be careful to prepare our young people for the world that they will live in, as best we can forecast that world, rather than the one we grew up in. Figure 10.1 illustrates a role of the library media specialist which is not likely to go out of style in the 1980s, the 1990s or beyond. It contains the single statement, "Helping teachers teach concepts is more important than teaching library skills."

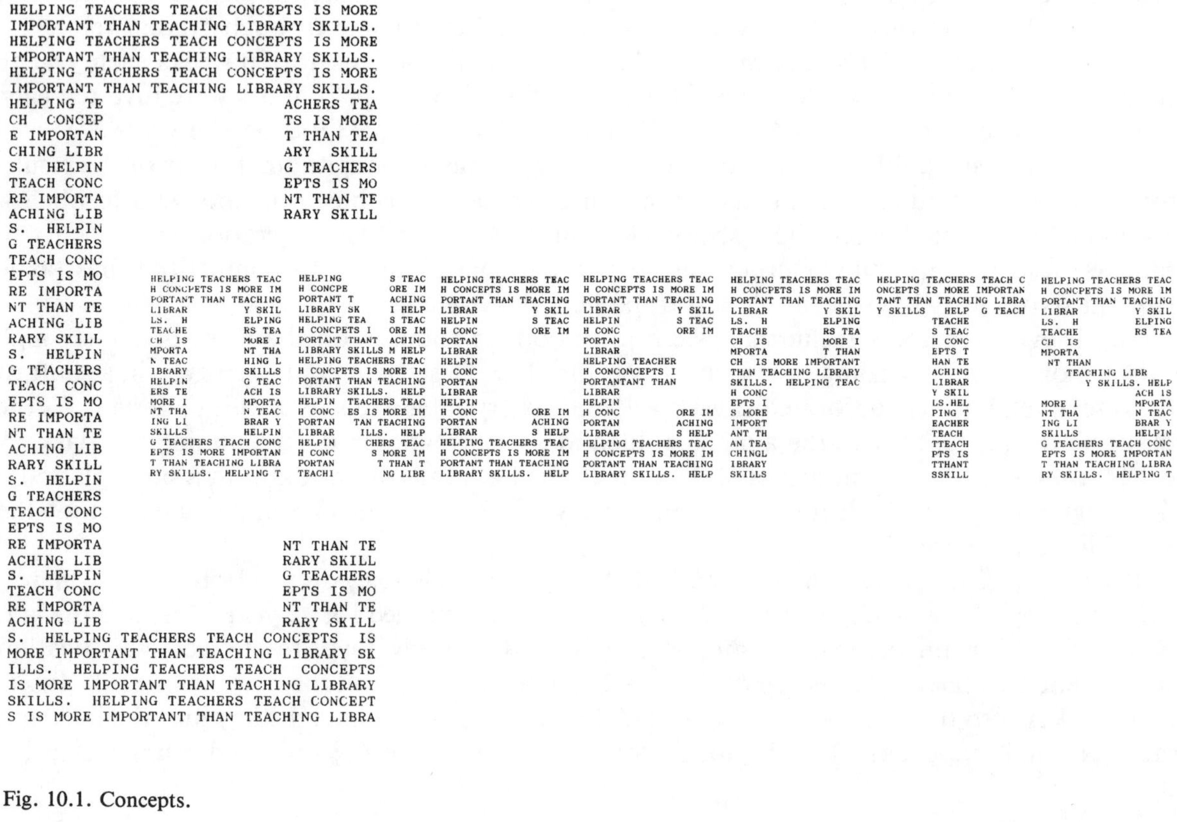

Fig. 10.1. Concepts.

The articles and figure contain a harsh indictment for those who allow any program, be it library skills, reading motivation, or technology skills to crowd out the central function of the library media program which is the support of resource-based teaching. Care must be taken by library media specialists not to get caught up in a fad which will not only crowd out that central function, but will imprison them.

The remainder of this chapter focuses on some of the best programs available to library media specialists, gives examples of these programs in the schools, and provides a few simple ways in which to evaluate the impact of these programs.

LIBRARY SKILLS

Concept

A program of library skills teaches students to orient themselves to an LMC facility, and how to find, select, and use the resources of the center to good advantage. There are numerous checklists or continuums of library skills in the literature, and most suggest a grade level for teaching and reviewing the skills. *Partners in Action* contains a sample list, an excerpt of which is in figure 10.2.

Topic	Awareness	Mastery	Maintenance
A. Library-Resource-Centre Orientation			
1. Know location of LRC	K	1	2-13
2. Identify LRC personnel	K	1-2	3-13
3. Observe LRC rules and manners	K	1-2	3-13
4. Identify specific terms for LRC furniture	K	1-3	4-13
5. Check out own books(s)	K	1	2-13
6. Check out all other material	1	2-3	4-13
7. Know how to renew material	1	2	3-13
8. Identify areas of LRC	K-2	3-4	5-13
9. Identify kinds of media	K-2	3-4	5-13
10. Handle material properly	K-2	3-6	7-13
B. Organization of Resources			
1. Know the location and arrangement of the following:			
a. picture books	K	1	2-13
b. fiction books	2	3-5	6-13
c. non-fiction books	K-3	4-8	9-13
d. general reference material	1-3	4-9	10-13
e. audio-visual materials	K-3	4-10	11-13
f. periodicals	K-3	4-8	9-13
g. vertical-file material	3-4	5-10	11-13
h. specialized reference materials	3-10	9-12	13
i. periodical indexes	7-10	11-12	13

(Figure 10.2 continues on page 144.)

Topic	Awareness	Mastery	Maintenance
2. Identify author, title, and subject cards in the card catalogue	3	4-8	9-13
3. Locate materials according to call number	1-3	4-8	9-13
C. Selection of Resources			
1. Distinguish between fiction and non-fiction	K-3	4-8	9-13
2. Select materials from resources outside the school	K-3	4-10	11-13
3. Use the card catalogue as a selection tool	3-6	7-8	9-13
4. Distinguish between Canadian and non-Canadian material where relevant	K-6	7-10	11-13
5. Select desired materials independently	K-8	9-10	11-13
6. Proceed from general to specific or vice versa when researching a subject	5-8	9-10	11-13
7. Select general reference material	3-8	9-10	11-13
8. Select specialized reference material	3-10	9-12	13
9. Evaluate material for currency	4-8	9-10	11-13
10. Identify stereotyping, bias, and prejudice	K-13	9-13	
11. Select material that presents alternative points of view	5-10	11-12	13
12. Use a bibliography to select additional information	7-10	11-12	13
13. Identify primary, secondary, and tertiary sources	7-11	12-13	
D. Utilization of Resources			
1. Know parts and aspects of a book:			
a. front, back, spine, cover	K	1	2-13
b. name of author, illustrator, and/or editor	K	1-2	3-13
c. table of contents, title page, index	1-2	3-6	7-13
d. name of publisher, copyright date	3-4	5-11	12-13
e. bibliography, glossary, footnotes	5-8	9-12	12-13
2. Use and compare material appropriate to reading level and need:			
a. audio-visual material	K-3	4-10	11-13
b. vertical-file material	3-4	5-10	11-13
c. periodicals	2-8	9-10	11-13
d. general reference material	3-8	9-10	11-13
e. specialized reference material	3-10	9-12	13
f. periodical indexes	7-10	11-12	13
g. different levels of sources: primary, secondary, tertiary	7-11	12-13	

Fig. 10.2. Teaching and reviewing library skills. From *Partners in Action: The Library Resource Centre in the School Curriculum* (Toronto: Ontario Ministry of Education, 1982), 30-31.

Library media specialists in the state of Minnesota summarized these skills under the heading "Accessing Information," and created the following objective:

Learners will become familiar with and understand the potential of the wide variety of information sources and personnel available in their schools, communities, state, nation, and global society. Learners will be able to locate and use information from these sources. Learners will actively pursue information according to their particular academic and individual needs. The learner will understand that there are a variety of formats and materials available to accommodate all ability levels and learning styles.[1]

The Connecticut LMC manual provides a sample unit entitled "Understanding Electricity" which demonstrates how a library media specialist and a teacher work as a team to teach both the concepts of electricity and several library skills (location of materials, use of indexes, and preparation of bibliographies). What is particularly interesting about this unit is the note at the end. A previously jointly planned unit had failed, necessitating a complete redesign by the library media specialist and the teacher.

Example: Understanding Electricity*

Grace Roche
Guilford Public Schools

Competency Area II
Grade Level 5 - 6
Subject area: Science

I Objectives

Subject Area Objectives

1. To identify pertinent biographical data on an assigned scientist, focusing on the individual's background in relation to scientific discovery.

2. To communicate orally basic knowledge about the scientist's life and scientific discovery.

3. To demonstrate understanding of basic principals of electricity used by the scientists in their work.

Library Media Skills Objectives

1. To select appropriate nonfiction and reference materials for obtaining information.

2. To utilize indexes in order to locate specific information within a book.

3. To prepare a simple bibliography.

---

*From *Instruction in Library Media Skills: A Supplement to "A Guide to School Library Media Programs"* (Hartford, Conn.: Connecticut Department of Education, 1984), 63-65. Reprinted with permission.

II Activities

A. The teacher will assign students the names of scientists who have made major contributions in the field of electricity and will explain that there will be class time for library research. The teacher also explains that the following will be expected of each student:

1. Oral presentation in the format of a news broadcast or show. Limited to most important aspects of individual's life and events relating to scientific discovery.

2. Written script of the oral presentation.

3. Bibliography with a minimum of two sources (with only one encyclopedia).

4. Model or chart relating to experiment or discovery.

B. Research activities

1. Suitable book collection assembled by library media specialist and put on reserve.

2. Class is held daily in the library for one week.

3. Students are assigned to work in pairs in order to provide the opportunity to discuss ideas and therefore help to understand concepts.

4. During library class time, the teacher and the library media specialist work with students to check:

-- their selection of reference books and books from the reserve collection

-- their ability to use indexes to find information on the specific topics.

5. Library media specialist distributes bibliography sample and instructs individual students on the proper bibliographic form.

C. Making of Models and Charts

1. Complete in science lab under direction of the teacher.

2. Student's assignment sheet suggests projects.

3. Reserve collection of library books is placed in the lab for this part of the unit.

D. Oral Presentation (in form of news broadcast or talk show)

1. Presented in library media center with props (including models and charts). K-12 science coordinator attends.

2. Can be videotaped for later sharing with students and to keep as a reserve to use with future students.

III   Resources/bibliography

1.   Appropriate information sources in science and biography.

2.   Multiple copies of annotated booklist of key sources.

3.   Bibliography sample.

4.   Post board, construction paper, scissors, glue, markers, etc. for charts.

5.   Materials needed for science models.

6.   Videotape recorder, camera, monitor, tapes.

IV   Evaluation

Each student (working in pairs) is expected to complete the projects listed under activities. The projects are to demonstrate pertinent knowledge of a key scientist's life as well as knowledge and understanding of the concepts which his/her discovery or experiment involved.

The teacher will evaluate the accuracy and comprehensiveness of the student's knowledge and understanding. The library media specialist and the teacher will jointly assess the student's use of sources and the way in which learning is expressed through the oral presentations, charts, and models.

Note: This unit is a revision of a previous unit that both the teacher and the library media specialist felt needed to be improved. The original unit required students to write a short "research paper" on a scientist who had made a major contribution in the field of electricity. Because most students did not understand the complexity of the scientist's work or theory, students usually copied insignificant biographical information. Important electrical concepts and experiments were also copied with little comprehension. The research paper was not an effective method for understanding basic concepts of electricity. The activities described above have proved to be more effective.

Evaluation

Library media specialists may consider their library skills programs a success if the students can demonstrate a degree of independence in locating and using information and materials. Progress can be noted through observation as the teacher and library media specialist involve students in the location of materials and information. In addition, a number of printed tests can be administered which measure some aspects of library skills.

RESEARCH SKILLS

Concept

A program of research skills teaches students search strategies for finding the materials and information they need. Some library media specialists include study skills as a part of research skills since it often takes hard work and persistence to ferret out what is needed. *Partners in Action* lists a few of these skills under the heading "comprehension and study skills" (see figure 10.3).

Topic	Awareness	Mastery	Maintenance
1. Identify main idea, facts, and/or concepts in material appropriate to level of comprehension:			
a. orally presented materials		K-13	
b. audio-visual material		K-13	
c. written material	2-3	4-13	
2. Use audio-visual clues to aid in understanding material	K-1	2-3	4-13
3. Know how to work independently and in small groups	1-2	3-6	7-13
4. Record facts:			
a. by completing a sentence or a simple outline	1-2	3-6	7-13
b. visually	K-8	4-8	9-13
c. by making jot notes	3-6	7-10	11-13
d. orally	K-7	8-13	
e. by writing an outline using prescribed standardized procedures	5-8	9-10	11-13
5. Use alphabetical order	1-6	4-8	9-13
6. Use table of contents	1-5	6-8	9-13
7. Record bibliographical information	3-5	6-11	12-13
8. Use key words	2-6	7-8	9-13
9. Use index	2-6	7-8	9-13
10. Skim to get overview and to select relevant material	4-6	7-10	11-13
11. Use cross references	6-9	8-10	11-13
12. Recognize the use of and prepare footnotes	7-10	11-13	

Fig. 10.3. Comprehension and study skills. *Partners in Action: The Library Resource Centre in the School Curriculum* (Toronto: Ontario Ministry of Education, 1982), 31.

A fine example of a research system has been produced in the Information Skills in the Curriculum Research Unit of the Inner London Education Authority in England. Their inquiry framework is printed here (see figure 10.4).

The Stages of Your Project

- **what do I need to do?**

  what topic should I choose?

  what is the topic?

  what do I already know about this topic and what must I find out?

- **where could I go and when?**

  what sources exist?

  how accessible are they?

  how appropriate is each one to the topic?

  where do I go first?

  do I need to create my own information?

- **how do I get at what I want?**

  what procedures should I follow?

- **which shall I use?**

  how should I choose?

  what resources are there?

  how can I tell which to select?

  what other sources could they lead me to?

- **how shall I use them?**

  what will help me to find the information I'm looking for?

  what strategies could I use?

- **what should I make a record of?**

  what is important?

  how could I record it?

  how should I arrange it?

- **have I got the information I need?**

  what have I got?

  what do I think?

  what does it all add up to?

  have I got what I need?

  should I look further?

- **how should I present it?**

  in what form could I present it (if choice allowed)?

  who is my audience?

  how should I report it?

  how could I structure it?

- **how have I done?**

  in my opinion?

  according to others?

  what knowledge have I learned?

  what skills have I learned?

  what should I improve and how?

Fig. 10.4. The stages of your project. From *Information Skills in the Secondary Curriculum* by permission of the Schools Council and Methuen Educational Ltd., London, England. Also printed in Terence Brake, *The Inquiry Framework* (London: Information Skills in the Curriculum Research Unit, Inner London Education Authority, 1983). See also Ann Irving, *Study and Information Skills across the Curriculum* (London: Heinemann Educational Books, 1985).

One of the best categorizations of the research process has come from two library media specialists in Fayetteville, Arkansas. Barbara Stripling and Judy Pitts, working as a team, have posed dual taxonomies which link the research and the thinking process together. Their taxonomies and brief examples are given below.

Teaching a Library Research Process That Develops Critical Thinking Skills*

CONSIDERATIONS IN PLANNING A RESEARCH UNIT:

Thoughtful Research

At the beginning of each library research project, librarians and teachers must decide how much they want the students to think about their research. Library research may be performed at many different levels of thought from very simple fact-finding to complex conceptualizing.

Thoughtful Reactions

Students must be required to react to their research in some way. Their reactions may vary in the amount of thinking required from simple recalling to complex model building or hypothesizing, and their reactions may be in a variety of formats (written and visual).

LEVELS OF THOUGHT IN RESEARCH AND REACTIONS:

The following taxonomies represent the levels of thought in research and in reactions to research. Through practice, students can develop the skills necessary to succeed at more complex levels of research and reactions.

* *

RESEARCH TAXONOMY	REACTIONS TAXONOMY
Fact-finding	Recalling
Asking—Searching	Explaining
Examining—Organizing	Analyzing
Evaluating—Deliberating	Challenging
Integrating—Concluding	Transforming
Conceptualizing	Synthesizing

* *

*From Barbara Stripling and Judy Pitts, *Brainstorms and Blueprints: Teaching Library Research as a Thinking Process* (Englewood, Colo.: Libraries Unlimited, 1988).

* *

LEVEL 1

RESEARCH

REACTION

Fact-finding

Figuring out prior knowledge and feelings about subject

Finding simple facts using simple locating skills

Recalling

Recalling and reporting the main facts discovered

Making no attempt to analyze the information or reorganize it for comparison purposes

Sample Assignment: Math
Students will:
Research—
— be given a list of famous mathematicians.
— use reference books such as *McGraw-Hill Encyclopedia of World Biography* to discover each mathematician's contribution.
Reaction—
— use the researched information to construct a *crossword puzzle.*

* *

LEVEL 2

RESEARCH

REACTION

Asking—Searching

Figuring out general area to investigate

Defining the specific problem or questions

Pursuing answers to questions using research strategies

Explaining

Recalling and restating, summarizing, or paraphrasing information

Finding examples, explaining events or actions

Understanding the information well enough to be able to put it in a new context

Sample Assignment: History
Students will:
Research—
— be assigned a specific historical event.
— write questions about the main points they want to find out.
— use a research process to find information about their event in one reference book and one regular book.
Reaction—
— dramatize their information in the form of an *on-the-spot radio report* such as the famous Hindenburg crash description. Incorporate into the dramatization background information about the topic.

* *

* *

LEVEL 3

RESEARCH

REACTION

Examining—Organizing

Deciding whether information is appropriate, whether it answers questions

Grouping information by categories/questions

Analyzing

Breaking a subject into its component parts (causes, effects, problems, solutions)

Comparing one part with another

Sample Assignment: Health

Students will:

Research—

— choose a specific communicable disease (for example, polio) to research.
— write questions that will lead to finding out about the history of the disease and important social and political events around the time a cure/vaccine for the disease was discovered.
— use a research process to find information about the topic in reference and regular books and periodicals if appropriate.
— categorize every item of information by the question it answers and by the time or year in which it occurred.

Reaction—

— construct a *timeline* to correlate the medical research to social and political events.

* *

LEVEL 4

RESEARCH

REACTION

Evaluating—Deliberating

Deciding value of material

Judging bias, inaccuracy

Weighing evidence on both sides of issue

Challenging

Making critical judgments about subject based on internal or external standards

Sample Assignment: English

Students will:

Research—

— read a novel published since 1940.
— use a research process to find critical information about the author and novel.
— assess the quality of the novel according to standards established in class and judge the quality of the criticisms found in reviews of the novel.
— combine their own critical opinions with those of the critics they judge to be most reputable.

Reaction—

— produce one of the following:
    — a *book review* for the school or local newspaper.
    — a videotaped review for local public access TV or viewing by other English classes.
    — an audiotaped review in the style of those aired on National Public Radio for playback on the local radio station or to English classes.

* *

* *

LEVEL 5

RESEARCH   REACTION

Integrating—Concluding

Pulling the information together and integrating it with previous knowledge

Drawing own conclusions from information found

Transforming

Bringing together more than one piece of information, forming own conclusion, and presenting that conclusion in a creative new format

Sample Assignment: Science
Students will:
Research—

— choose an ecological problem facing our country such as smog, acid rain, litter, chemical waste dumps, etc.
— use a research process to investigate and evaluate that problem and solutions that have been tried.
— draw their own conclusions about the best solution to the problem and be able to support those conclusions with evidence.

Reaction—

— use the researched information and conclusions to design and produce an *advertising campaign* to convince viewers and readers to act on the "best solution" proposed by the researcher. The campaign could include a brochure, television commercial, bumper sticker, etc.

* *

LEVEL 6

RESEARCH   REACTION

Conceptualizing

Forming own concept, model, or theory based on the evidence collected, evaluated and integrated

Synthesizing

Creating an entirely original product based on the new concept or theory

Sample Assignment: Psychology/Sociology
Students will:
Research—

— use a research process to investigate an adolescent problem (drinking, suicide, crime, dropouts).
— investigate community programs that treat or attempt to alleviate that problem.
— evaluate the extent of the adolescent problem and the successes and failures of the community programs.
— design a *model program* to be instituted in the school, community, or church which would address the adolescent problem in a new way or would improve the services offered by the community programs already in place.

Reaction—

— generate a presentation on the model program to be delivered to the appropriate agencies. Include visuals and handouts with the presentation.

* *

There are several other student guides to the research process which provide students with a very clear outline of how to do research and write up the result in a report or term paper. The first, *Write It*, was written by a team of library media specialists and an English teacher at the Cherry Creek, Colorado, High School under the direction of Betty Bankhead.[2] The second set of guides, one each for social studies, literature, and science, detail research in subject specific areas. These guides are by Robert Skapura, library media specialist at Concord High School in California and a former English teacher, John Marlowe, now principal in Danville, California.[3] Library media specialists and teachers now have excellent tools available to make the research process a coordinated and meaningful experience.

Two sample units of instruction are provided here. The first is a typical research unit, in which students select an author, find information about that author, and then produce some sort of product, which in this case is an oral report.

The second comes close to a test of research skills. A math teacher and the library media specialist together have created a research contest with math implications. In this unique unit, students are creating the questions for which research skills would be required. In an extension of this unit, other students might use the products created by their peers in an actual research question test. Students might be divided into groups for their "hunt for information." One trained student would be assigned to each group to observe the research skills used by the group. The winners of the information hunt would be the group who not only solved the equation, but whose information searching strategies were the best.

Example #1: Researching Foreign Authors*

Maureen Reilly
Regional School District # 10

Competency Area II
Grade Levels 11 - 12
Subject Area: Foreign Language (e.g., Spanish or French)

I Objectives

Subject Area Objectives

1. To identify for an author whose work has been read in class:
    — basic facts of his/her life;
    — interesting personal information;
    — types of literature written (e.g., novels, drama, poetry);
    — important works, dates and brief descriptions of these works;
    — literary reputation/what the critics have said.

Library Media Skills Objectives

1. To demonstrate competence in previously taught skill of using card catalog.

2. To independently use special references especially in the area of literature and biography.

3. To extract pertinent information for a specific topic.

*From *Instruction in Library Media Skills: A Supplement to "A Guide to School Library Media Programs"* (Hartford, Conn.: Connecticut Department of Education, 1984), 97-100. Reprinted with permission.

II   Activities

1. The teacher will assign an author to each student and explain that a 5-10 minute oral report will be required which covers the information listed above under Subject Area Objectives. The report should be given in French or Spanish if research materials written in the target language are available to the students. Accompanying hand-outs indicating some of the required facts will also be expected.

2. The teacher and library media specialist discuss the assignment and schedule class time in the media center.

3. During the initial session, the library media specialist will quickly note the use of the card catalog and suggest how students should determine headings under which to search. For example, the cataloging of literature under country of origin (e.g., "French Literature") can be briefly indicated.

4. Also during the initial session, the library media specialist will point out and explain the use of special references such as:

Twentieth Century Authors	*World Authors*
European Authors (1000-1900)	*Contemporary Authors*
Contemporary Literary Criticism	*Biography Index*
Magill's Author Criticisms	*Encyclopedia of Drama*
Current Biography	*Encyclopedia of World Biography*

5. As a partial alternative to the above, students can also be given a copy of a guide to literary research which the library media center has prepared for student use. An example of this type of "customized guide" is included at the end of the description of this activity.

6. The students will proceed to locate at least three sources, read through information on the selected author, and extract information that covers subject area objectives.

7. Students take appropriate notes and organize and write information needed for oral report and accompanying hand-out.

III   Resources

Reference titles such as those listed in Exhibit A (following).

IV   Evaluation

Each student will locate and use three appropriate sources on the selected author and extract specified information. The successful identification of this information and use of sources will be demonstrated in the culminating report which is shared with classmates. A bibliography will also be submitted.

Exhibit A
Researching Foreign Authors

To: Students doing research on literature

From: The Library Media Center

The "helpful hints" below will hopefully be of assistance to you in completing your research.

1.   Locating sources in the Nonfiction area

The first category of materials from which you will probably want to find sources is the nonfiction collection. To locate a book about an author, look under that writer's last name in the card catalog. Books about the author will have the name printed in all *capital letters* on the top of the card. If the name is in small letters, the book described on the card is written *by* the writer you are searching. (Of course, you may also be interested in reading works by an author as well as sources written about him/her.)

To expand your resources, you will also want to look under headings that are broader than just the individual author. In other words, think of the "larger literary topic" of which your author may be a part. For example, if you are researching F. Scott Fitzgerald, you could also look under AMERICAN FICTION. Through doing this, you may find a book such as one on American novels of the twentieth century that has a whole chapter or section on Fitzgerald. To find this out, you will most likely have to locate the book on the shelves and look up your topic in the index.

2.   Great American Writers microfiche series

This series consists of reprinted *New York Times* articles on quite a range of American authors. Subject cards for all the writers covered are individually filed in the card catalog, so source material from this series can be located in the same way as other nonfiction.

3.   Magazines

Magazines may have included articles on different authors. Writers covered may often be more current, but "retrospective" articles on authors from the past may also have appeared.

Magazine articles can be located through using the *Readers' Guide to Periodical Literature*.

The Reference Area

Finally, you will probably find valuable material on literature in our special subject reference books. Titles which may be helpful include:

803/c272e	*Cassell's Encyclopedia of World Literature*—biographies, histories, special articles
803/C	*Columbia Dictionary of Modern European Literature*—includes analytical articles on authors
803/D	*Dictionary of Literary Biography*—8 volumes with lengthy articles on individual authors/includes:
	American Renaissance in New England
	Antebellum Writers in New York and the South
	American Writers in Paris 1920-1939
	American Poets since World War II
	American Novelists since World War II
803/V	*Great Writers of the English Language*—3 volumes of scholarly articles on Dramatists, Novelists, and Poets
809.2/M	*McGraw-Hill Encyclopedia of World Drama*—lengthy articles on individual playwrights
820.3/H262	*Oxford Companion to English Literature*—handbook of short articles
	Twentieth Century American Dramatists
	Twentieth Century American Science Fiction Writers
	American Novelists; 1910-1945
	American Humorists; 1800-1950
810.3/H441	*Reader's Guide of American Literature*—dictionary of terms, authors, etc.
810.9/A	*American Writers*—8 volume set with lengthy articles
810.9/B	*Fifteen Modern American Authors*—survey of research and criticism
810.9/C	*History of American Literature*
810.9/C	*Modern American Literature*—collection of criticism organized by author
820.3/B266	*New Century Handbook of English Literature*—dictionary of authors, characters, terms
820.9/S48	*Concise Cambridge History of English Literature*

822.33/C153r   *Reader's Encyclopedia of Shakespeare*—one volume "dictionary" dealing just with topics related to Shakespeare

840.3/H2620   *Oxford Companion to French Literature*—handbook of short articles

880.3/H2620   *Oxford Companion to Classical Literature*—handbook of short articles

920/E139c   *Contemporary Authors*—multi-volume set with biographical and critical information on current writers

920.3/v786c   *Contemporary Poets*—critical articles on current poets

920.3/v786c   *Contemporary Novelists*—critical articles on current novelists

Also shelved in the 920.3's are a series of reference books, published by the H. W. Wilson Company, with biographical and critical articles on authors. Books in this series include:

European Authors 1000-1900

British Authors of the Nineteenth Century

American Authors 1600-1900

Twentieth Century Authors

World Authors 1950-1970

World Authors 1970-1975

Greek and Latin Authors

Example #2: Math Scavenger Hunt:
A Contest in Mathematics*

Emma Lou Benedict
Ridgefield Public Schools

Competency Area I
Grade Level 7
Subject Area: Mathematics

I Objectives

Subject Area Objectives

1. To perform mathematical operations using a calculator.

2. To perform computations accurately and in the correct order.

Library Media Skills Objectives

1. To locate special areas in the library media center.

2. To locate the center's special reference materials particularly in the area of mathematics.

3. To become motivated to use such materials not only for the contest but also for assigned work, independent study and leisure reading.

II Activities

The activity described here is a mathematics contest, co-sponsored by the Library Media Center and the Mathematics Department, open to all students.

Students will be given an algebraic expression to evaluate. It is suggested that there be 3 different expressions of varying difficulty, to provide for different levels of ability and achievement. The value of the expression will be found by determining the value of each variable which may be found by completing mathematical computations, locating certain areas in the LMC, or by finding the answers to specific research questions. The following is an example of a simple question:

Find the value of X if:

$$X = \frac{(B+D)(C-A)}{F} - G^E$$

---

*From *Instruction in Library Media Skills: A Supplement to "A Guide to School Library Media Programs"* (Hartford, Conn.: Connecticut Department of Education, 1984), 71-76. Reprinted with permission.

and

A = Number of moons of Mars

B = Largest 3 digit palindromic number not ending in 9

C = Birth year of Tony Randall

D = Number of white keys on a piano

E = Number of Presidents who have served less than one year

F = Number of primes less than eleven

G = Number of countries that border Hungary

Math teacher responsibilities

1. Teach the students the mathematics skills necessary to perform the computations and to solve the equation.

2. Prepare the equations and determine the values of the variables.

3. Determine the correct answer.

4. Check contest entries for correct solution.

Library Media Specialist responsibilities

1. Introduce the students to the types of materials to be used.

2. Introduce specific materials and areas of the LMC.

3. Prepare bibliography, entry blanks, rules, etc.

4. Check answer sources if a disagreement arises as to the correct answer for a variable value.

The library media specialist and the math teacher will jointly publicize the contest and seek to provide prizes for the winners from school or PTA/PTO funds. They will prepare joint news releases to school and local papers and other appropriate media outlets.

III Materials/resources

Suggested rules. (These can be attached to the contest entry forms.)

1. You may use computers, calculators, textbooks, reference books, maps, fingers, toes, etc.

2. All answers should be *your* answers—no help.

3. Entry blanks must be filled out completely, including not only the value for X but also each variable and the source of the answer if a reference source was used. The value of X should be expressed as an integer or a mixed number.

4. For each of the problems the winning entry will be the one that correctly states the value for X. If no entry correctly states the value of X, the winner will be the entry with the greatest number of correct values for the variables. Ties will be broken by random drawing.

5. There will be first prizes in each expression — (state prizes).

6. Entries must be placed in the contest box in the LMC by _____ on _____.

7. State which ability and grade levels should use which of the 3 problems.

GOOD LUCK!

Math Scavenger Hunt

Name _____

Math grade or level _____

Math teacher _____

Answer X = _____

Problem 1

$$X = U(E+G) + \frac{K}{P} - H^A + BVF - \frac{ST}{A} + M(D + W) + TOM + WS - B - C + Q(R - L) + JN + C^H$$

Variable Source	Variable Source
A =	M =
B =	N =
C =	O =
D =	P =
E =	Q =
F =	R =
G =	S =
H =	T =
I =	U =
J =	V =
K =	W =
L =	

*Be sure to give the title of the book you used for the reference question and the page on which you found your answer.

Sample variables

A. What is the number of primes less than twenty five?
B. What is the largest three-digit palindromic number?
C. Give the number of degrees in each central angle of a regular octagon?
D. What is the number of edges on one face of a parallelepiped?

E. $X^2 + 5X + 6 = 0$ X = ?

F. How many drawers in the SUBJECT side of the card catalog have cards beginning with the letter "S"?

G. How many paperback racks does the LMC have?

H. How many stairs are there to climb when you go from the main floor to the balcony?

I. How many computers are there in the Computer Lab?

J. What is the numerical value of the 7th key from the left on the top row of the keys of the Apple II computer?

K. How many home runs did Mantle hit in the year Maris hit 61?

L. What is the atomic number of krypton?

M. How many sides of a trapezium are parallel?

N. In what year was Leonardo Fibonacci born?

O. How many barometers did Pascal's brother-in-law carry up the sides of the Puy-de-Dome mountain?

What is/are:

P. The number of miles between Hartford and New Haven?

Q. The number of thieves Ali Baba had to contend with?

R. The first three digits of the zip code of Custer City, Oklahoma?

S. The street number of the White House?

T. The number of years Robinson Crusoe was alone on his island before Friday arrived?

U. The number of landlocked countries in South America?

V. The number of card catalog drawers on the SUBJECT side of the card catalog in the ERJHS library?

W. The year in which the Alamo fell?

Bibliography

East Ridge Junior High School Library Mathematics Contest
Sample Sources

"Arithmetic is numbers you squeeze from your head to your hand to your pencil till you get the answer."
                                                                          Carl Sandburg

811.08 Plotz, H.   IMAGINATION'S OTHER PLACE: POEMS OF SCIENCE AND MATHEMATICS

Types of Reference Materials

R031   *Encyclopedias*—multivolume sets of general information on all subjects. Good place to start when researching a subject. USE THE INDEX!

(For scientific subjects try:)

R503	SCIENCE AND TECHNOLOGY ENCYCLOPEDIA
R510.3	Newman UNIVERSAL ENCYCLOPEDIA OF MATHEMATICS
R031.03	*Almanacs*—the most useful single volume, yearly collection of facts, statistics, tables and general information. USE THE INDEX! For other sources of statistics, try:

R	STATISTICAL ABSTRACT OF THE UNITED STATES
R973.2	HISTORICAL STATISTICS OF THE UNITED STATES
R551.6	Huffner THE WEATHER ALMANAC

R423	*Dictionaries*—for word meanings, derivation, often brief encyclopedic information. Ex.—American Heritage DICTIONARY OF THE ENGLISH LANGUAGE. For specialized words, try:

R510.3	James MATHEMATICS DICTIONARY

R920	*Biography*—for information about people—past and present, including birth and death dates and, often, addresses. Ex.—CURRENT BIOGRAPHY—people currently in the news. Use index volumes 1950, 1960, 1970, 1979. For scientists and mathematicians, try:

R925	Asimov BIOGRAPHICAL ENCYCLOPEDIA OF SCIENCE AND TECHNOLOGY

ENJOY THESE FROM THE MATHEMATICS SECTION   510 - 519

510	Abbott, E. FLATLAND—a story in two dimensions
510.7	Kadesch, R. MATH MENAGERIE—math projects
510.9	Rogers, J. STORY OF MATHEMATICS FOR YOUNG PEOPLE—math history

IV Evaluation

1. Students are expected to be able to perform the computations correctly.

2. Students are expected to be able to find the correct answers to the research and location questions in the resources of the LMC. Achievement will be measured by the number of correct answers to each variable and the number of correct solutions to the equation.

The math teacher and the library media specialist will also evaluate the overall success of the contest on the basis of:

1. The number of participants.

2. The number of correctly completed variable values.

3. The number of correct solutions to the equation.

Evaluation

Library media specialists and teachers might set up a number of strategies to evaluate whether progress is being made in research skills. Paper and pencil tests are one means; simulated research quests are another. In the latter test, students are given an information problem. They must detail their research process and are evaluated upon the quality of their search strategy.

INFORMATION ANALYSIS (SKILLS)

Concept

Information analysis (skills) have not been as well defined as other types of skills. The ballooning of information in the past twenty years has presented great problems to information seekers who are looking for the "needle in the haystack."

The Minnesota manual uses the term *processing information* and defines the goal as follows:

> The learner will comprehend and apply concepts presented in media. The learner will apply critical reading, viewing and listening skills in resource selection and in analyzing available resources. The learner will apply thinking processes in organizing, analyzing, and interpreting information and developing evaluative skills in order to become an intelligent consumer of information for the purpose of solving problems and making decisions.[4]

Partners in Action provides a sequence for some of these skills which they label "critical reading, viewing and listening" (see figure 10.5).

Topic	Awareness	Mastery	Maintenance
1. Compare sources for differing viewpoints and to verify facts	3-4	5-6	7-13
2. Formulate questions (content and reasoning type)	4	5-6	7-13
3. Distinguish among fact, fantasy and opinion	K-9	10-13	
4. Recognize the effect of sound and colour on mood and content	K-9	10-13	
5. Recognize and interpret symbolism	K-9	10-13	
6. Recognize stereotyping in all forms	K-10	11-13	
7. Recognize bias and prejudice	K-11	11-13	
8. Recognize the effect of juxtaposition of images	K-10	11-13	

Fig. 10.5. Critical reading, viewing and listening. From *Partners in Action: The Library Resource Centre in the School Curriculum* (Toronto: Ontario Ministry of Education, 1982), 32.

Other scholars have added to the list the following:

1. Determining the reliability of a source.

2. Distinguishing relevant from irrelevant information, claims or reasons.

3. Identifying unstated assumptions.

4. Identifying ambiguous or equivocal claims or arguments. Recognizing logical inconsistencies or fallacies in a life of reasoning.

5. Thinking about one's own thinking process (metacognition).

6. Knowing how to tackle difficult materials or ideas.

7. Questioning one's own understanding of a concept.

8. Building problem solving skills.

9. Knowing how to learn by sharing ideas with others.

10. Knowing how to ask the right questions.[5]

There is a great deal of work to be done to define information skills needed by children which will effectively prepare them for the information society. Evaluative measures of a student's information skills are only hinted at in the literature.

The Connecticut manual includes a sample information skills unit which helps students to interpret information on graphs and tables. Students are involved in the collection of data about themselves and then this information is used to create charts. An alternative activity which has become quite popular is to have students create a computerized database from which they can do many different analyses, charts, diagrams, and graphs, and from which they can draw conclusions.

Example: Graphs and Tables*

Betty V. Billman
Connecticut State Department of Education

Competency Area III
Grade Level 4
Subject Area: Mathematics

I Objectives

Subject Area Objectives

1. To construct information tables.

2. To read tables and find information from them.

3. To demonstrate ability to construct bar graphs in which information is labeled on two axes.

Library Media Skills Objectives

1. To interpret data from maps, graphs and charts.

2. To develop an awareness and evaluation of his/her own television viewing habits.

II Activities

1. Library media specialist records (or locates) "Problem Solving: Making a Table" and "Using Bar Graphs" episodes from the *It Figures* instructional television series.

2. Library media specialist provides teacher with an accompanying teacher guide and student worksheets.

3. Teacher shows "Problem Solving: Making a Table" to the math class and does all or part of the activities with the class.

4. Library media specialist conducts a class discussion in the library media center on television viewing and how it fits into the students' lives. This may involve the use of a TV fact quiz, asking what students' favorite TV shows are and why, and estimating how many hours a day they spend watching television.

5. Media specialist asks students to design a chart to help them evaluate their viewing habits.

6. Students are asked to record their viewing activities for one week using the chart.

7. After one week the teacher shows "Using Bar Graphs" and does worksheet activities with students.

---

*From *Instruction in Library Media Skills: A Supplement to "A Guide to School Library Media Programs"* (Hartford, Conn.: Connecticut Department of Education, 1984), 45-54. Reprinted with permission.

8. Students are asked to make a bar graph of their viewing habits using the data they have collected over the past week. A bar graph of cumulative data for the entire class might also be done.

III   Materials/Resources

Agency for Instructional Television. "It Figures: Teacher's Guide." Bloomington, Indiana, 1982.

Baratta-Lorton, Mary. *Mathematics Their Way*. Massachusetts, Addison-Wesley, 1976.

Connecticut State Board of Education. *A Guide to Curriculum Development in Mathematics*. Hartford, Connecticut, 1981.

Connecticut State Board of Education. *A Guide to School Library Media Programs*. Hartford, Connecticut, 1983.

Far West Laboratory for Educational Research and Development. "A Family Guide to Television." California, 1979.

Hilliard, Robert L. and Hyman H. Field. *Television and the Teacher: A Handbook for Classroom Use*. Hastings, Pennsylvania, 1975.

Singer, Dorothy and Jerome and Diane Zuckerman. *Getting the Most Out of Television*. Goodyear, California, 1981. (There are also seven video tapes that can be purchased that accompany *Getting the Most Out of Television*, from ABC Wide World of Learning, New York.)

The local school math curriculum and adopted text should also be consulted. Equipment resources necessary include a videotape recorder and television set.

IV   Evaluation

Effectiveness of the lessons can be determined by evaluating the student's ability to:

1. Transfer TV viewing data to a bar graph.

2. Make and use charts and/or bar graphs successfully on classroom math tests.

3. Apply the use of charts and graphs to other problem solving situations and activities in other subject areas.

4. Identify information given on graphs and charts found in books, television, newspapers and magazines.

5. Understand and accurately describe his/her television viewing habits.

A more subjective evaluation should be based on a conversation between the teacher and the library media specialist as to their perceptions of student enthusiasm for the projects, increased use of the library media center, and the adequacy of the library media center collections to provide in-depth information and to reinforce the classroom activities.

Exhibit A
Graphs and Tables

Using Bar Graphs

*This program shows how bar graphs
present information visually, and shows the function of each component.*

16

Before the Program

Suggest to students that during this program they watch for what Andy, David, and Kris learn about making a bar graph.

The Program

Linda is in the hospital recovering from a bicycle accident. She was hit by a car at an unmarked corner on the way to school. Her classmates think that a crosswalk is needed at that corner, but their teacher, Mr. Martinez, knows they will need to prove their case to get action from the traffic commission.

The class collects evidence—counting cars that pass the spot during the day—and Mr. Martinez shows them how to put their data on a bar graph to make it easier to understand. However, when Andy, David, and Kris bring the graph to Linda, she isn't able to understand it. They have forgotten to label the parts of the graph. (*Animation occurs here.*)

Realizing the problem, the youngsters first add a title, then label the axes and the scale. Now Linda can understand the bar graph, and when Mr. Martinez sees it the next day he thinks they have proved their point.

Animation—The Queen of Hearts has been making delicious tarts. In fact, they are so good that someone has been stealing a number of them. To help solve the crime, the King keeps track of how many tarts are eaten each day, and when the information is put on a graph the culprit's identity is obvious.

Questions

1. When Andy, David, and Kris brought their information to Mr. Martinez, why did he suggest that they make a bar graph?
2. Why wasn't Linda able to understand the bar graph when her friends first showed it to her?
3. What did the Queen of Hearts tell the King to do to make his graph understandable?
4. How did a graph help the Queen of Hearts figure out who was eating the tarts?
5. What did Linda's friends add to the graph to make it easier for her to understand?

Activities

1. LABELING AND READING A GRAPH.
On the chalkboard draw the unlabeled graph from the program. (Graph 1 below.) Have students label the parts of the graph as in Graph 2, describing the function of each label. When the graph is completed, discuss how the graph shows that a crosswalk is needed.

GRAPH 1

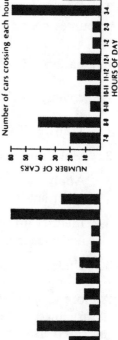

GRAPH 2

Number of cars crossing each hour

NUMBER OF CARS

HOURS OF DAY

2. LOOKING FOR GRAPHS.
Have students find samples of bar graphs in newspapers, magazines, or books and bring them to class. Display all the graphs, and then discuss:

What the graphs have in common
How the graphs are titled and labeled
The scales used on the graphs
The different kinds of information presented
Why some graphs are easier to read than others

3. GRAPH INTERPRETATION.
On the chalkboard draw the graphs shown below. Then read the following problem to students:

The manager of the local bank wanted to make sure that she had enough people working at the bank to wait on customers. She did not want the customers to have to wait in long lines. She also did not want to have too many people working each day, since that would cost the bank money.

Ask students to look at the graphs and try to answer these questions.

On which days does the bank manager need to have the most people working?
On which day can she have the fewest people working?

WEEK 1
Customers per day

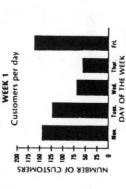

NUMBER OF CUSTOMERS

DAY OF THE WEEK

WEEK 2
Customers per day

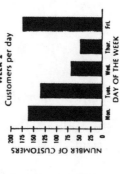

NUMBER OF CUSTOMERS

DAY OF THE WEEK

4. COLLECTION OF DATA AND GRAPH CONSTRUCTION.
Materials. Students will need graph paper, pencils, and time to collect data.
Have each student make a graph using the following steps:

Select a topic. Each student should select his or her own topic. Possible topics include: favorite fruit, favorite time of day, normal bedtime, or chores done at home.

Decide on data sources. Students should decide what group of people they are going to poll, and pick a realistic number of informants to interview.

Collect data. Suggest to students that when they collect their information they should use a tally chart similar to the one used in the program.

Make a graph.
  a. Using graph paper, draw the bottom scale. Label it.
  b. Draw the side scale and label it.
  c. Fill in the bars.
  d. Title the graph.

Analyze the graph. When students have completed their graphs, discuss the results that are shown on them.

Using Bar Graphs

16 Student Worksheet

The Queen of Hearts took a survey to see what kind of tarts she should make. These are the data she collected:

FLAVORS

Apple	⁷⁷ ⧵⧵	Blueberry	⧸⧸⧸ ⧸⧸⧸ ⧸⧸⧸⧸	Strawberry	⧸⧸⧸ ⧸⧸⧸ ⧸⧸⧸ ⧸⧸⧸⧸
Banana	⧸⧸	Cherry	⧸⧸⧸ ⧸⧸⧸ ⧸	Peach	⧸⧸⧸

Apple: **7**

1. Write the total for each flavor in the squares on the tally chart above.

2. The Queen made a graph using the data she collected. Help her finish labeling the parts of the graph. Add the title and label the side and bottom.

   Use the graph to answer the rest of the questions for the Queen.

3. What flavor is liked the most?

   _____

4. What flavor is liked the least?

   _____

5. If the Queen wants to make only the four most popular flavors, which ones should she make?

   _____
   _____

6. Take a survey of your, class, family, or other group and see which flavor tart they like best. Make a graph using the data.

APPLE

0   1

From *Teacher's Guide to "It Figures."* Bloomington, Indiana: Agency for Instructional Television, 1982.

Sample Viewing Log

DAY	NAME OF PROGRAM	MINUTES WATCHED	TOTAL FOR THE DAY
Monday	_____	_____	
	_____	_____	
	_____	_____	
	_____	_____	
	_____	_____	_____
Tuesday	_____	_____	
	_____	_____	
	_____	_____	
	_____	_____	
	_____	_____	_____
Wednesday	_____	_____	
	_____	_____	
	_____	_____	
	_____	_____	
	_____	_____	_____
Thursday	_____	_____	
	_____	_____	
	_____	_____	
	_____	_____	
	_____	_____	_____

DAY	NAME OF PROGRAM	MINUTES WATCHED	TOTAL FOR THE DAY
Friday	_____	_____	
	_____	_____	
	_____	_____	
	_____	_____	
	_____	_____	_____
Saturday	_____	_____	
	_____	_____	
	_____	_____	
	_____	_____	
	_____	_____	_____

TOTAL TIME FOR THE WEEK _____

Evaluation

Evaluating information skills can be done much like reference skills. A combination of paper, pencil test, observation, and performance tests will provide library media specialists and teachers with signs of progress toward the objectives planned.

READING MOTIVATION

Concept

In the second edition of the widely circulated *What Works*, created by the U.S. Department of Education, a number of commonsense principles supported by research findings dealt with both the importance of reading and the methods for promoting it. Those which have implications for school library media centers follow:

- The best way for parents to help their children become better readers is to read to them—even when they are very young. Children benefit most from reading aloud when they discuss stories, learn to identify letters and words, and talk about the meaning of words.

- Children improve their reading ability by reading a lot. Reading achievement is directly related to the amount of reading children do in school and outside.

- Children get more out of a reading assignment when the teacher precedes the lesson with background information and follows it with discussion.

- Telling young children stories can motivate them to read. Storytelling also introduces them to cultural values and literary traditions before they can read, write, and talk about stories by themselves.

- Hearing good readers read and encouraging students repeatedly to read a passage aloud helps them become good readers.

- The use of libraries enhances reading skills and encourages independent learning.[6]

For a number of years, library media specialists have been worried about their contribution to standardized test scores. If the statements from *What Works* are true, and if the library media specialist has a joint program of reading motivation, then librarians can certainly claim credit for better readers. What portion of the reading score is attributable to the library media program is impossible to isolate, but teachers and parents cannot isolate their part of the score either. There are lots of reasons why young people learn to read successfully, and many can take partial credit for this success.

The creators of basal readers have gone overboard on the teaching of isolated and extremely precise reading skills—so much so, that many of the young people of the United States know how to read but don't enjoy it and don't do it unless required. Library media specialists have been and will continue to be interested in building the life-long reading habit. The task is to join hands with classroom teachers, reading specialists, and parents to promote and build this trait. This effort must span both the elementary years and secondary schooling, for there are many pressures on young people for their time and interest and attention. Every teacher in the school should know that the library media specialist is interested in a reading motivation program and will conduct one with or without the teacher. To be sure, cooperative efforts will produce better results, but if the LMC must go it alone, so be it.

In a recent survey of reading research, the author found several principles to guide library media specialists in their reading motivational programs. They were to:

1. Involve parents in the reading motivational program if possible.

2. See that every child is read to every day (grades K-12).

3. Have a period of sustained silent reading on a regular basis.

4. Flood children and young people with good books.

5. Use many and varied techniques to interest and involve young people in reading`and don't give up.

There has never been a better time in the history of the world to flood young people with great literature. Every year, more than 2,000 new picture books are published and hundreds of books written specifically for young adults are becoming available. Libraries that can afford to buy at least one book a year per student can provide for the needs and interests of each student. But once purchased, the books must be put into the hands of the students.

Many people and organizations are interested in building the reading habit and promoting books to children and young people. Library media specialists and teachers should participate in many of these programs. Just a few of the ideas are to:

1. Participate in a "Reading Is Fundamental" (RIF) program.

2. Work with a local business such as Pizza Hut in a reading motivational program.

3. Start a reading Olympics program.

4. Participate in national programs sponsored by the American Library Association, The Children's Book Council, The National Council for Teachers of English. Such programs include National Library Week, National Children's Book week, Library Media Month, The Year of the Reader, and many other celebrations.

Recently, the author wrote a brief article for *School Library Media Activities Monthly* urging library media specialists to flood children and young people with good books. The article and a little saying from Arkansas are reprinted here.

Recreating the Flood*

Airplane wings are magical things
That work on such plain, simple law.
You already know it; I'm certain I could show it,
If you'd just drink that juice through this straw.

Likewise, dear Corrigan, my favorite librarian,
There's a plain, simple rule about reading.
You can teach kids to do it, and thoroughly enjoy it,
If you'll immerse them in good books morn' 'til evening.

One of the most delightful findings of a recent study of elementary school library media centers in the 270 schools listed by the U.S. Department of Education as "exemplary" in 1986, was that the encouragement of reading is still the foundation of quality LMC programming.

But many of us may be accused and should be strung up from the nearest coat rack for preventing children from interacting with books! Could it be that we are shooting ourselves in the foot? Consider the following:

One librarian I know does not allow kindergarten children to touch books—only adults may do so.

A principal on the east coast does not allow any of the children in the school to check materials out of the library!

Thousands of other library media specialists allow children only one book to be checked out per visit and can now enforce this rule rigidly through automated circulation control.

Recently, one library media specialist remarked: If a child will read 40 books, the reward is being allowed to check out *two* books at a time.

In practice, library media specialists seem to be saying that two principles are in conflict:

1. Children and young adults need large quantities of reading material available if they are to learn to enjoy reading.

2. Children and young adults should be taught responsibility and respect for public property.

Stated negatively, we might say: It is the disposition of almost all children and young adults, when given the opportunity to check out all the materials they can carry, they will lose track of most, never return many, and will become careless in handling this precious and often scarce commodity.

Or there's the argument: Our collection is too small to allow readers to take all they want.

Or the question: How would we handle the circulation and reshelving of the entire LMC collection every day if patrons were allowed to rape the shelves?

What advice should we give to the new library media specialist in a 90% Black, urban middle school library when she realizes that every title of remote interest to her patrons has been stolen?

*From David V. Loertscher, "Recreating the Flood," *School Library Media Activities Monthly* 3, no. 6 (February 1987): 46, 48. Reprinted with permission from LMS Associates, *School Library Media Activities Monthly*, © 1987.

When the only books that are left on the shelves are titles enjoyed by critics or suburban, affluent children, what should she do with the 100 high interest titles she has just purchased?

In the face of discouragement, we must face the fact: Every child deserves to learn how to read and to enjoy it. If we really believe that, then we must plan our regulations to carry out its mandate.

If we think about it, every child or young person comes to us with a varying sense of responsibility. Could our regulations reflect that variability and also encourage responsibility? Suppose we allowed every child to have a library bank card and encouraged each to establish a credit history. But our credit history would have one major difference from bank credit histories—library credit cards would be much more liberal. We would make sure that our automated circulation systems would alert us to poor credit risks, but these young people would be referred to the library media specialist who would work with that student individually to improve responsibility, yet stress accessability.

Used negatively, automated circulation systems can tighten the noose around the child's neck who doesn't handle materials well and will cut off access to materials entirely. Who among us wants to be known as a deterent to reading?

If we are to win the war of television vs. reading with our young people, we must shovel materials at these budding adults. We *can* work out ways to allow materials use to vary in direct proportion to demonstrated responsibility, BUT FOR READERS' SAKE, LET'S NEVER TURN OFF THE FAUCET.

THINK FLOOD!

EVEN THE INMATES OF TUCKER PRISON CAN CHECK OUT THREE BOOKS EVERY TIME THEY VISIT THE LIBRARY.

Shirley A. Carmony, Chair of the English Department at New Castle Chrysler High School in New Castle, Indiana, details how she and the library media specialist worked together to incorporate young adult novels into the reading curriculum as a way of promoting life-long reading. Her brief article is reprinted here from *Voice of Youth Advocates*.

Example: "... I've Never Read So Much in My Life, But It's Not Bad!"*

In the past 20 years I have heard again and again the sad lament of the English teacher and the librarian: "These kids just won't read anymore." For years it seemed to me, too, that this was a fair assessment of what we were seeing. It seemed regrettable but also undeniable. However, some recent additions we have made to our sophomore English program have resulted in differences that have changed my viewpoint. In the past two years we have developed and written into our curriculum a reading program that has far exceeded our expectations.

The beginnings of this program were really quite ordinary. First of all, we were called upon to develop a new sophomore program in between book adoptions. What this meant in reality was that the teachers had to define objectives, write curriculum, and create their own teaching materials; we literally had to write our own textbooks to fit the needs we had identified because no books would be purchased for four years. This situation was both a curse and a blessing because while we were desperately trying to fill the time with worthwhile activities, we also began to see some possibilities for a program other people never seemed to have time for.

One of the needs these students had was in reading; the scores were low, and we were trying to address the problem with instruction in study skills and vocabulary development. As we looked for answers, we began to see that we wanted a reading program that did several things. We wanted a program that would: 1) provide an activity that allowed for individual differences in rate of completion of classroom activities, 2) provide for the great volume of reading practice so badly needed, 3) provide enough structure to allow even poor readers to be successful, 4) allow the teacher to direct and administer the program with a minimum of extra work, and 5) provide a means of increasing the student's overall pleasure in reading.

To implement such a program, we knew that we needed multiple copies of a wide selection of titles. This would have been absolutely impossible had it not been for our librarian, who used Title funds towards such a purchase. We ordered Perma-Bound and EconoClad books that were short, relatively easy to read, and high interest. We ordered romances like *P.S. I Love You*, *Love Is Never Enough*, and *Mr. & Mrs. Bo Jo Jones* for the girls. We chose books like *The Contender*, *Tuned Out*, and *Deathwatch* to appeal to the boys. Whatever books one of us could personally recommend or which looked promising, we tried to include. Our primary goal was not literary appreciation but a collection of titles that would interest a wide variety of rather reluctant readers.

As the novels came in, we made further preparations for implementing the program. We wrote a study guide and a 15-point quiz for each so the collection could be easily used by the classroom teacher. Eventually we supplemented these first novels with Scholastic Unit paperbacks once used in classes now no longer taught. For these books, too, we did study guides and

---

*From Shirley A. Carmony, "... I've never read so much in my life, but it's not bad!" *Voice of Youth Advocates* 7, no. 3 (August 1984): 135, 138.

quizzes. One way or another, we acquired enough novels to use in our sophomore non-college-bound classes. At present we have quizzes for approximately 92 different titles.

In actual practice there are several classroom libraries of these books. The teacher has a set of books, a file of study guides for most of these titles, and a file of ten-to-15 point quizzes for each. In order to provide the initial motivation to read, we make 1/5 of the student's grade each six weeks reflect the number of books he has read and passed quizzes on (4 = A, 3 = B, 2 = C, 1 = D). All students do a study guide on the first book of the year, and after that only those students who have difficulty need do a study guide. Some students simply prefer the security of the study guide and will ask for one each time to help assure the A or B on the quiz. Whatever other requirements there are in class for the six weeks, the student knows he is always to be in the midst of reading one of the books.

The program has met our needs in several ways. First of all, it has certainly provided for individual differences in completion of classroom activities. Whenever a student finishes the daily assignment, she knows she is expected to read. The program has also dramatically increased the amount of reading done by students. During the fourth six weeks of the year in a non-college-bound sophomore English class, eight of the 26 students read at least four books for the A. A total of 52 books were read in that section in one six week period. In a college-bound sophomore section where the requirement for an A is five books, 14 of 22 students read at least five books in six weeks. Without a doubt more of their time is spent in reading than we would have seen otherwise.

Another practical need the program has met is ease of handling for the teacher. There are no lengthy book reports to evaluate and no uneasy feelings that the students are getting by with reading only small portions of the books. Quizzes are easily given and graded during class study time. The teacher is not asked to do more work than the student in order to determine credit or noncredit. As a result, the teacher can demand a great deal more reading from all of the students.

Perhaps the most important need the program has addressed is in the area of attitude. For more of these students than ever before, the experience of reading is a positive one. The quizzes are purposely designed to be easily passed if the student has read with basic understanding. Those students who do have particular trouble do study guides. The result is that the student is almost always successful if he has indeed read the book. For some it is a totally new experience to read one book after another successfully, and they seem genuinely pleased to be able to control 1/5 of their grade in this way.

One girl in particular comes to mind as an example of success. At the beginning of the year Amy was identified as a student with reading problems—reading stanine of three. She was placed in a special section for students who did not read well. However, that class was particularly large, and she was transferred to my regular English class. She did a study guide on the first book but failed the quiz. I talked with her about filling out the guide chapter by chapter rather than all at the end. That first six weeks she read only that one book and failed the quiz. The second six weeks she read another book and got a C on the quiz. The third six weeks she read three books and got A + 's on all of the quizzes. It is interesting to see that the fourth six weeks she read five books and received no lower than a C on any quiz. Amy is a different reader than she was at the beginning of the year. She is confident and interested; she even stopped me in the hall one day to ask if the new books had come in and then wanted to check one out right then to read in study hall. Amy's attitude has undergone an enormous change, and it has been rewarding to watch that change slowly come about.

Other students, too, have changed because of the nature of the program. Many of my students started out reading only one kind of book. Girls in particular seem to want nothing but romances. We have a number of these in the collection, and the first few weeks there is a rush on *P.S. I Love You*, *Falling in Love Again*, *Mr. & Mrs. Bo Jo Jones*, *Distant Summer*, and *Love Is Never Enough*. However, because the collection is limited, they eventually run out of these. I am always glad they enjoy reading; it does not matter particularly to me that they stick to the romances. I know that by the end of the first semester they are probably going to be reading something else. Inevitably they come to the end of the romances. Then because they must read for 1/5 of their grade, and because reading has become something of a habit, and because they have begun to trust me, they ask for some advice about other books. Several of these girls have found that they enjoy the more complex books *A Shining Season* or *Death Be Not Proud*. Others have read *And Then There Were None* or other mysteries by Agatha Christie. Still others have even come to some science fiction like *Alas Babylon*. Whatever the direction they go, they will have at least found some alternatives to the first few books they read because the collection they choose from is limited.

I have come to believe that part of the reason kids won't read is that we have not really expected and provided for it. One thing we have found as the program has grown is that when we have really expected and planned a workable structure for it, the kids have responded. This year we even had juniors inquiring about where the books were they would read; they assumed the demand would be made. The most rewarding comment came from a student of mine as she hurriedly checked out a book at the end of class. She said, "You know, I've never read so much in my life." Then she added the words that would warm any English teacher's heart, "But it's not bad!"

Evaluation

Evaluating the effects of reading motivational programs is time consuming and sometimes difficult. Early school librarians and teachers had each student keep a reading diary where every book read was recorded and comments were made. This record accompanied the student throughout the elementary school years. Such a record, if accurately kept and then analyzed by researchers, would provide a true picture of the effects of reading motivational efforts. Library media specialists could analyze the results of booktalks, contests, efforts to promote breadth in reading many genres, and a whole host of other effects. Reading records and diaries were discouraged many years ago because adults found that they were not accurate. Students would forget to record items they had read, recorded items they had not read, and lost the diaries. If the library media specialists could dream up a way to accurately record a student's reading, a wonderful evaluative analysis could be made.

Polly Jean Wickstrom has created an alternative method to check student's reading. Her idea is to build a reading record and check on its accuracy by providing brief multiple choice tests for students to take, so that teachers can check whether or not the student has read and comprehended the book. The tests are easy for the student who has read the book, and a simple recording system keeps track of progress.[7] Another common check on how much students read is to send notes home with each book. Parents certify that the child has read the book and then teachers give credit for the item. This method's success depends on good communication and cooperation with the parents.

TECHNOLOGY SKILLS

Concept

Many library media specialists have discovered that students not only need to be able to communicate in a variety of media, but enjoy doing it. Teachers often include audiovisual production activities because they are highly motivating and require an understanding of the topic before an effective product can be created.

The Minnesota guide provides a succinct goal for this area, which is titled "Communicating Information." "Learners will select the most appropriate technology to communicate their messages. The learner will design, produce, and present information in a variety of formats appropriate to the message being communicated. The learners will use multicultural, gender-fair concepts in the design of the production. Learners will evaluate the presentation of information produced by themselves and others."[8]

Partners in Action lists a few of the possible competencies under the category of "modes of presentation" (see figure 10.6).

Topic	Awareness	Mastery	Maintenance
1. Experience chart	K-1	2-3	4-13
2. Pictures and other artistic activities	K-3	4-8	9-13
3. Dramatization, puppet show	K-3	4-8	9-13
4. Booklet	1-3	4-8	9-13
5. Oral presentation	K-3	4-10	11-13
6. Charts, tables, diagrams	1-5	6-13	
7. Maps and graphs	1-5	6-13	
8. Audio-visual presentation	3-6	7-10	
9. Report on a given topic	3-6	7-11	11-13
10. Interview	1-6	7-11	12-13
11. Model	K-8	9-13	12-13
12. Essay	7-10	11-13	
13. Research paper using standardized procedures	7-10	11-13	
14. Seminar on a given topic	10-13		

Fig. 10.6. Modes of presentation. From *Partners in Action: The Library Resource Centre in the School Curriculum* (Toronto: Ontario Ministry of Education, 1982), 32.

The Connecticut guide lists the following audiovisual competencies for grades 7-8:

Competency IV   Students should demonstrate the ability to communicate through oral, written and visual modes.

Skills

- Use photography to communicate an idea:
    black and white still photos
    super 8 film
    filmstrips
    slides

- Combine print and nonprint elements in a presentation of a single theme.

- Begin interviewing as a communication tool.

- Prepare a slide/tape, videotape or filmstrip using a story-board.

- Prepare simple graphs and charts.

- Determine the most appropriate method or medium for presenting specific information.

- Produce a photo essay.

- Give and take clear directions (written and oral) when working in group activities and audio visual productions.[9]

Many states have media fair competitions for the audiovisual or computer products that students produce. These media fairs often match science fair competitions for excitement and competitive spirit.

The Connecticut guide has an excellent example of how production activities are integrated into a language arts topical study of biography. The outline is instructive for its exemplary merging of the LMC and the classroom for its joint teacher-library media specialist cooperation, and the methods used to capitalize on the resources of the LMC. Library skills are used in preparation for the production skill. The unit has been designed to do preliminary work on video skills, not camera skills. Drymounting and laminating skills are reviewed.

Example: Video Book Reports*

Wilma Narciso
Regional School District #14

Competency Area III
Grade Level 3
Subject Area: Language Arts

I Objectives

Subject Area Objectives

1. To identify specific information and present it in an organized fashion.

2. To develop a distinctive and natural style of oral and written communication.

Library Media Skills Objectives

1. To understand the characteristics of biographies.

2. To understand how biographies are classified and arranged.

3. To locate a biography for a book report.

4. To identify main ideas from a book.

5. To learn how to prepare materials for video production.

II Activities

1. The teacher will discuss what it means to be a famous (or infamous) person.

2. Students will name famous (or infamous) people.

3. The teacher will define the term "biography."

4. The teacher will explain that each student is to select and read one biography.

5. The teacher will list important facts which are to be identified for each famous person—i.e., birth, death, famous deeds, family, contributions.

6. The student will record these important facts on 3x5 index cards.

7. During class time in the library media center, the library media specialist will explain further the nature of biographies; e.g., accuracy, authenticity, design, etc. Examples of biographies will also be shown and described to students.

---

*From *Instruction in Library Media Skills: A Supplement to "A Guide to School Library Media Programs"* (Hartford, Conn.: Connecticut Department of Education, 1984), 43-44. Reprinted with permission.

8. The library media specialist will also show students where biographies are located and how they are classified and arranged.

9. The teacher and library media specialist jointly assist students in selection. Students are encouraged to use knowledge of biography call numbers and arrangement to find books on persons in whom they are interested.

10. The teacher and the library media specialist will assist students in locating pictures relating to biographies; e.g., George Washington at Mount Vernon.

11. Students will be shown how to make a study print: Picture on one side of oaktag and 3x5 note card with facts on opposite side of oaktag sheet.

12. Study prints are then drymounted and laminated with student assistance.

13. Students then do an oral report by using the study print which is held up in front of a video camera while student shares facts with audience.

III   Materials/resources

1. Biographies selected for appropriate grade

2. Oaktag sheets 12x18 or 9x12

3. Dry mount, laminating materials

4. Pictures (of/from/about biography)

5. 3x5 cards

IV   Evaluation

Each student is required to

— select and read one biography for a book report

— identify specific information and organize it on cards

— make a study print

— share information orally on videotape

The library media specialist and the teacher will jointly assess students.

Evaluation

Evaluation of audiovisual production skills can be a very simple matter or a rigorous activity. The library media specialist and the teacher may just observe the progress of students so that the fun and enjoyment of the production activity are emphasized. If a more detailed evaluation is desired, a set of criteria can be shared with the students and used as the basis for judging excellence. These criteria would include:

1. The technical quality of the production.

2. The soundness of the information presented.

3. The organizational structure of the presentation.

4. The creativity demonstrated in the product.

CULTURAL LITERACY

Concept

Library media collections are the repositories of culture. They span a wide diversity of ideas and contain the products of the creative and talented minds of the world. If children can experience the breadth and diversity of these collections, they are well on the road to a liberal education. From time to time, there are many calls by scholars for a liberal vs. a narrow and focused education. E. D. Hirsch, in *Cultural Literacy*, is one of the many voices pleading that young people be educated more broadly.[10]

Working with teachers and administrators, library media specialists can help to create a special program which will ensure that every student while in the school would experience every type of cultural experience, either vicariously or directly, which would build a "cultured individual." The best of every form of literature, art, music, drama, and great ideas can be coordinated and intertwined into the curriculum. Many things can be done. A few suggestions follow:

1. The library media specialist and the art teacher purchase an art print collection and sculpture replicas for the school and see that they hang or are exhibited throughout the building.

2. The music teacher and the library media specialist purchase a collection of music of many cultures and plan ways to see that students hear the best as part of not only music classes, but in social studies, humanities, and literature classes.

3. Teachers and library media specialists work to see that all children visit local cultural events and places: museums, zoos, dramatic theaters, concerts, famous persons who come to the community, and any other significant place or event. When field trips cannot be taken, persons and groups are invited to the school.

4. Library media specialists promote or "booktalk" the best from their collections, including plays, books of paintings, classical music, ethnic music, recorded drama, poetry readings, great short films, television specials, and other special items in the collection.

Parents and local business partners can be a tremendous help in keeping the school informed when cultural events are coming to the local area. Many of these events can be enjoyed by both parents and their children through special showings and at reduced prices.

Sandra Novik of Fairfax County, Virginia, described a cultural arts program which she helped organize for her school in an article published in *School Library Media Activities Monthly*.

Example: Planning and Organizing Cultural Arts Programs for Students: An Extension of Library Media Services*

The school library media center is the central resource and information center of the school. In addition to supporting curriculum needs of faculty and providing print and nonprint materials for its users, learning may be extended through cultural arts programs scheduled and arranged by the library media department. Cultural arts programming may be considered an extension of the library shelf. Arranging for the guest appearances of storytellers, authors, dancers, artists, and musicians is a natural outgrowth of library media services. To consider introducing cultural arts, the following topics should be addressed:

1. Philosophy and rationale for maintaining a cultural arts program in your school.

2. Planning, scheduling, and supervising programs.

3. Selecting guest artists, writers, and performers appropriate to a grade level or curriculum unit.

4. Securing guest artist fees.

5. Providing publicity.

6. Getting feedback and evaluations from participants.

Cultural arts programming at Rocky Run Intermediate School (grades 7 and 8) in Fairfax County, Virginia has been implemented, and a precedent established for its continuation. A checklist was developed to serve as a guide to planning and implementation.

There are those in our profession who say that school library media specialists have more than enough tasks and responsibilities, and do not need the additional responsibilities of a cultural arts program. Who can deny that the demands of the library profession are becoming more complex as we move into the era of high technology? However, if we believe that the library media center is an extension of the classroom learning experience, the justification for taking on another role (cultural arts coordinator) is evident and the payoff real.

School library media specialists are in a key position to extend learning by providing enrichment programs for students. These programs can be considered a form of publicity since they frequently lure students and faculty to the library media center and stimulate curiosity and a desire to learn.

Among the guest authors and performers who have enriched the learning experience of students at Rocky Run School are:

*From Sandra Novik, "Planning and Organizing Cultural Arts Programs for Students: An Extension of Library Media Services," *School Library Media Activities Monthly* 3, no. 10 (June 1987): 30-31. Reprinted with permission from LMS Associates, *School Library Media Activities Monthly*, © 1987.

Alice McGill, poet, folklorist, and actress, who transformed herself into Sojourner Truth, an 83-year-old ex-slave who became one of the most powerful speakers of the nineteenth century. This program provided a glimpse into the post Civil War period in American history.

Vsevolod Lezhnev, Russian cellist, demonstrated the extraordinary versatility of the cello in classical, folk, and jazz music, and talked about contemporary life in the Soviet Union.

Jon Spelman, a professional actor and storyteller, wove tall tales and commented on the art of storytelling.

James Getty portrayed Abraham Lincoln in a unique program that focused on Mr. Lincoln's childhood and his entry into politics.

Candice Ransom, author of young adult historical romances, shared her experiences as a young writer trying to publish.

Other visiting authors who spoke about the craft of writing and the agonies and ecstasies of research include Larry Callen, Phyllis Naylor, Milton Lomask, and Colby Rodowsky.

Librarians are in the business of information and ideas, and these can be presented through stimulating arts programs that support curriculum goals and school objectives.

Checklist for Planning a Cultural Arts Program in Your School or District

☐ 1. Determine the type of program you want. WHO, WHAT, WHEN, WHERE, and HOW.

☐ 2. Identify your audience.

☐ 3. Contact the guest artist and establish a tentative date.

☐ 4. Confirm date and time with school or district administrator.

☐ 5. Order books and other resources so they will be available at the time of the visit.

☐ 6. Provide biographical and other pertinent information about the guest artist.

☐ 7. Make suggestions for pre- and post-visit activities or lessons.

☐ 8. Schedule classes and other interested groups.

☐ 9. Invite special guests including parent volunteers, administrators, and district officers.

☐ 10. Arrange for publicity, such as flyers, PTA news, community newsletters, radio spots, exhibits, displays, and handouts.

☐ 11. Reserve necessary equipment including podiums, video recorders, and microphones.

☐ 12. Prepare a seating chart for class groups and other members of the audience.

☐ 13. Photograph or videotape the program if possible (seek permissions).

☐ 14. Plan a reception or autograph session.

☐ 15. Review and evaluate the program by asking faculty to respond to a brief questionnaire.

☐ 16. Write a letter of thanks to the guest artist.

Evaluation

A group of library media supervisors in Indiana developed a cultural quotient test which would be a fascinating test/game for students in grades 4, 8, and 10.[11] The idea was to assemble a collection of slide images and recorded sounds such as a picture of Frederick Douglass, a picture of the Eiffel Tower, a reproduction of the Mona Lisa, a few bars from Beethoven's Fifth Symphony, a picture from a Caldecott award-winning book, etc. It could be presented as a nontrivial test/contest/game event to see how many students could identify the collection. In addition, a short answer survey/test could be developed with questions such as:

When I think of MUSEUMS, I remember *our trip to see the dinosaurs in Indianapolis*.

When I think of DRAMA, I remember *the play the senior class produced*.

When I think of CLASSICAL MUSIC, I remember *the movie "Amadeus"*.

When I think of GREAT SPEECHES, I remember *listening to the tape of King's "I have a Dream" speech*.

TARGETED STUDENT GROUPS: GIFTED AND TALENTED SAMPLE

Concept

The library media specialist can join forces with any special teacher on the staff such as the gifted teacher, the reading teacher, the special education teacher, the art teacher, the music teacher, the counselor, the nurse, or physical education teacher to provide a special program for certain students in the school. In the absence of special teachers, the library media specialist should cooperate with the classroom teacher to determine which students need special assistance and how that help can be provided. The library media center provides a perfect laboratory for individuals with special needs. Realizing that fact and doing something about it takes time, cooperation with classroom teachers and other specialists, an organizational structure which encourages attention to individuals, and a willingness on the part of the library media specialist to lead or cooperate with others in building opportunities for special children.

Jerry Flack, a professor of gifted and talented education in the School of Education at the University of Colorado, Colorado Springs, provides some recommendations to library media specialists who are either leading programs for the gifted or are cooperating with gifted and talented teachers to create one. He provides some pointers to library media specialists embarking on a gifted program:

1. Promote a sense of independence gained from self-directed learning through self-initiated searches. That means that a program of individualized research skills needs to be taught. The student will not only need to know how to find materials but how to evaluate those resources once obtained.

2. The gifted student might be encouraged to explore advanced ideas and do research on advanced topics far beyond what textbooks and curriculum guides generally suggest.

3. A program of individual reading guidance is a must for the gifted student to draw a path through great literature, share the love of good books, help develop a sense of literary criticism and analysis of great ideas, sampling the classics of the past and the best of contemporary writers, and introducing great authors as human beings.

4. Special programs might be provided to the gifted which might include:
   a. A study of philosophy through the reading of great books.
   b. An Odyssey of the Mind program
   c. A Future Problem Solving team
   d. A Junior Great Books discussion group[12]

Flack quotes this sage advice which can guide both teachers and library media specialists in creating programs for the gifted: "Gifted students should not be viewed as silent partners in their relationships with library media specialists," and adds that librarians and teachers "should strive to be 'not the sage on the stage, but the guide on the side.'"

Example: *The Tasaday:* A Non-Primitive Culture

The Tasaday: A Non-Primitive Culture

Subject: Honors History

Grades 7-8

Objectives: To explore a primitive culture known widely to the world until it is discovered a hoax. To explore the nature of primary and secondary source materials. To explore the ethics of historical and anthropological research.

Method: Teach students the difference between primary and secondary source materials. Working as a team with the library media specialist, learn how to determine the authenticity of primary sources and secondary sources. Can students discover a conflict between what a primary source actually says and a secondary resource reports about that document?

Have students explore the culture of the Tasaday peoples as they were known before 1986. Use the library media center and networks to uncover as many sources of information about the Tasaday peoples as possible. Start with the *National Geographic* article by Kenneth MacLeish in the August 1972 issue (pp. 219-49). Find filmstrips, books, articles and any other sources of information. Scrutinize each source as a primary or secondary source. Can students reconstruct that primitive society?

Hint: In 1971, in the Philippines on the island of Mindanow, a small group of primitive people were discovered in rain forest country who were living as their ancestors had done 50,000 years before. The world was fascinated by the discovery of a primitive society.

After students have reconstructed the Tasaday society, allow them to research information in the library media center that was produced after 1986. They should uncover stories, articles, and perhaps books written about the hoax of the Tasaday society.

Re-analyze the documents from before 1986. Were there clues of a fraud? Had any of the students suspected a fraud? Explore the reasons for the hoax. What are the ethics involved? Were any laws broken? What are the consequences of poor or misleading scholarship? What are the consequences of purposeful misinformation?

Have the students produce an audiovisual presentation in the library media center which shows how they researched a primitive society that later turned out to be a hoax. Allow them to share their work with other groups in the school and perhaps a group of parents.

Note: Such a unit is probably good only if it is a surprise. Usually there are enough hoax examples from the world of scholarship to do such a study in a different area if students already know about this one.

Evaluation

Evaluation of targeted student group programs is done by judging whether the objectives of the program have been met and whether learning has taken place. Some affective measures/observations should also be used to judge the impact.

ENJOYMENT

Concept

One danger in any library media center is to be so well organized, so structured that the LMC is as businesslike as is the classroom. Many library media specialists make special efforts to build enjoyment and relaxation into the program, the facilities, and the ambience of the center. They realize that there is no better place in the school to relieve tension and the pressure of course demands than an inviting and attractive LMC.

Examples

In order to create an atmosphere of enjoyment, many library media specialists:

1. Provide an area of comfortable chairs for lounging. This often becomes a place for quiet conversation with friends, enjoyment of materials, or just a place to sit and rest.

2. Provide individual spaces to "get away from it all." It is not uncommon to find private spaces to curl up and read or enjoy a favorite magazine. Fur-lined bathtubs, reading

row boats, large "reading houses" with space big enough for a pillow and a person, and reading nooks and crannies with soft pillows are just a few of the spaces provided.

3. Provide plenty of interesting do-it-yourself centers or displays which can be used by anyone and which are changed regularly.

4. Provide small group conference areas for groups planning events, doing small group projects, or just socializing.

5. Provide plenty of materials on display which entice visitors to "try me out."

6. Provide areas to view the best of what students have created in the school (paintings, awards, projects, etc.).

Students feel free to browse, use the materials of the center, engage in activities provided, taste a little culture, explore an interest, and just be themselves. To provide a sense of relaxation, the library media specialist might make one and only one rule (see figure 10.7).

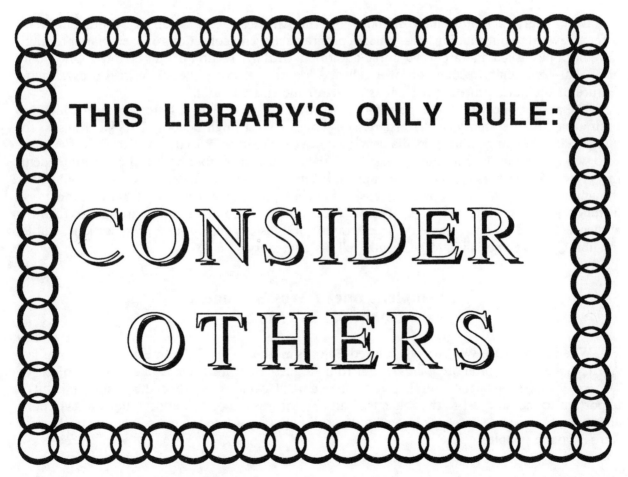

Fig. 10.7. Center fold-in from *Emergency Librarian* 14, no. 2 (November/December 1986): 32-33. Reprinted with permission of Ken Haycock.

OTHER POSSIBILITIES

The array of special programs, projects, threads, themes, and vertical program features sponsored as a part of the library media programs wherever there is a creative person is absolutely astounding. If one wants to be impressed with the creativity and imagination of library media specialists, look around, visit, read applications for a national library media program award, or watch the professional literature.

No matter how dismal the outlook for the world is, or what financial constraints local districts seem to have, creative people keep building and doing wonderful things with children and young people. Just a few of the possibilities for vertical program features include:

1. Oral history/community heritage themes and projects.

2. Career exploration as a guidance/teacher/LMC program.

3. A schoolwide self-image building program.

4. Year-long emphasis studies involving the total school program.

5. Building a whole language movement.

Every year, *Encyclopaedia Britannica* and the American Association of School Librarians offer an award to outstanding library media programs. Several collections of exemplary programs have been published and are listed in the additional readings section of this chapter. One would hope that community recognition of excellence is a part of every special vertical programming feature of the library media program as a part of the entire school.

The author once had the opportunity to visit an outstanding oral history project which has been a part of the library media program of Topeka West High School, Topeka, Kansas, for many years. The huge library media center had been turned into a large auditorium. Everyone who was anyone in the community was there: the mayor, the school board, the superintendent, the principal, teachers, parents, community business leaders, and students. One would have thought it was the state championship basketball game, the excitement was so high. Student oral history teams were in formal dress. Formal presentations were made to the group and then the audience divided up and sampled a wide array of oral history slide/sound presentations. But let the library media specialist, Mike Printz, tell his own story.

Example: Topeka West's Students Honor "E.T." Mom*

When actress Dee Wallace, who played Elliott's mother in "E.T.," came home to Kansas last April, it was not to promote a movie, but to be a guest of honor. She is one of the subjects of Topeka West High School's oral history program. "I came in just for this," she said. "It is important to me, not just to the students. This project was the best interview that was ever done about me; now people know me instead of the roles I play. I wanted to put something back in for Kansas young people."

---

*From Mike Printz, "Topeka West's Students Honor 'E.T.' Mom," *School Library Journal* 30, no. 8 (April 1984): 33-34. Reprinted with permission from *School Library Journal*. © A Cahners Magazine/R. R. Bowker Company.

Topeka West's oral history program was developed in 1976 as a Bicentennial project by the library staff. We wanted a new way to make history come alive for students, and also to give them a clearer understanding of their local—Kansas—heritage. Initial funding came from the school system—a grant of $2,500 was provided for purchasing cameras, copy stands, copy lenses, film, tape recorders, and tape. When the program received a Bicentennial citation from the American Association for State and Local History, the school administration decided to continue the project, and it was made part of the curriculum.

The subjects to be researched, chosen by Topeka West Librarian Jane Beasley and myself, offer a wide range from which the oral history students can choose. They have researched the lives of: Nancy Kassenbaum, Republican Senator from Kansas; poet Gwendolyn Brooks; naturalists Marlin Perkins and Martin and Osa Johnson; astronaut Joe Engle; aviator Amelia Earhart; and actors such as Ed Asner, Elizabeth Taylor, and the reclusive Louise Brooks—all of whom either grew up in Kansas or had spent a major part of their lives here.

Students work in pairs on the chosen subject. Each class begins with an all-day orientation workshop in which students learn to use the cameras, audio recorders, and videotape equipment loaned to them for the term. A local TV talk show host teaches interviewing techniques, and a TV cinematographer demonstrates basic photography procedures and videotape recording.

Research begins at the local level. Students are taught the use of biographical directories, newspaper indexes, and other basic tools for biographical research. Field trips are made to the Kansas State Historical Research Center as well as to other places within the state. Students research historical collections in public libraries, universities; newspaper morgues and archives, cemetery records, courthouses, high school yearbooks, and historical museums.

The students arrange their own interviews, and they are usually successful—seldom have they been refused. Interviews generally take place at the subject's home, whether it is with Dee Wallace in Hollywood or with Senators Nancy Kassenbaum and Robert Dole in Washington, D.C. The funding for the trips—approximately $12,000 to $15,000 annually—is raised by the students themselves. They solicit contributions, which have ranged from $5 to $1,000, and meet personally with each potential donor. It's very difficult to refuse an enthusiastic, highly motivated 17- or 18-year-old. Additional funds, earmarked for the purchase of equipment and for in-state travel, are provided by the Shawnee County Historical Society and the Topeka West Booster Club.

The organization of each project is the students' responsibility. The result is a 30-minute slide/tape or videotape presentation. For example, the project on Amelia Earhart was a slide/tape presentation that included showing government documents and newspaper clippings related to her career and mysterious disappearance, photographs of her family and home in Atchison, and pictures of statues and places bearing her name. The narration included interviews with her family and her childhood friends.

The final presentations are screened at an "Opening Night" gala in mid-April. Invitations are sent to Topeka area teachers of grades 3 through 12, and to officials of civic and service organizations. Oral history students explain their projects, and some are asked to make presentations in area schools and for community groups during the last month of school. Following the program, the students' parents hold a reception for participants and honored guests. Our 1983 preview drew some 1500 individuals. As a result, 815 appearances were scheduled during the last weeks of school—starting with 7 A.M. breakfasts and proceeding through lunches, school sessions, dinners, and late evening programs.

Projects are duplicated so that one set can be retained by the Topeka West Library, and another by the Kansas Historical Society. Thus the students' work remains a part of the community's permanent heritage.

Since the inception of this program, we have attempted to expand its focus in various ways. Each year we include two oral history projects by foreign exchange students about their homelands. Upon completion these are used extensively by the school district's social studies departments.

Another departure from the usual Kansas oral history presentations featured now ex-Marine Rocky Sickmann, who was one of the Iranian hostages. This came about when Topeka West's oral historians, through their interviews, learned of a diary that Marine Sergeant Sickmann had kept during his captivity. They pursued the lead and were eventually instrumental in getting it published (*Iranian Hostage: A Personal Diary of 444 Days in Captivity*, Crawford Press, 1982). We also did a special group oral history highlighting the twentieth anniversary of the school. We interviewed and taped many graduates of Topeka West, including Doug Wright, Mayor of Topeka, and Marilyn Schreffler, the voice of "Olive Oyl" in the Popeye cartoons.

Since 1976, the year of the Bicentennial, 157 students have been involved in eighty-nine oral history projects on significant events or important persons in Topeka, Shawnee County, or Kansas history. These oral historians have gathered 1,770 hours of recorded interviews—two-and-one-half months of listening for 24 hours a day. They have preserved 19,000 documents, photographs, and newspaper clippings on 35mm slides or videotapes. They have raised nearly $40,000 in contributions from members of the Topeka community. Many of the taped interviews are extremely valuable. One is the last interview with world-famous clown Emmett Kelly. Another is the only known interview with Amelia Earhart's sister, Muriel Morrisey (who, incidentally, believed her sister crashed into the sea during her last flight).

The benefits of this project to students are many. Our students have learned to do careful, detailed research, and have acquired problem-solving techniques that will aid them in many endeavors. Also, career choices have been influenced by the oral history experience.

We believe that whatever they do, or wherever they live, these students will continue to support local historical societies.

And last, our students have developed a fierce pride in the rich heritage of Kansas, as well as an appreciation of the wisdom they have gained from adults and senior citizens whom they have interviewed and learned to know.

It was a natural thing that I once and that long ago wrote about how Iowa differed from Kansas and Kansas from Ohio and Ohio from Illinois and Illinois from Michigan and that I called that writing "Useful Knowledge." That is what Gertrude Stein believed, and we believe it too. Our students have acquired the same "Useful Knowledge."

Resources

Baum, Willa K. *Transcribing and Editing Oral History*. American Association for State and Local History, 1971.

Davis, Cullom. *Oral History: From Tape to Type*. American Library Association, 1977.

Grele, Ronald J., ed. *Envelope of Sound: Six Practicioners Discuss the Method, Theory, and Practice of Oral History and Oral Testimony*. Precedent Publishing, 1975.

Hoopes, James. *Oral History: An Introduction for Students.* University of North Carolina Press, 1979.

Moss, William W. *Oral History Program Manual.* Praeger, 1974.

Neunothwarder, John A. *Oral History: As a Teaching Approach.* National Education Association, 1976.

Wigginton, Eliot. *I Wish I Could Give My Son a Wild Raccoon.* Anchor Books, 1976.

Wood, Pamela. *You and Aunt Arie: A Guide to Cultural Journalism.* Idea, 1975.

NOTES

1. Mary Dalbotten, ed., *Model Learner Outcomes for Educational Media and Technology* (White Bear Lake, Minn.: Minnesota Department of Education, 1986), 13.

2. Betty Bankhead and Ann Richards, et al., *Write It!* (Englewood, Colo.: Libraries Unlimited, 1988).

3. Robert Skapura and John Marlowe, *History: A Student's Guide to Research and Writing*; *Literature: A Student's Guide to Research and Writing*; *Science: A Student's Guide to Research and Writing* (Englewood, Colo.: Libraries Unlimited, 1988).

4. Dalbotten, *Model Learner Outcomes*, 13.

5. See Jacqueline C. Mancall, Shirley L. Aaron, and Sue A. Walker, "Educating Students to Think: The Role of the School Library Media Program," *School Library Media Quarterly* 15, no. 1 (Fall 1986): 18-27. Reprinted in Francis McDonald, *The Emerging School Library Media Program: Readings* (Englewood, Colo.: Libraries Unlimited, 1988).

6. William J. Bennett, *What Works: Research about Teaching and Learning*, 2nd ed. (Washington, D.C.: U.S. Department of Education, 1987).

7. Polly Jean Wickstrom, *Quizzes for 220 Great Children's Books* (Englewood, Colo.: Libraries Unlimited, 1988).

8. Dalbotten, *Model Learner Outcomes*, 13-14.

9. *Instruction in Library Media Skills: A Supplement to "A Guide to School Library Media Programs"* (Hartford, Conn.: Connecticut Department of Education, 1984), 20.

10. E. D. Hirsch, *Cultural Literacy* (New York: Houghton, 1987).

11. An unpublished evaluation document done for the Indiana State Department of Public Instruction, 1987.

12.   Jerry Flack, "A New Look at a Valued Partnership: The Library Media Specialist and Gifted Students," *School Library Media Quarterly* 14, no. 3 (Summer 1986): 174-79.

ADDITIONAL READINGS

Library Skills

Cutlip, Glen W. *Learning and Information: The Secondary Classroom and Library Media Skills Instruction*. Englewood, Colo.: Libraries Unlimited, 1988.
   An integrated approach to the topic.

Dalbotten, Mary, ed. *Model Learner Outcomes for Educational Media and Technology*. White Bear Lake, Minn.: Minnesota State Department of Education, 1986.
   An elaborate scope and sequence charting of library skills, production skills, selection of media formats, media literacy, thinking and research processes, and presentation skills.

Kuhlthau, Carol Collier. "A Process Approach to Library Skills Instruction." *School Library Media Quarterly* 13, no. 1 (Winter 1985): 35-44.
   Kuhlthau explores the stages of research coupled with feelings, thoughts, and actions of the student. Readers should follow Kuhlthau's work in the next several years as her model develops and is supported by research.

Facilities

Lamkin, Bernice. "A Media Center for the 21st Century." *School Library Journal* 33, no. 3 (November 1986): 25-29.
   Lamkin provides a description of the total process of building a new high school library media center from architectural plans through establishing a program in the facility.

Library Learning Resource Facilities: New and Remodeled. Dallas, Tex.: Texas Education Agency, 1982.
   This pamphlet contains numerous floor plans of Texas school library media centers—more than any other publication of its type.

Reading Motivation

Cullinan, Bernice, ed. *Children's Literature in the Reading Program*. Newark, Del.: International Reading Association, 1987.
   A collection of essays by prominent educators and experts which promote the use of literature to teach reading and lifelong reading habits.

Goodman, Ken. *What's Whole Language?* Jefferson City, Mo.: Scholastic, 1986.
   Goodman provides an excellent framework for the language arts into which a reading motivational program can fit.

Graves, Ruth, ed. *The RIF Guide to Encouraging Young Readers.* New York: Doubleday, 1987.
A sourcebook of over 200 reading activities plus an annotated list of books and resources.

Polkingharn, Anne T., and Catherine Toohey. *Creative Encounters: Activities to Expand Children's Responses to Literature.* Littleton, Colo.: Libraries Unlimited, 1983.
Extremely creative ideas for making books come alive.

Polkingharn, Anne T., and Catherine Toohey. *More Creative Encounters.* Englewood, Colo.: Libraries Unlimited, 1988.
More of the best for younger children.

Thimmesch, Nick, ed. *Aliteracy: People Who Can Read But Won't.* Washington, D.C.: American Enterprise Institute for Public Policy Research, 1984.
An excellent analysis of the problems of nonreading readers, with recommendations for what might be done.

Wilkens, Lea-Ruth C. *Supporting K-5 Reading Instruction in the School Library Media Center.* Chicago: American Library Association, 1984.
Roles and ideas for reading involvement. Must reading.

Exemplary Programs

Baker, D. Philip. *School and Public Library Media Programs for Children and Young Adults.* Syracuse, N.Y.: Gaylord Professional Publications, 1977.
Baker provides information about fifty exemplary programs which he surveyed in 1976.

Schmidt, William D. *Learning Resources Programs That Make a Difference: A Source of Ideas and Models from Exemplary Programs in the Field.* Washington, D.C.: Association for Educational Communications and Technology, 1987.
Schmidt surveys programs in schools and colleges which are exemplary in terms of educational technology.

Seager, Andrew J., Sarah J. Roberts, and Carol Z. Lincoln. *Check This Out: Library Programs That Work.* Washington, D.C.: U.S. Department of Education, 1987.
Sixty-two library media programs which underwent an analysis by the National Diffusion Network staff are described briefly.

Information Skills

Irving, Ann. *Study and Information Skills across the Curriculum.* London: Heinemann Educational Books, 1985.
This valuable book lists nine important steps that lead students through assignments involving library media materials and activities.

Alternative Views of the Library Media Program

A number of other theorists have presented their views of the evolutionary role of the library media program. These persons have promoted a healthy discussion of issues, focused attention on change, and forecast ways in which the library media program could respond to the curriculum of the school.

EXAMPLES OF DIFFERENT VIEWPOINTS: THE HAYCOCK MODEL AND THE TURNER MODEL

Several important philosophical positions are presented in this chapter which differ somewhat from the author's, but are significant in their own right.

The first is from Ken Haycock. He and his wife, Carol Ann, have made a wonderful contribution to the creation and development of resource-based teaching in Canada and the United States. Ken is an assistant superintendent for the Vancouver School Board in British Columbia, Canada. He and Carol Ann edit the periodical *Emergency Librarian*, which presents many good ideas for building and promoting school library media programs. Carol Ann is also a traveling consultant, doing workshops across the United States and Canada.

Ken printed a model of the school library media program in his periodical which provides a three-step approach to a library media program. His model is shown in figure 11.1.

Phil Turner, in *Helping Teachers Teach*, concentrates on the process used to create resource-based teaching units known as instructional design consultation. Turner begins by presenting two models. The first is an instructional design model which shows the steps of planning and preparing a topical unit of study. The second shows four levels of involvement by the library media specialist in each step of the unit design. Both models are shown in figure 11.2, page 198.

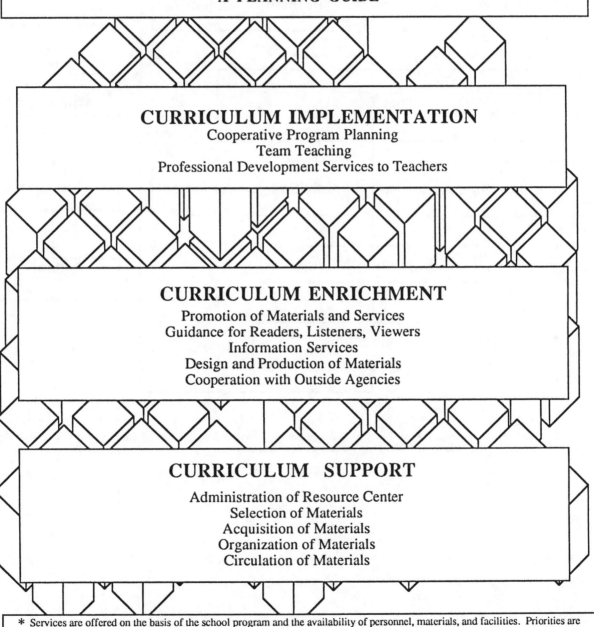

SERVICES OF SCHOOL RESOURCE CENTERS

A PLANNING GUIDE*

CURRICULUM IMPLEMENTATION
Cooperative Program Planning
Team Teaching
Professional Development Services to Teachers

CURRICULUM ENRICHMENT

Promotion of Materials and Services
Guidance for Readers, Listeners, Viewers
Information Services
Design and Production of Materials
Cooperation with Outside Agencies

CURRICULUM SUPPORT

Administration of Resource Center
Selection of Materials
Acquisition of Materials
Organization of Materials
Circulation of Materials

* Services are offered on the basis of the school program and the availability of personnel, materials, and facilities. Priorities are determined by the individual school since not all services will be offered in every school or to the same extent in all schools.

Fig. 11.1. Services of school resource centers. From Ken Haycock, "Services of School Resource Centers," *Emergency Librarian* 13, no. 1 (September/October 1985): 28-29. Reprinted with permission.

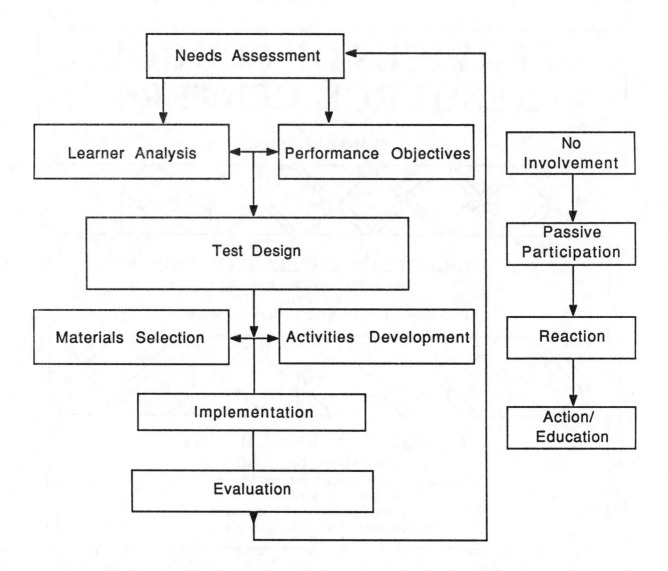

Fig. 11.2. Basic instructional design. From Philip M. Turner, *Helping Teachers Teach: A School Library/Media Specialist's Role* (Littleton, Colo.: Libraries Unlimited, 1985), 14-15. Reprinted with permission.

Turner's concept of intervention with the teacher at each stage of unit planning is further explained as follows:

1. *No Involvement.* Perhaps no intervention is required. Perhaps the teacher has not requested involvement by the center. Perhaps the library/media specialist is unwilling or unable to intervene.

2. *Passive Participation.* This level of intervention at a given step involves little or no interaction between the library/media specialist and the faculty member. The library/media specialist selects and maintains materials, equipment, and facilities which assist the faculty member in implementing a particular step.

3. *Reaction.* As a teacher performs a particular step, he/she may randomly request some sort of assistance from the library/media center program. This intervention would be informal and not designed to increase the teacher's ability to perform the step more effectively at a later date.

4. *Action/Education.* This level of intervention by the library/media specialist most closely resembles formal instructional design consultation as described in the literature. At this level, the library/media specialist often works as part of a team, implementing a number of the steps in the instructional design process. The library/media specialist might present an inservice on one or more of the steps. Often the purpose of involvement at this level is to increase the teacher's ability to perform one or more of the steps subsequent to the intervention.[1]

To further illustrate his point, Turner has created a whole book of sample units which might be of interest to the reader.[2] But as a brief example of some of his levels, Turner provides an interesting example (see figure 11.3).

STEP 1: NEEDS ASSESSMENT

Level	Sample Activity
Action/Education—Participates as an active team member in the goal-setting process at all stages. Implements inservice on needs assessment.	Conducts inservice for English teachers on the process of setting unit goals.
Reaction—Upon request, helps identify and prioritize goals and needs.	Mrs. Jones, the second-grade teacher, says, "I'm supposed to teach a unit on plants, but I'm not sure what to include." The L/MS responds by providing, from the files, a unit developed at another elementary school.

(Figure 11.3 continues on page 200.)

STEP 1 (*continued*)

Level	Sample Activity
Passive Participation—Maintains a collection of works on needs assessment. Maintains sources of potential goals.	Purchases copy of *Needs Assessment* for the professional collection in the media center.
No Involvement—Not involved at this step.	

STEP 2: PERFORMANCE OBJECTIVES

Level	Sample Activity
Action/Education—Acquaints teachers through workshops and consultations with the writing of objectives and their use.	Makes regular visits to the social studies faculty meetings to assist with the writing of objectives.
Reaction—Upon request, assists in any aspect of creating and using objectives.	After being informed by the principal that her objective, "The students will *really* understand the value of good citizenship," is not adequate, the new social studies teacher asks for help. The L/MS helps her rewrite the objective.
Passive Participation—Maintains a collection of works on objectives and previously formulated objectives.	Purchases a copy of *Writing Objectives* and places it in the media center.
No Involvement—Not involved at this step.	

STEP 3: LEARNER ANALYSIS

Level	Sample Activity
Action/Education—Acquaints teachers through workshops and consultations with learner analysis processes and uses.	Conducts an inservice for math teachers on the *Learning Style Inventory*.
Reaction—Upon request, assists teachers in selection appropriate learner analysis methods and categorizes student(s) in terms of learner characteristics.	Returning a filmstrip after school, the science teacher says, "A few of my students can't seem to locate important information in a visual. What is wrong with them?" The L/MS discusses the characteristic of field dependence.

Passive Participation—Maintains a collection of works on learner analysis. Maintains hardware/software necessary for learner analysis.

Obtains the *Learning Style Inventory* and puts it in the professional collection.

No Involvement—Not involved at this step.

STEP 4: TEST DESIGN

Level	Sample Activity
Action/Education—Acquaints teachers through workshops and consultations with the design and implementation of criterion tests.	Conducts a workshop for the history department on deriving test items from objectives.
Reaction—Upon request, assists in any aspect of test design and implementation.	Mr. Jones asks whether the L/MS thinks that multiple-choice or essay questions are best for a history unit. The L/MS responds by presenting pros and cons of each type.
Passive Participation—Maintains a collection of works on test construction and administration. Maintains a pool of test items and hardware/software for analysis.	Maintains files in media center on performance measurements other than tests.
No Involvement—Not involved at this step.	

STEP 5: MATERIALS SELECTION

Level	Sample Activity
Action/Education—Conducts workshops on the materials selection process and production techniques. Regularly designs/produces/selects instructional materials based upon consultation.	Implements a program to train new teachers in design and production of slide presentations.
Reaction—Acts as a clearinghouse for preview requests. Produces/obtains instructional materials upon request.	The third-grade teacher mentions that she is teaching a unit on planets. The L/MS sends her an instructional kit on the solar system that has just arrived.

(Figure 11.3 continues on page 202.)

STEP 5 (*continues*)

Level	Sample Activity
Passive Participation—Maintains a collection of instructional materials. Maintains a production area. Maintains a collection of works and facilities required to produce/select/preview materials.	Unilaterally selects, orders, and catalogs a filmstrip for the general collection.
No Involvement—Not involved at this step.	

STEP 6: ACTIVITIES DEVELOPMENT

Level	Sample Activity
Action/Education—Acquaints teachers through workshops and consultation with the process of matching learning activities with objectives and learners.	L/MS works with third-grade teachers in designing group activities.
Reaction—Upon request, discusses methodologies and options to meet a given objective for a specific learner type.	The social studies teacher mentions that he is having difficulty thinking of an activity to use in teaching the concept of economy. The L/MS helps him design a simulation exercise.
Passive Participation—Maintains a collection of materials on activity design.	Starts a vertical file of descriptions of activities for teaching the kindergarten units.
No Involvement—Not involved at this step.	

STEP 7: IMPLEMENTATION

Level	Sample Activity
Action/Education—Acquaints teachers with effective compensating activities and proper use of materials, equipment, and facilities through workshops and consultation.	Works with ninth-grade remedial math teacher to develop teacher activities to help students benefit from audiovisual materials.
Reaction—Upon request, demonstrates operation of and delivers items of equipment. Upon request, assists with assigning of tasks and scheduling of facilities.	Arranges to have a 16mm projector delivered to the third-period art class.

Passive Participation—Maintains a collection of works on equipment operation and on teacher activities including information and classroom control. Maintains a collection of equipment. Maintains media center for group and individual use.

Purchases a listing of evaluations and descriptions of computer-managed instruction.

No Involvement—Not involved at this step.

STEP 8: EVALUATION

Level	Sample Activity
Action/Education—Acquaints teachers through workshops and consultation with evaluation techniques and use.	Helps seventh-grade social studies teachers evaluate their unit on cities.
Reaction—Upon request, advises on the design of evaluation strategies, implementation of evaluation, or interpretation of results.	The science teacher says, "I just finished my taxonomy unit, but I'm not really sure whether it was successful or not." The L/MS provides assistance in setting up an evaluation strategy for the next implementation.
Passive Participation—Maintains a collection of works on evaluation and hardware/ software necessary for evaluations.	Purchases a statistical program for the microcomputer for use by the faculty.
No Involvement—Not involved at this step.	

Fig. 11.3. Steps and levels of instructional design consultation and sample activities performed by school library/media specialists. From Philip M. Turner, *Helping Teachers Teach: A School Library/Media Specialist's Role* (Littleton, Colo.: Libraries Unlimited, 1985), 219-22. Reprinted with permission.

NOTES

1. Philip M. Turner, *Helping Teachers Teach: A School Library/Media Specialist's Role* (Littleton, Colo.: Libraries Unlimited, 1985), 14-15.

2. Philip M. Turner, *Casebook for "Helping Teachers Teach"* (Englewood, Colo.: Libraries Unlimited, 1988).

ADDITIONAL READINGS

Haycock, Ken. "Strengthening the Foundations for Teacher-Librarianship." *School Library Media Quarterly* 13, no. 2 (Spring 1985): 102-9.

Haycock's keynote address to the 1984 Conference of the International Association of School Librarianship in Honolulu, Hawaii. An important statement on the role and change of directions for the library media center.

Liesener, James W. "Learning at Risk: School Library Media Programs in an Information World." *School Library Media Quarterly* 13, no. 4 (Fall 1985): 11-20. Reprinted in Frances McDonald, *The Emerging School Library Media Program: Readings*. Englewood, Colo.: Libraries Unlimited, 1988.

This paper was presented for a series of seminars, held January through March 1984, sponsored by the U.S. Department of Education and was one of the papers in response to *A Nation at Risk*.

Vandergrift, Kay E., and Jane Anne Hannigan. "Elementary School Library Media Centers as Essential Components in the Schooling Process: An AASL Position Paper." *School Library Media Quarterly* 14, no. 4 (Summer 1986): 171-73.

An important and succinct statement about the purpose of the elementary school library media center, backed up with an extensive bibliography.

Evaluating the Success of the Library Media Program

If you were charged with contributing to the education of a minor, would there be enough evidence to convict?

In the white expanse of blowing snow on a typical winter morning, the school bus driver from Bone, Idaho, has only one hope of delivering the children safely and on time to Idaho Falls Schools—steer between the lodgepole pine poles at 300-yard intervals, for that is where the road lies. One misjudgment and it's in the ditch. Time to call for help on the CB radio.

Library media specialists need some lodgepole pine poles to stand as markers along the road to success, indicators that will mark progress or regression along the way. The purpose of this chapter, which could be a book in and of itself, is to provide a glimpse at measures which will supply information for decision making to the library media specialist, the principal, and board of education.

The author has met a few library media specialists who had little need for evaluative instruments and techniques. These were people who not only knew where they were going with their program, but whose minds were always analyzing every situation, picking up constant clues of failure and success, and translating negative signals into positive steps for action. The rest of us need more direct evidence. In fact, good analytic library media specialists need them too, perhaps not for themselves, but for others who are charged with making administrative and budgetary decisions.

Library media centers are service organizations and like all service organizations, the perceptions that people have of them, true or not, have far-reaching consequences. Old and outdated perceptions die hard. Many principals and teachers only remember what the library did for them as a child and that may be exactly opposite of what the profession intends for the students of today. Library media specialists have battled an image problem for many years, bemoaning the fact that administrators and teachers really do not understand the function of the library media program. How could they understand? Did they have a great library media center as a child? Did they learn the function of a library media program in their college preparation courses? Do they have any models locally which they can visit to see exemplary programs in operation? When they read national, regional, or state standards for school libraries, do they believe what they read and do what the standards recommend? The answers to all the above questions might well be no.

The premise of this chapter is that informed decision making is preferable to decisions made on personal perceptions or political whims. The impossible dream? Perhaps. This chapter is not for persons who make judgments without consulting evidence or data. The author remembers a library media specialist who documented everything he did for the principal. Every meeting attended, every consultation, every hour of the day was accounted for. The administrator was not convinced of worth. Certain decisions about the destiny of the library media program and staff had been made in the political arena and no amount of data was going to change the outcome. In another tragic situation, the author collected data about a certain library media program and the library media specialist lost her job because the data confirmed the suspicions of the administrator.

Collecting data about a library media program can be a very negative or a very positive experience, a growing or a threatening situation. The best that any of us can hope is that data we collect will be interpreted fairly and used in a positive manner. We trust that most people, given the facts, will act in a rational manner; that the interest of quality education and children will be paramount as program directions are decided upon. Such will not always be the case.

Another assumption of the profession is that quality programs have a future and mediocre ones do not. That is, if you demonstrate your worth to a student body, a faculty, and a principal, you will have a job tomorrow, next year, and for another decade. Generally, that is true, but many times, overriding political conditions and situations dictate policies, cuts in budget and staff, and other negative effects which have little to do with a quality LMC program. A whole host of political and economic factors has devastated many school districts in the past ten years. Library media specialists who have built programs over a period of twenty years have watched that progress melt away almost overnight and have given up rather than watch all they have worked for die.

Not long ago, there was a documentary on television about Soviet society. Soviet citizens were expressing their amazement at the insecurity of the capitalistic society. The commentator said that the Soviet citizen had a secure future. Everyone had a job. It may not be a job you liked doing; it may not pay very well. But the government would always provide you with work. But the capitalist? How do we deal with the uncertainty of whether we will have a job, whether we can build programs, improve conditions? In this case, neither society admires the other.

Trying to reach out and build a quality library media program is taking a chance. It is taking a chance because it often involves making people change. It's tough. It requires knowing where you want to go, documenting where you are, making decisions, and documenting both the progress and the problems.

Over the years, a number of evaluative systems have been tried by library media specialists to show worth, to demonstrate where we'd like to go, to show gaps, and to illustrate problems. Library media specialists should realize that some evaluative data will convey an impressive message over and over again. Other data will be effective only once or just a few times. We must all be astute enough to select measures and report data which will accurately reflect what is really happening, but do so within the political climate of the local community.

To ask for major collection renewal efforts in a time of district financial exigency would be unwise, but more than one library media specialist has been courageous enough to sell major program improvement when others in the organization are being cut. One state library media supervisor had the vision and the political clout to get her legislature to appropriate $3 million for direct grants to school libraries. The program became so popular with the many small school districts that when a huge state budget crunch faced the state legislature, one legislator said, "We probably won't touch the library grants—it would make too many people mad." And they didn't.

What is the point of all this? Simply that it would be wise for all library media specialists to document what they do—to be prepared, not only to defend what they are doing, but to advance the cause of the LMC program. Manna from heaven is not all that common.

Few persons would dispute the fact that library media specialists are busy all day. All should realize that the degree of tiredness at the end of the day is no measure of the effectiveness of the LMC program. The documentation of a day's activities may indicate that the library media specialist rarely poked a nose up out of the warehouse all day long.

WHAT SHOULD BE EVALUATED?

Most of the evaluative measures of school libraries over the last twenty years have concentrated on measuring things, people, and space. Figures have been compared to what standards or accreditation documents have recommended. If a gap was evident, the library media specialist would request additional funding to "bring us up to the standard." Comparing library media programs against standards documents will always be important if they are what decision makers want and use. But a wide variety of other measures that are at least, if not more effective, are available.

There are four general areas of a library media program which can be measured. The wise library media specialist collects data in each of the areas for decision makers. These four areas form an acronym for easy recall and are illustrated in figure 12.1, page 208.

Area 1: *Goals and objectives.* Measure where you think you are in relation to where you think you ought to be, or evaluate whether the goals you have are worthy ones.

Area 2: *Resources.* Do you have the materials, space, facilities, budget, and staff to operate an effective program?

Area 3: *Operations.* Do the many warehousing routines of the LMC run smoothly and efficiently?

Area 4: *Worth/Results/Impact.* Does the LMC program make a difference in the way teachers teach and how much students learn?

Each of the evaluative measures recommended in this book is classified in figure 12.2, page 209. It would be instructive to compare the definitions listed above to each measure.

G oals / Objectives

R esources

O perations

W orth / Results / Impact

Fig. 12.1. GROW. Adapted from Daniel J. Stufflebeam and Anthony J. Shinkfield, *Systematic Evaluation: A Self-Instructional Guide to Theory and Practice* (Boston: Kluwer-Nijhoff, 1985).

Chapter	Measure	Type	Page
3	Library media staff role	Goals	17-18
4	Self-evaluative checklist for the teacher taxonomy	Goals	28-34
5	Self-evaluative checklist for the student taxonomy	Goals	41-45
6	Principal's taxonomy self-check test	Goals	55-58
7	Cooperative evaluation of resource-based teaching	Worth	76
7	Curriculum involvement of the library media center	Worth	77
7	Library-based teaching units	Worth	78-79
7	Student questionnaire: French cultures	Worth	81
7	Student questionnaire: French government	Worth	82
8	Reference success/failure	Operations	88
8	Judging online searching recall and precision	Operations	89-90
8	Reader's advisory measure	Operations	91
8	Gathering materials log	Operations	91
8	In-service evaluation	Operations	92
8	Public relations	Operations	92
9	Collection maps	Resources	98-99, 103-6
9	Recency analysis	Resources	102, 108-11
9	Collection quality evaluation form	Resources	112
9	Technology evaluation form	Resources	114-20
9	Materials cost analysis	Resources	122
9	Library media budget allocation form	Resources	123
9	Budgetary report card	Resources	125-27
9	Time saved with computerization	Operations	131-33
9	Success/failure measure (general)	Operations	134-35
9	Periodical success rate form	Operations	136
10	Library skills paper/pencil or observation tests	Worth	147
10	Research skills paper/pencil tests, simulated research quests	Worth	164
10	Information skills paper/pencil tests, observations, and performance tests	Worth	171
10	Reading diaries/logs, parent notes	Worth	178
10	Evaluation of audiovisual projects	Worth	182-83
10	Cultural literacy test/game	Worth	186
10	Targeted student groups measures	Worth	188
12	An orderly warehouse	Operations	214
12	A "living" collection	Resources	214
12	Good materials and equipment access	Operations	214
12	Reliable equipment services	Operations	214
12	Response of reference collection	Worth	214
12	Positive impression on patrons	Worth	214
12	Successful cooperative unit involvement	Worth	214
12	Library media specialist as an idea fountain	Resources	214
12	LMC materials are integral to a unit	Worth	214
12	Book and media talks influence student choice	Worth	214
12	Progress made toward self-motivated use	Worth	214
12	Instructional planning time analysis form	Operations	215
12	Library media center observational form	Operations	217
12	Ohio standards evaluation	Goals	218
12	Circulation survey	Worth	219
A	All instruments	Goals/Operations/Worth/Resources	229
B	PSES	Goals/Operations	295

Fig. 12.2. Evaluative measures.

CRITERIA FOR SELECTING AN
EVALUATION MEASURE AND PROGRAM

Before one begins to use any evaluative measure or program of evaluation, some important questions need to be asked and answered. No evaluation effort should be taken lightly.

1. What will the evaluation instrument really measure? People's perceptions or opinions? Hard data? Generally, hard data will be preferable to an opinion if such hard evidence can actually be collected. For example, an actual circulation count is preferable to people's opinions about whether the library circulates many, some, or few items. But, is a circulation count a measure of use? No, it merely indicates how many items were checked in and out through the official circulation system. If I want a true measure of use, then I must check on in-house use, multiple use of items circulated once, and items circulated but not actually used. By analyzing carefully what a measure would actually tell me, I would know whether or not to collect the data in the first place and what conclusions I could draw from the data.

2. How easy will it be to collect the data and analyze them? Any measure must fit in the routine of the day and it must not take an inordinate amount of time to collect. One could spend the majority of the day measuring but not actually doing. For example, tallies are easy to keep if tally sheets are in the location of the activity being measured. A magazine success/failure measure is easily kept if it is at the magazine desk and is a part of the normal check-in/check-out procedure.

3. Is the measure accurate? If the staff forgets to record data or fudges on tallies, the measure may not only be inaccurate, but counterproductive.

4. If you were an outsider who knew little about the internal operations of a library, would you be able to understand the data which would result from an evaluation instrument? Some measures should be taken within the organization for the staff's use only. Other measures need to be taken with an outsider in mind, particularly as the data are interpreted and displayed in tables, graphs, or charts.

5. Is the measure within ethical guidelines? There are many concerns about rights of privacy and the use of evaluative data to take into consideration. Some of them include withholding the true nature of the study from participants; exposing participants to stress, anguish, or harm; invading participants' privacy; and withholding benefits from persons in the control groups. Many school districts have committees which must approve research or evaluation instruments to ensure that the measures will not endanger the physical, mental, or emotional health of students. For example, an experiment which would deprive some students of library books in order to test how much library book shoveling contributes to the reading scores of an experimental group would be unacceptable.

6. Is the measure cost effective? Taking into consideration the amount of staff time to collect, analyze, and interpret the data, how much will it cost? Is it worth the effort and cost?

7. Do all the measures being taken provide a cross section view of the library media program? It is easy to concentrate on resource measures but ignore those for worth. As stated previously, the best evaluation plan is to include a variety of measures which look at various parts of the program and which provide the basis for demonstrating progress as well as charting the needs of the program for the future.

HOW SHOULD A MEASURE BE TAKEN?

Conducting an evaluative program is much like launching a program of formal research. In fact, evaluation is a branch of research, since many research techniques are used in the evaluation design. Does one need a course in research and statistics to conduct evaluations? A course would help, but with some general guidelines and a pot full of common sense, some excellent measures can be taken, analyzed, and interpreted. There are five steps to consider in conducting an evaluation:

1. Deciding on an evaluation plan. This will include deciding what to measure, who will do the measuring, when the evaluation will be done, how it will be done, and how and to whom the data will be reported.

2. Designing the evaluation measure. There are many evaluation measures which can be used or adapted easily to the local needs and situations. Care should be taken to assure that the instrument will really measure what the school needs.

3. Collecting the data. Collect the data according to the guidelines given by those who designed the instrument, but temper those instructions with common sense. Practicalities of collecting the data, coupled with concern for accuracy, are important considerations. Remember that random samples are often as good as measuring every occurrence or person.

4. Data analysis and interpretation. Generally, instructions for analysis and interpretation will be given by the creator of the instrument. If not, simple totals, averages, and percentages are a good place to start. Persons with a statistical background can often suggest some interesting comparisons and provide a simple microcomputer package that will analyze the data.

5. Communicating the information. It will do no good to collect data which are not communicated to decision makers clearly, accurately, and succinctly.

WHAT KINDS OF DATA ARE
USUALLY COLLECTED?

Most evaluative instruments call for the collection of similar types of data in various subject areas. Each type of data has its own advantages and disadvantages as interpretations are made.

1. Direct data. This type of data measures a service or objects exactly. The number of books in a collection, the number of items circulated, a list of copyright dates, the amount of money spent on audiovisual equipment, and the number of square feet in the LMC are all examples of direct measures. Direct numbers are always the best if they can be obtained; however, no one can directly measure the amount of enjoyment a child experiences listening to a storyteller or the attitude teachers have toward library media services.

2. Opinion data. Most of the answers to questionnaires measure opinion on rating scales. The most popular data of this type are collected using the Likkert Scale which measures perceptions on a sliding scale (Disagree 1 2 3 4 5 Agree). Measuring attitudes, feelings, and perceptions, and making judgments and ranking items are all examples of opinion data. This type of data is commonly collected because there is no way to measure opinion directly—there is no thermometer we can stick in someone's mouth and say, "she agrees at the 76.359 level." Sometimes, we convert opinion data into more direct data by constructing the scales so that only two options are possible. For example, we make a statement such as, "I like the librarian." Respondents either must agree or disagree. Then we report the number and percentage of the respondents: 80 percent like the librarian; 10 percent don't like the librarian; 10 percent have never met her, so they have no opinion.

3. Observational or interview data. If a trained person looks for the occurrence of certain things and keeps track on a tally sheet, or if an interviewer asks questions of teachers or students, either direct or opinion data can be collected. Both methods are expensive because they require a great deal of time to collect compared to a questionnaire or taking a few moments to tally the circulation for the day. Generally, these data are superior to questionnaire opinion data because the person being questioned can clarify what is wanted before answering.

Scientists often scoff at the data that social scientists and educators collect as lacking precision. No one has learned how to accurately measure the number of facts memorized, the attitude toward a teacher, the amount of learning, or whether a life-long reading habit is developing at a constant rate. We have not planted computerized data sensing devices in students brains nor fed them "reading pills," nor planted hidden television cameras to record the effects of reading pornography. Progress has been made in the last thirty years in measuring what people believe and feel (predicting winners in national elections is frightfully quick and even controversial), but we are likely to live with a margin of error for some time to come.

The challenge for library media specialists is to select the most appropriate and best measuring devices they can to ascertain the worth of their programs. Such a skill is developed with experience, by trial and error, by looking at what others do and borrowing their successes and avoiding their failures. Probably the best advice is to start simple and collect a wide variety of measures. Some measures will emerge as good thermometers of the program, others will seem irrelevant. The best measures are those which make sense to decision makers as they weigh both evidence and political or policy information. This means that data which have the potential for the most use and which are likely to make the biggest difference should be collected.

If decision makers are tired of seeing data on collection size or comparing one district's budget against the national standards, collect and use different data. Principals might be much more interested in the number of resource-based teaching units which were conducted cooperatively between teachers and library media specialists than they would be in circulation data. The former gives them some feeling for progress in the instructional program as a whole—something they may have to report to a school board interested in educational excellence. Circulation data may be uninteresting.

Figure 12.3, page 214, illustrates some of the important data that might be collected to match parts of the taxonomies presented in this book.

SAMPLE EVALUATIVE INSTRUMENTS

It is very instructive to look at a variety of evaluation instruments and to begin categorizing them by the type of data they collect and their potential for making a difference in library media programs. An instrument which may be very effective in one situation may not be in another, so flexibility is the key. Samples of many instruments are given in this chapter. Longer and more complete measures are provided and discussed in the appendices.

Resource-Based Teaching Involvement

One of the most effective tools to keep which can chart progress toward and involvement in resource-based teaching is a log which tracks the time spent in planning, executing and evaluating cooperative teaching activities. Such a log is presented in figure 12.4, page 215.

The log asks for a teacher's name and the number of minutes consulting on resource-based teaching. A column for topic or unit discussed might be helpful. The log is a direct measurement of people and time. If reported to the principal monthly, support of particular curricular areas could be discussed, which teachers are and are not doing joint planning, methods for attracting more teachers to resource-based teaching, the need for in-service or summer workshops to boost cooperation, planning which units to showcase for the school board, deciding which units to feature in local news stories, changes in library media schedules to boost the amount of resource-based teaching being done, and a whole host of other concerns.

Sucess Factor by Taxonomy Level	Measuring Tool
LMS Taxonomy Level 2:	
1. An orderly warehouse.	Interview, questionnaire, observation.
2. A "living" collection. (the collection is constantly renewed and regenerated toward curricular aims)	Collection map; evaluation after units of instruction; age, replacement, inflation factors.
3. Good materials and equipment access (patrons get what they need when they need it)	Success/failure measure, interview, survey.
4. Reliable equipment services (it works, it's there when they need it)	Success/failure measure, interview, survey.
LMS Taxonomy Level 3:	
1. Reference collection responds to patron's needs.	Success/failure measure, failure analysis leading to purchase plans.
LMS Taxonomy Level 7:	
1. A positive impression on patrons.	Interview, survey, observation.
LMS Taxonomy Level 9-10:	
1. Successful cooperative unit involvement.	Anecdotal records on every jointly planned unit, collection evaluation sheet on every unit.
Teacher Taxonomy Level 4:	
1. The library media specialist is a fountain of ideas.	Tally sheet, survey, interview.
Teacher Taxonomy Level 6:	
1. LMC materials are integral, not always supplementary to a unit.	Interview, anecdotal record, observation.
Student Taxonomy Level 4:	
1. Book and media talks influence student choice.	Tally sheet, interview, survey.
Student Taxonomy Level 7:	
1. Progress is made toward self-motivated use.	Observational checklist in LMC of student behavior when assignments are given; observational checklists when no assignment pressing, paper/pencil tests, performance tests (can operate computer, can find periodical articles, etc.).

Fig. 12.3. Measuring tools for the taxonomy.

Instructional Planning Time Analysis Form

Assistance with Planning Instructional Units (Instructional Design)		Carrying out of Teacher/Library Media Specialist Planned Activities		Evaluation of LMC Activities with Teacher	
With whom:	Number of minutes:	With whom:	Number of minutes:	With whom:	Number of minutes:
# of teacher contacts: _____ # of different teachers: _____	Total minutes: _____ % of total day: _____	# of classes: _____ # of different teachers: _____	Total minutes: _____ % of total day: _____	# of teacher contacts: _____ # of different teachers: _____	Total minutes: _____ % of total day: _____

Fig. 12.4. Instructional planning time analysis form.

General Evaluative Measures of Staff Performance

There have been numerous efforts over the last twenty years to provide an overall evaluation instrument to be used by district library media supervisors and principals to either substitute for, or be used in addition to, regular yearly evaluation procedures. These efforts have varied from simple to complex depending on the degree of formalization of the evaluation process in the district.

One example is a simple form to be used by an observer, most likely the principal or the district library media supervisor, who visits the LMC on an occasional basis and who has a handy checklist of items to look for. The rating for each activity on the checklist is either "observed" or "not observed," and there is some space for comments. The completed evaluation form is generally discussed in an individual conference. Figure 12.5 illustrates the brief form.

The problem with using the above form is twofold. First, the items may not apply to a local situation, and two, the ratings are imprecise. The advantage is that the checklist is simple, fast, and provides the stimulation for discussion in a personal interview.

Other instruments are much more in-depth and often are a part of district negotiations or even state contracts. Appendix A contains a number of such instruments with accompanying discussion.

Library Media Center Observational Form

	Observed	Not Observed	Comments
Decorum:			
1. Multiple groups use the LMC and work harmoniously.			
2. Private and quiet individual use is evident.			
3. Purposeful group use is evident.			
4. Relaxed individual and small groups use the center without undue disturbance of other groups.			
Instructional Impact:			
1. Teacher/library media specialist planning is a regular occurrence.			
2. The library media staff plans regularly with a wide cross section of the faculty.			
3. The library media staff serves every segment of the student population.			
4. Students consider the LMC as the primary source for instructional materials.			
5. When large groups are using the LMC, both the teacher and the LMC staff are helping.			
6. The materials in the LMC support the curriculum of the school in addition to the recreational and personal interests of the students.			
7. All kinds of materials and equipment are used and used wisely.			
Other impressions:			
1. Students seem satisfied with the library media services they receive.			
2. Teachers seem satisfied with the library media services they receive.			
3. Students and teachers feel that they can make suggestions for improving LMC services.			
4. The types of complaints received indicate minor problems rather than major policy or personnel flaws.			
5. The LMC is a cultural center in the school.			
6. The LMC is a showplace for visitors to the school.			
7. The ambience of the LMC attracts patrons.			
8. The administrator and the library media specialist agree on the role of the LMC and are partners in decision making.			

Fig. 12.5. Library media center observational form. Developed by David V. Loertscher and Blanche Woolls.

The Ohio Standards Evaluation

The Ohio Library Association published their *Standards for Public Library Service in Ohio* in 1986. Most of the measures in the book are of little value to school library media programs because they address issues of a different audience. However, their method of combining standards with evaluative reporting is unique and could be adopted by library media specialists. Their document lists each standard and asks whether that standard has been achieved, is being worked on, or has not yet begun. Then at the conclusion of the standard statement, the percentage of Ohio libraries which reach that standard is reported. A sample standard follows:

All Ohio residents should receive information and materials in a reasonable time regardless of location or format of the information and materials.

Ohio residents should:
> receive correct answers to their questions, with 80% of those questions answered by the end of the business day.

A library is considered to achieve this standard if it:

1. conducts a reference fill rate study at least every three years using the procedures in *Output Measures for Public Libraries*. (Procedures for measuring accuracy have not been developed as yet.)

   Reference fill rate measures the number of reference transactions *completed* by the end of a working day, in proportion to the total number of reference transactions for that day.

2. achieves an 80% reference fill rate.

In 1986, over 50% of 31 responding Ohio public libraries exceeded this standard in terms of completing questions by the end of the business day.[1]

This method of reporting progress might well be adopted by a district for a school board meeting. Goals for a year or five years could be listed very succinctly and progress noted for each goal. Note how the evaluative instrument defines each standard and explains how a particular standard is to be measured.

The Indiana Student Survey

One of the measures created by a group of Indiana district library media supervisors was designed to measure student attitudes regarding the materials they check out of the LMC. These supervisors selected the survey method of measuring attitude, but they gave the questionnaire a new twist. Their measure is reprinted in figure 12.6.

Outcome 2; Evaluation 1: CIRCULATION SURVEY

Objective:

Measure students' attitudes regarding materials they check out from the school library media center.

Method:

Create a bookmark questionnaire [see below] to be distributed in outgoing materials. The questionnaire could be placed in randomly chosen items, for instance every tenth item checked out, or in specifically chosen items such as all the materials pertinent to a particular instructional unit.

Have a fishbowl/box for questionnaires returned *after* the material has been used. In payment for a returned, completed questionnaire, offer a really nice bookmark, or conduct a raffle with winners being drawn from the bowl of returned questionnaires.

Plan when and how often to use this measure. Tailor the questions to a specific purpose.

Check responses to curricular assignments, motivational reading efforts, and natural circulation. Use this measure as one strategy to measure how well the collection is responding to student needs.

Sample Bookmark/Questionnaire:

For curricular materials . . .

For recreational materials . . .

Your Name: Your Room #: Title of Material: What did you need this material for? Did this material answer that need? Was this material easy, difficult, or just right? Would you recommend this material as a good source of information?

Your Name: Your Room #: Title of Material: Did you check this out for pleasure? How did you select this material? (suggested by teacher; recommended by friend; etc.) Was this material easy, difficult, or just right? Did you enjoy this material? Would you recommend this material to a friend?

Fig. 12.6. Circulation survey. Reprinted from "Draft Evaluation Measures for School Libraries" (Indianapolis, Ind.: Indiana Department of Public Instruction, 1987. Reprinted with permission.

COMMUNICATING EVALUATION DATA

Collecting evaluative data, then burying their
meaning in jargon or mystical tabular form

Generally, a principal, a school board, or a parent has little time to spend analyzing reports or evaluative data produced by the library media center staff. In many cases, the data collected are really for internal staff use and would neither be understood nor appreciated by an outsider.

If the information collected would be of interest to an outsider, then a good deal of time should be spent deciding how to communicate that information to the people who need to examine it.

We all live in an information-rich society. From every corner, via every medium, people and organizations are trying to get our attention. Try to answer the following questions.

1. "Where's the beef" refers to _____ .

2. Jerry Lewis wants us all to contribute to _____ .

3. The major reason our government says it must have nuclear weapons is to support its policy of _____ .

4. The newspaper most widely read is _____ .

5. The candy which will melt in your mouth, but not in your hand, is _____ .

6. When Neil Armstrong set foot on the moon, he said _____ .

7. The two old farmers who advertise wine coolers are pushing the products of _____ .

Advertising or propaganda campaigns bring much to the public's attention. Oftimes, this is done through humor, shock, and fancy graphics, and most of the time, through repetition. The American Library Association has been very successful in the past decade in getting out its message by the use of posters with famous people pictured on them. There's Bill Cosby telling us that reading is a neat idea. Or there is Dan Marino or Lee Iacocca saying "Get a head start at the library." George Burns, Miss Piggy, Goldie Hawn, Bette Midler, Mikhail Baryshnikov, or Sting saying "READ." "E.T. reads at home." "Discover new worlds: Explore your library." "Library: a word to the wise." "Jog your mind: run to your library"—are all familiar poster products.

Should library media specialists hire a Madison Avenue firm to get the word out? Sounds like a good idea, but we can't afford it. Anyway, why hire Madison Avenue when we can study their tactics for free every day of our lives. That doesn't mean be a copycat, such as using "Where's the beef? The library of course!" but there is much we all can learn just by paying attention.

How many complex concepts or results of sophisticated research are communicated to us every day in ways we can all understand? Plenty. The news broadcasts tell us the results of complex experiments published in the *New England Journal of Medicine*, pollsters communicate the results of their latest polls, and *U.S.A. Today* uses pictograms in the lower lefthand corner of the front page to communicate to us some piece of data. All of these communicators tell us their message in thirty seconds or less and most of us can understand what they mean.

Throughout this book, principles and data have been pictured in ways to suggest to the readers different ways to communicate information. Mark Loertscher, the illustrator of the book, used the programs Super Paint, Cricket Draw, and Adobe Illustrator on a Macintosh Plus computer connected to a laser printer to produce the drawings. There are a number of computer programs available which do graphing using data from spreadsheets or databases, or the data can be entered by hand. Many students might be pleased to help create such computer graphics or they might help discover ways to present a complicated piece of library information to a novice.

The most common ways of communicating data are bar charts, line graphs, circle graphs, or pictograms. All these techniques have been used in this book, but the author and illustrator have only scratched the surface of possibilities. One of the fun things to do for an in-service session of library media specialists would be to take a district report, a library media report, a research study, and a state research report and translate the findings into a few simple pictograms which could be interpreted by a layperson in thirty seconds or less. The author has done this on several occasions, and the group often comes up with some great ideas.

To begin, start with a simple line graph, change the scale, and redraw the graph. Example: graph the federal deficit for the past five years in billions of dollars. Now in trillions of dollars. Now in millions of dollars (can't be done). If you are a Democrat, which chart would you use in your campaign speech? If you are a Republican, which chart would you use? Now chart the library media budget for the past five years in dollars per student using one dollar increments. Using ten dollar increments. Using ten cent intervals. Then chart the library media budget for the past five years in constant dollars using the price of a book five years ago as the base.

There was a book published many years ago entitled *How to Lie with Statistics*. That book taught many ways to deceive any audience by using facts and figures. Library media specialists might well dig up that book and read it, not with the intention of misleading the public, but to jog our creative minds that there are many ways to look at facts and figures, depending on our motives. Not long ago, *Harper* published a thin paperback of some of the statistics they publish in their monthly "Index" page. Their idea is to juxtapose certain statistics which will make the reader laugh, consider, and think. Four examples are given here:

Amount the Reagan administration budgeted for military bands in 1987:
$154,200,000.

Amount it budgeted for the National Endowment for the Arts:
$144,900,000.

Number of videocassettes rented in 1985:
1,200,000,000.

Number of books checked out from public libraries:
1,197,000,000.[2]

While the creators of the "Index" leave it to the reader to make their own conclusions, the intent of the authors is usually apparent, as the above examples show.

Statistics can be used to sway many minds if used creatively. In the early 1960s when readers of *McCall's* read that Americans spent more on dog food than on library books for children, the nation was outraged and we got ESEA Title II, which pumped money into every school library in the country. The statistic itself was not the prime reason for the legislation, but it certainly helped.

As a final piece of advice for those who are collecting and using statistics with the object of improving the conditions of library media programs, it would be wise to read the road sign posted just as you enter Snowmass Village, Colorado. It teaches a great lesson about statistics (see figure 12.7): If you are going to use statistics to support a position, for heaven's sake, use good sense and judgment! Also, it doesn't hurt to tell the truth!

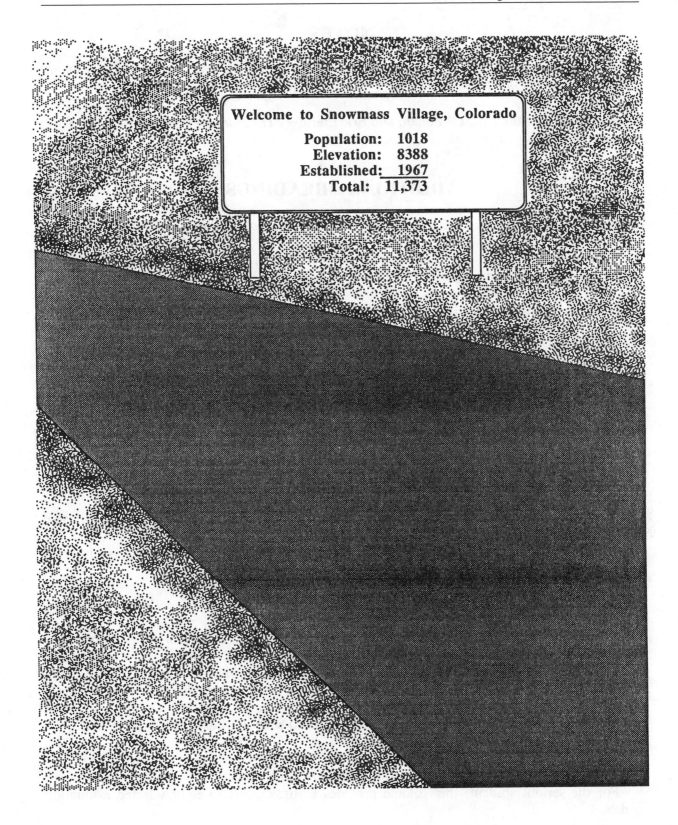

Fig. 12.7. Welcome to Snowmass.

NOTES

1. Ohio Library Association, Library Development Committee, et al., *Standards for Public Library Service in Ohio* (Columbus, Ohio: The Association, 1986), 8.

2. Lewis H. Lapham, Michael Pollan, and Eric Eteridge, *The Harper's Index Book* (New York: Henry Holt and Co., 1987), xi, 28.

ADDITIONAL READINGS

Bruning, James L., and B. L. Kintz. *Computational Handbook of Statistics*, 2nd ed. Glenview, Ill.: Scott, Foresman, 1977.
  Still one of the best and clearest statistical cookbooks which clearly illustrates how to compute a statistical measure, with some hints on interpretation.

Isaac, Stephen, and William B. Michaels. *Handbook in Research and Evaluation*. San Diego, Calif.: Robert R. Knapp, 1971.
  Still one of the best handbooks on research design and methods of conducting evaluations.

Joint Committee on Standards for Evaluation. *Standards for Evaluation of Educational Programs, Projects, and Materials*. New York: McGraw-Hill, 1981.
  For the serious evaluator, these standards set the stage for quantitative and ethical considerations when conducting educational evaluations.

Klein, M. Frances. *How to Study a School*. West Lafayette, Ind.: Kappa Delta Pi, 1983.
  Gives brief but valuable guidelines for conducting evaluation and research studies.

Liesener, James W. *A Systematic Planning Process for School Media Programs*. Chicago: American Library Association, 1976.
  Liesener's technique for planning is to involve teachers in a systematic prioritizing of library media services.

Morris, Lynn Lyons, and Carol Taylor Fitz-Gibbon. *Program Evaluation Kit*. Beverly Hills, Calif.: Sage Publications, 1978.
  The kit consists of eight volumes with the following titles: *The Evaluator's Handbook*, *How to Deal with Goals and Objectives*, *How to Design a Program Evaluation*, *How to Measure Program Implementation*, *How to Measure Attitudes*, *How to Measure Achievement*, *How to Calculate Statistics*, and *How to Present an Evaluation Report*. Each volume is well written and is understandable by a person somewhat knowledgeable in research methods. The last volume of presenting the evaluation report is particularly helpful to school library media specialists.

Stufflebeam, Daniel L., and Anthony J. Shinkfield. *Systematic Evaluation: A Self-Instructional Guide to Theory and Practice*. Boston: Kluwer-Nijhoff, 1985.
  For the serious student, this volume provides a study guide to eight selected evaluation models.

Yesner, Bernice L., and Hilda L. Jay. *The School Administrator's Guide to Evaluating Library Media Programs*. Hamden, Conn.: Library Professional Publications, 1987.

Yesner and Jay provide the principal with numerous topics, mostly warehousing and operational parts of the LMC program. Rather than evaluative instruments or methodologies, the approach is to provide summary statements or points to consider as the principal looks for positive elements, negative elements, missing elements, and possible solutions to problems.

Zweizig, Douglas L., Joan A. Braune, and Gloria A. Waity. *Output Measures for Children's Services in Wisconsin Public Libraries: A Pilot Project, 1984-85*. Madison, Wis.: Wisconsin Division for Library Services, 1985.

A few of the measures in this publication could be adapted for use in school libraries, but most measure only direct services. Measures include circulation, in-library use of materials, number of library visits, program attendance, reference fill rate, and turnover rate of materials.

Epilogue

It was the year 2000. The old and ornate ballroom of the Palmer Hotel in Chicago was filled to overflowing for the fortieth anniversary of the publication of the 1960 *Standards for School Libraries*. President Marilyn Miller, who had been called from the ranks to serve her third term, was busily putting the final touches on her program. The AASL Board had invited the membership to this important occasion and it seemed that everyone had responded.

Forty years! It had been four decades filled with elation and challenges for school libraries and public education as well. President Miller was about to do two important things. The first was to distribute copies of the seventh edition of national standards to the eager crowd. The copies were piled all along the head table and one could barely see the faces of the board over the books. The second event of the morning was a report of a ten-year longitudinal study of school libraries.

In 1990, the Knapp Foundation had offered AASL a third major grant to study the impact of school libraries on children, teachers, and education. Long-term effects were to be measured by studying the best LMC programs in the country. Participating schools had given assurances that LMC programs would be encouraged to flourish over the period of the study and grant funds were available to ensure that excellence was maintained.

President Miller made one last check of the ten-foot computer monitor on which the results of the study would be made known to the audience. The researchers had been working feverishly for the past six months in Washington, D.C., and because of the deadline were merely going to flash their findings electronically to the conference.

The first part of the program went smoothly. Copies of the 2000 standards were distributed and their features explained. The audience had received their copies with appreciation, but were really anticipating the results of the research. They were thinking, which of all the things librarians do make the most difference? Which part of the program the 2000 standards propose should be emphasized?

During the coffee break, President Miller called the research team. Yes, they were ready to transmit the findings and were just awaiting the signal. Sounding her gavel, Marilyn brought the audience back to attention. An air of expectancy spread over the crowd as she described the study. Marilyn then raised her telephone and dialed the appropriate number and signal to the Washington Office.

Suddenly over the giant screen came an array of numbers, not words. President Miller was stunned. The audience was puzzled. So deep was the shock, that they all just sat quietly trying to figure out whether the message was garble, or code, or just preliminary data transmission. Suddenly a ten-year-old boy from the audience stood up (his mother had brought him to the convention as a reward for getting straight As on his report card) and said, "I know what it says!"

President Miller asked the boy to come to the podium and whisper what it meant in her ear. He did so, first revealing that the message was in a common code that every computer hacker knows backward and forward. He whispered the decoded message in her ear. "I thought I had guessed the message," Marilyn said over the microphone, and was just about to announce it when a fire alarm sounded and the room had to be cleared.

A grease fire in the kitchen was quickly brought under control, but upstairs, the old ornate ballroom was still a little smokey. Over in the corner, still brightly lit, was the computer message, which read:

82 101 115 111 117 114 99 101 45 98 97 115 101 100 32 116 101 97 99

104 105 110 103 32 104 97 115 32 109 97 100 101 32 116 104 101 32 108

105 98 114 97 114 121 32 109 101 100 105 97 32 99 101 110 116 101

114 32 116 104 101 32 104 101 97 114 116 32 111 102 32 116 104 101 32

115 99 104 111 111 108 33

Appendix A: Instruments for Evaluating School Library Media Specialists and Programs

This appendix contains six evaluation instruments of school library media specialists and programs which are in use in states and school districts. The first three, the Iowa, Iowa City and Tennessee models, include the role of the school library media specialist as presented in this book. All of the techniques represented here have merit and each could be easily modified for use in a local school. For those instruments lacking a resource-based teaching section, one could easily be added. All have been reprinted with permission.

THE IOWA MODEL*

The Professional Growth Committee of the Iowa Educational Media Association began in the fall of 1982 to create a model task list for library media specialists. This blue-ribbon panel not only accomplished its task, but created a draft evaluation instrument to match the task list. The entire instrument is based not only on the original taxonomy of the author, but on the work of notable people such as Dr. Evelyn H. Daniel, Donald P. Ely, and Dr. James Liesener. The entire task list and draft evaluation document are reprinted here.

A Model Task List for
School Media Specialists

Iowa Educational Media Association, 1985

FOREWORD

The role of the librarian who once spent the day typing, filing and checking out books has changed. The rapid expansion of information technology during the last decade placed the demands upon instruction in schools, propelling the librarian into a new role as school media specialist.

The transformation from librarian to media specialist and library to media center has not evolved smoothly. Many colleges of education, professional associations, school boards and parents continue to struggle with the role of the media specialist in the educational process.

Many media specialists have difficulty in grasping a concept of their role in schools. They are pressured to understand state-of-the-art technology and apply that knowledge to instruction and information retrieval. Increasingly, they find themselves involved in the instructional development process, while they still retain the traditional role as keeper of books. Media specialists must understand their role in the instructional program and assess the skills required to perform their professional duties. Therefore, the Professional Growth Committee of the Iowa Educational Media Association has developed a model task list to:

1. Guide media specialists in developing the "higher level" media services—those services which involve planning with the teacher to facilitate efficient, effective learning.

2. Help media specialists understand their role in the instructional program, to assess their professional performance and to set goals for improvement.

3. Be used as one tool for performance evaluation of the media specialist, and/or as a basis for developing job descriptions for media specialists.

Incorporated in this list is a taxonomy of tasks related to curriculum based upon the work of Dr. David V. Loertscher.

---

*Professional Growth Committee, Iowa Educational Media Association, "A Model Task List for School Media Specialists," 1985.

In his article, "The School Library Media Center, A New Force in American Education," Loertscher discusses the successive stages in the development of the media center. His discussion places the current identity crisis of media specialists and the role of media programs in perspective.

Briefly stated, Loertscher divides the development into two revolutions. The first revolution introduced audiovisual materials as a resource for learning. The multi-media concept—learning from film, transparencies, slides, prints, audio, as well as books—evolved. The first revolution resulted in:

1. Classroom collections merged into a single, central collection.

2. The addition of audiovisual media and equipment as part of the media center.

3. Improved collections.

4. Hiring of professional and clerical staff.

The second revolution involves the media program as part of the curriculum. To Loertscher, the ideal media program is part of the curriculum and the media specialist is an integral part of the teaching team. Certainly not every curricular unit will require use of the media center staff and facilities, but the idea of the media center only as a warehouse for resources is as obsolete as the wire recorder and the box camera. The ideal program combines the first and second revolutions. Loertscher summarizes the role of the media program in the educational process.

> The first revolution (which still is continuing) brought into existence the library media center. This is a central facility in the school which serves as the repository for books, pamphlets, magazines, filmstrips, films, videotapes, videodiscs and computer programs. These materials must be accompanied by equipment and space for use by individuals, small groups and large groups. To build and interpret this collection as a curricular force, there is a professional library media specialist who has technical, clerical and volunteer assistance. This LMC staff performs a wide range of tasks including housekeeping chores, dynamic services and program activities.

> The second revolution seeks to take this resource—the LMC—into the heart of the curriculum—to teach educators how to base their learning activities upon the bedrock of media experience. The second revolution seeks to make the collection, the equipment and the staff used—not isolated—not neglected—not like a trophy in a trophy case. The second revolution promotes the concept of instructional development and shows how this can be integrated with traditional LMC services to produce a total program.

MODEL TASK LIST

A. CURRICULUM TAXONOMY

1. NO INVOLVEMENT

The media specialist:

1.1 Assesses whether the media center staff or facilities need to be involved with a unit of instruction.

2. SELF-HELP WAREHOUSE

The media specialist:

2.1 Selects and maintains a collection.

2.2 Plans use of media facilities by allocating space according to the needs of the students, staff, and program.

2.3 Uses a variety of sources to obtain current reviews and information about material and equipment.

2.4 Develops policies and guidelines for storage and retrieval systems.

2.5 Organizes and maintains accurate storage and retrieval systems.

2.6 Organizes and maintains accurate accession and inventory records of materials and equipment.

2.7 Compiles and organizes orders for materials and equipment.

2.8 Supervises receiving and processing of materials for storage and circulation.

2.9 Supervises circulation of materials and equipment.

2.10 Arranges for inspection, maintenance, replacement, and repair of equipment.

3. INDIVIDUAL AND GROUP REFERENCE ASSISTANCE

The media specialist:

3.1 Guides staff and students in the use of reference materials.

3.2 Teaches retrieval skills.

3.3 Provides students and staff with appropriate experiences in reading, listening, and viewing.

4. SPONTANEOUS INTERACTION AND GATHERING

The media specialist:

4.1 Responds positively to spur-of-the-moment requests for materials and assistance.

5. CURSORY PLANNING

The media specialist:

5.1 Recommends alternative media formats.

5.2 Takes advantage of informal situations to offer teachers recommendations of teaching strategies and/or instructional materials.

6. PLANNED GATHERING

The media specialist:

6.1 Meets with staff to identify needs for instructional materials.

6.2 Identifies, in advance, materials appropriate for classroom instruction.

6.3 Prepares selective bibliographies.

7. EVANGELISTIC OUTREACH

The media specialist:

7.1 Plans and provides media in-service.

7.2 Initiates programs to motivate students to read, view, and listen.

7.3 Teaches design and production of media.

7.4 Disseminates results of research related to the media program.

7.5 Plans and implements a public relations program.

7.6 Establishes regular communication channels between the media center and students, teachers, administrators, parents, and the school board.

7.7 Initiates use of media center materials and facilities in spontaneous situations.

8. SCHEDULED PLANNING IN THE SUPPORT ROLE

The media specialist:

8.1 Supports teacher and student goals and objectives by supplying appropriate resources.

8.2 Uses basic principles of instructional design to produce media that meet learning objectives.

8.3 Initiates use of media center materials and facilities in planned situations.

9. INSTRUCTIONAL DESIGN

The media specialist:

9.1 Analyzes learner characteristics.

9.2 Elicits and clarifies objectives of teacher and/or learner.

9.3 Assists in determining instructional content.

9.4 Cooperates with other staff to integrate the teaching of media skills into the curriculum.

9.5 Teaches media skills where appropriate.

9.6 Teaches analysis, synthesis, and evaluation of information.

9.7 Shares with the teacher in evaluation of students' progress.

10. CURRICULUM DEVELOPMENT

The media specialist:

10.1 Serves on curriculum committees as an information resource for curriculum development.

10.2 Participates in selection and evaluation of instructional materials.

B. ADMINISTRATION

The media specialist:

1.1 Establishes and implements philosophies and goals of the media program.

1.2 Prepares and administers the building media center budget.

1.3 Seeks information about local, state, and federal policies, standards, legislation, regulations, additional funding sources and certification.

1.4 Assesses whether the daily operation of the media center meets program goals.

1.5 Writes job descriptions for the media staff.

1.6 Provides for the training of media staff.

1.7 Supervises and evaluates the performance of media staff.

1.8 Designs facilities and establishes policies for operation of these facilities.

1.9 Adapts space to meet current needs.

1.10 Determines the need for conducting research activities related to the media program.

1.11 Designs and conducts research studies for the development of the media program.

1.12 Develops a plan for evaluating the media program based upon stated objectives according to recognized, accepted standards.

1.13 Cooperates with other media service agencies.

C. PROFESSIONAL GROWTH

The media specialist:

1.1 Evaluates and identifies areas of personal strength and weakness and seeks improvement of skills and professional performance.

1.2 Participates in district, county, regional, state, and national organizations.

ACKNOWLEDGEMENTS

The Professional Growth Committee of the Iowa Educational Media Association (IEMA) began in the fall of 1982 to create a model task list for media specialists. The professional work of Dr. David Loertscher, Dr. Evelyn H. Daniel, Dr. Donald P. Ely and Dr. James Liesener provides the basis of the model program.

In addition, recognition needs to go to the members of the Professional Growth Committee, 1982-1985:

1984-1985

Dr. Robert Hardman, Chair, media director, University of Northern Iowa, Cedar Falls
Karlene Garn, media specialist, Ames
June Gross, media director, Iowa City
Joyce Hamilton, media specialist, Ames
Mary Jo Langhorne, media specialist, Iowa City
Larry McLain, media coordinator, Cedar Falls
Pat Severson, media specialist, Clear Lake

1983-1984	1982-1983
Pat Brown, Chair	Pat Brown, Chair
Jean Donham	Joyce Hamilton
Karlene Garn	Susan Hayes
Larry McLain	Kathy Parker
Pat Severson	Chuck Ruebling
	Pat Severson
	Russ Stahl
	Dianne Woodard

Acknowledgement of Assistance

Barb Beebe	Elizabeth Martin
Alisa Chapman	Jane Nagy
Lae Una DeWitt	Eva Otten
Lois Harker	Roger Volker
Carol Iverson	

IEMA Board of Directors, 1984-1985

Officers:

Pat Meier, President
Mike Simonson, Vice-President
Pat Severson, Past President
Karen Dole, Secretary
Don Powell, Treasurer

Directors:

Quentin Coffman
Karlene Garn
Tom Hoffman
Larry McLain
Lynn Myers
Ilene Rewerts
Paul Spurlock
Margaret White
June Wishman
Betty Yunek

DRAFT
MEDIA PROGRAM EVALUATION*

Directions: As a media specialist, rate how often you perform each of the following tasks using the scale:

1— Never
2— Rarely
3— Occasionally/Sometimes
4— Frequently
5— Always
N/A— Not applicable—subtract 1 from total for each N/A

After marking all of your ratings, compute the average rating at each of the summary points, and chart these means on the Summary Chart.

SELF-HELP WAREHOUSE

1 2 3 4 5   1. I select and maintain a collection of print and nonprint materials that supports the building curriculum.

1 2 3 4 5   2. I keep the shelf list up-to-date.

1 2 3 4 5   3. I weed the collection on a regular basis.

1 2 3 4 5   4. I consider for purchase materials recommended by faculty.

1 2 3 4 5   5. I consider for purchase materials recommended by students.

1 2 3 4 5   6. I encourage faculty involvement in the selection of materials by circulating reviews.

1 2 3 4 5   7. I encourage faculty involvement in the evaluation of materials.

1 2 3 4 5   8. I provide space for large groups in the media center.

1 2 3 4 5   9. I provide space for small group activities in the media center.

1 2 3 4 5   10. I provide space for individualized use of the media center.

1 2 3 4 5   11. I provide space for a professional collection.

1 2 3 4 5   12. I provide space for student production of materials.

1 2 3 4 5   13. I provide space for staff production of materials.

*Developed by the Professional Growth Committee, Iowa Educational Media Association. Reprinted by permission.

1 2 3 4 5   14. I use professional reviewing tools and recommended lists to select materials.

1 2 3 4 5   15. I use objective evaluations in the selection of equipment.

1 2 3 4 5   16. I provide media center orientation for students and new or returning teachers via classes, handbooks, consultations, etc.

1 2 3 4 5   17. I organize the media collection so that it is easily accessible to staff and students.

1 2 3 4 5   18. I make print and non-print materials accessible to staff.

1 2 3 4 5   19. I make print materials accessible to students.

1 2 3 4 5   20. I make non-print materials accessible to students.

1 2 3 4 5   21. I maintain a catalog of print and non-print materials that is accessible to users.

1 2 3 4 5   22. I schedule and distribute hardware.

1 2 3 4 5   23. I keep an accurate inventory of print and non-print materials.

1 2 3 4 5   24. I keep an accurate inventory of media hardware.

1 2 3 4 5   25. I order materials and equipment according to a long range plan.

1 2 3 4 5   26. I purchase materials as they are requested or needed.

1 2 3 4 5   27. I coordinate the selection and evaluation of learning materials and appropriate equipment.

1 2 3 4 5   28. I maintain a consideration file.

1 2 3 4 5   29. I arrange for materials to be processed.

1 2 3 4 5   30. I verify delivery of ordering materials.

1 2 3 4 5   31. I keep repair records for equipment.

1 2 3 4 5   32. I provide for the inspection and maintenance of equipment according to a plan.

1 2 3 4 5   33. I have a long range plan for the replacement of equipment.

Total of all ratings circled in questions 1-33 _____

Divide total of ratings by 33: _____

Graph the result on the chart under "Self-Help Warehouse."

REFERENCE ASSISTANCE

1 2 3 4 5   34.   I provide orientation on the use of the media center for staff.

1 2 3 4 5   35.   I provide orientation on the use of the media center for students.

1 2 3 4 5   36.   I provide individual guidance in research.

1 2 3 4 5   37.   I provide group instruction in reference skills when relevant to students' needs.

1 2 3 4 5   38.   I teach students the skills necessary for independent use of the media center.

1 2 3 4 5   39.   I provide storytelling experiences and introduce materials of special interest to class groups.

1 2 3 4 5   40.   I provide booktalk experiences and introduce materials of special interest to class groups.

1 2 3 4 5   41.   I provide reading guidance to students, considering both student interest and appropriate level of difficulty.

1 2 3 4 5   42.   I provide listening and/or viewing guidance to students, considering both student interest and appropriate level of difficulty.

Total of all rating circled in questions 34 to 42: _____
Divide total of rating by 9: _____
Graph the result on the chart under "Reference Assistance."

SPONTANEOUS SERVICE

1 2 3 4 5   43.   I provide materials and services in response to spur-of-the-moment requests.

Graph rating for #43 under "Spontaneous Service."

CURSORY PLANNING

1 2 3 4 5   44.   I recommend materials in a variety of formats appropriate to the activity, upon teacher request.

1 2 3 4 5   45.   I talk with teachers during unstructured times (breaks, planning periods, etc.) and suggest materials appropriate to their instructional needs.

1 2 3 4 5   46. I talk with teachers during unstructured times and suggest instructional strategies.

Total of all rating circled in questions 44-46: _____
Divide total of ratings by 3: _____
Graph the results on the chart under "Cursory Planning."

PLANNED GATHERING

1 2 3 4 5   47. I meet with teaching teams or individual teachers to identify their needs for instructional materials.

1 2 3 4 5   48. I allocate sufficient time to identify and gather materials for class room instruction.

1 2 3 4 5   49. I make use of a variety of sources (building district collections, public library, AEA, rental collections) to locate and procure materials in advance of classroom instruction.

1 2 3 4 5   50. I prepare selective bibliographies upon teacher request.

Total of all ratings circled in questions 47-50: _____
Divide total of ratings by 4: _____
Graph the result on the chart under "Planned Gathering."

EVANGELISTIC OUTREACH

1 2 3 4 5   51. I provide inservice sessions on topics related to print materials.

1 2 3 4 5   52. I provide inservice sessions on topics related to non-print materials.

1 2 3 4 5   53. I provide inservice sessions on topics related to instructional technology.

1 2 3 4 5   54. I develop special and/or on-going programs which provide students with incentives to read.

1 2 3 4 5   55. I develop special and/or on-going programs which provide students with incentives to utilize non-print materials.

1 2 3 4 5   56. I provide students with instruction in the design and production of print materials.

1 2 3 4 5   57. I provide students with instruction in the design and production of non-print materials.

1 2 3 4 5   58. I make available to the faculty, journal articles and other research related to the media program.

1 2 3 4 5   59. I use public relations devices to promote the media program.

1 2 3 4 5   60. I provide information to newspapers, television, and other mass media to promote the media program as an asset to the educational process.

1 2 3 4 5   61. I have established systematic procedures for communicating with students.

1 2 3 4 5   62. I have established systematic procedures for communicating with teachers.

1 2 3 4 5   63. I have established systematic procedures for communicating with administrators.

1 2 3 4 5   64. I have established systematic procedures for communicating with parents.

1 2 3 4 5   65. I have established systematic procedures for communicating with parent volunteers.

1 2 3 4 5   66. I have established systematic procedures for communicating with school board members.

1 2 3 4 5   67. I offer creative ideas for the use of the media center.

1 2 3 4 5   68. I offer creative ideas for the use of media materials.

Total of all ratings circled in questions 51-68: _____
Divide total of ratings by 18: _____
Graph the result on the chart under "Evangelistic Outreach."

SUPPORT OF INSTRUCTION

1 2 3 4 5   69. I schedule blocks of time at least fifteen minutes in length to meet with individual teachers to determine the specific objectives of instructional units.

1 2 3 4 5   70. I select materials at the appropriate levels and in the appropriate formats to meet the objectives of instructional units.

1 2 3 4 5   71. I design and produce media using basic principles of instructional development.

1 2 3 4 5   72. I initiate use of media center materials and facilities in planning situations.

Total of all ratings circled in questions 69-72: _____
Divide total of ratings by 4: _____
Graph the result on the chart under "Support of Instruction."

INSTRUCTIONAL DESIGN

1 2 3 4 5   73. I assist the teacher in identifying needs, interests, and abilities of individual students.

1 2 3 4 5   74. I conduct structured interviews to elicit and clarify objectives of the teachers.

1 2 3 4 5   75. I assist the teacher in identifying what the behavior of the learner will be.

1 2 3 4 5   76. I assist the teacher in identifying what the level of difficulty and cognitive complexity of the content.

1 2 3 4 5   77. I cooperate with other staff to integrate the teaching of media skills into the curriculum.

1 2 3 4 5   78. I teach media skills where appropriate.

1 2 3 4 5   79. I teach students to analyze information.

1 2 3 4 5   80. I teach students to synthesize information from a variety of sources.

1 2 3 4 5   81. I teach students to evaluate information.

1 2 3 4 5   82. I share with the teacher in evaluation of the student's progress.

Total of all ratings circled in questions 73-82: _____
Divide total of ratings by 10: _____
Graph the result on the chart under "Instructional Design."

CURRICULUM DEVELOPMENT

1 2 3 4 5   83. I participate in the planning of curriculum by providing ideas and suggestions.

1 2 3 4 5   84. I serve on curriculum development committees at the building and/or district level.

1 2 3 4 5   85. I provide guidance to curriculum committees by suggesting systematic approaches to curriculum development.

1 2 3 4 5   86. I participate in the evaluation and selection of instructional materials (textbooks, maps, curriculum units, etc.)

Total of all ratings circled in questions 83-86: _____
Divide total of ratings by 4: _____
Graph the result on the chart under "Curriculum Development."

PROGRAM

1 2 3 4 5   87. I have prepared a written philosophy for the media program.

1 2 3 4 5   88. I establish short and long term goals for the media program which are consistent with building goals.

1 2 3 4 5   89. I use the written philosophy of the media program as the basis for implementing program goals.

1 2 3 4 5   90. I keep informed about local, state, and federal policies affecting media centers.

1 2 3 4 5   91. I help to develop and implement proposals for projects and programs.

1 2 3 4 5   92. My school district has a board-adopted selection policy that includes re-consideration of materials, censoring.

1 2 3 4 5   93. I coordinate user's requests for service from other media service agencies, in order to provide the most effective, efficient services possible.

Total of all ratings circled in questions 87-93: _____
Divide total of ratings by 7: _____
Graph the result on the chart under "Program."

PERSONNEL MANAGEMENT

1 2 3 4 5   94. I prepare job descriptions for the media staff.

1 2 3 4 5   95. I review and revise media job descriptions to meet changing needs.

1 2 3 4 5   96. I provide training for media staff.

1 2 3 4 5   97. I formally evaluate the performance of the media staff.

Total of all ratings circled in questions 94-97: _____
Divide total of ratings by 4: _____
Graph the result on the chart under "Personnel Management."

BUDGET MANAGEMENT

1 2 3 4 5   98. I cooperate with my administrator in preparing a budget based upon the stated goals of the media program.

1 2 3 4 5   99. I manage the media budget effectively.

1 2 3 4 5   100. I keep records that indicate how the media budget is spent.

1 2 3 4 5   101. I spend the allotted budget amount.

Total of all ratings circled in questions 98-101: _____
Divide total of ratings by 4: _____
Graph the result on the chart under "Budget Management."

FACILITIES

1 2 3 4 5   102. I assist in the design of facilities throughout the school wherever media is to be used.

1 2 3 4 5   103. I design new or remodeled facilities for the media center.

1 2 3 4 5   104. I establish policies for the operation of facilities for the media program.

1 2 3 4 5   105. I adapt existing media facilities to meet current needs.

Total of all ratings circled in questions 103-106: _____
Divide total of ratings by 4: _____
Graph the result on the chart under "Facilities."

RESEARCH AND EVALUATION

1 2 3 4 5   106. I communicate with staff and students to assess media center services, materials and procedures.

1 2 3 4 5   107. I use written evaluations to assess the media program.

1 2 3 4 5   108. I identify areas of need for gathering information or statistics about the media program.

1 2 3 4 5   109. I design and conduct appropriate research relevant to the media program.

1 2 3 4 5   110. I develop plans for evaluating the media program based upon stated objectives according to recognized, accepted standards.

1 2 3 4 5   111. I work with personnel from other media service agencies (district, AEA, etc.) to determine effective methods for delivering media services to my staff and students.

Total of all ratings circled in questions 106-111: _____
Divide total of ratings by 6: _____
Graph the result on the chart under "Research and Evaluation."

PERSONAL DEVELOPMENT

1 2 3 4 5   112. I set challenging goals for myself and strive to manage my time to meet them.

1 2 3 4 5   113. I consult other media specialists to seek ways to improve my professional performance.

1 2 3 4 5   114. I attend workshops and inservices.

1 2 3 4 5   115. I read, view and listen to professional materials.

1 2 3 4 5   116. I enroll in graduate coursework.

Total of all ratings circled in questions 112-116: _____
Divide total of ratings by 5: _____
Graph the result on the chart under "Personal Development."

PROFESSIONALISM

1 2 3 4 5   117. I belong to media-related professional organizations.

1 2 3 4 5   118. I participate in the activities of media-related professional organizations.

1 2 3 4 5   119. I serve on decision-making committees in media-related professional organizations.

1 2 3 4 5   120. I share my knowledge and expertise through presentations at inservices, workshops and conferences.

Total of all ratings circled in questions 117-120: _____
Divide total of ratings by 4: _____
Graph the result on the chart under "Professionalism."

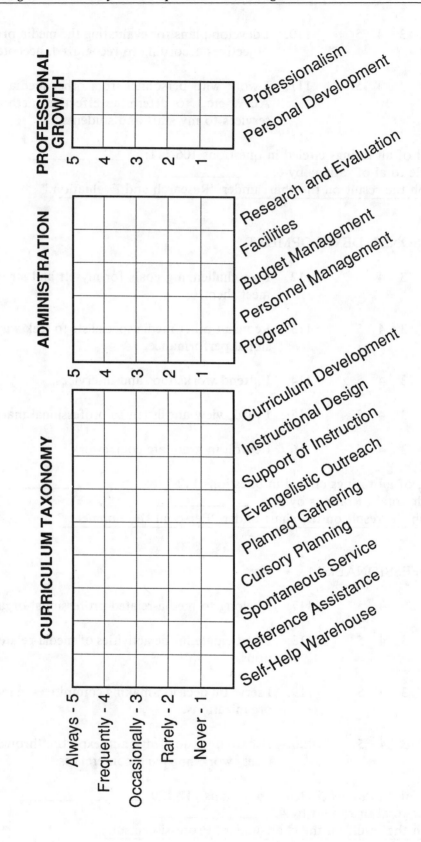

School Media Program Evaluation
SUMMARY

PROFESSIONAL GROWTH

- Professionalism
- Personal Development

ADMINISTRATION

- Research and Evaluation
- Facilities
- Budget Management
- Personnel Management
- Program

CURRICULUM TAXONOMY

- Curriculum Development
- Instructional Design
- Support of Instruction
- Evangelistic Outreach
- Planned Gathering
- Cursory Planning
- Spontaneous Service
- Reference Assistance
- Self-Help Warehouse

Always - 5
Frequently - 4
Occasionally - 3
Rarely - 2
Never - 1

THE IOWA CITY, IOWA, MODEL*

Jean Donham, the supervisor of library media programs in Iowa City, Iowa, developed an evaluation document which is used in the performance evaluation of library media specialists. The building principal fills out this form using evidence from observations and documentation collected by the library media specialist. This document does contain items which request evidence of an impact on the curriculum.

*Developed by Jean Donham for the Iowa City Community Schools, Iowa. Reprinted by permission.

IOWA CITY COMMUNITY SCHOOLS

PERFORMANCE EVALUATION

MEDIA SPECIALIST

NAME _____ GRADE LEVEL/SUBJECT _____

BUILDING _____ YEAR _____

KEY:

1
☐

Exceeds Expectations: Work receiving this mark is outstanding and above the standard that the district expects from teaching staff. This mark represents work clearly above and beyond that judged to meet district expectations.

2
☐

Meets Expectations: Work receiving this mark is the standard expected by the district. It represents high quality work and/or effective teaching.

3
☐

Needs Improvement: Work receiving this mark needs to be improved.

4
☐

Unacceptable: Work receiving this mark is clearly below the expectation of district. Work that is marked unacceptable must be brought up to district standard if continued employment is expected.

A. Teaching Strategies and Methodologies.

1. The Media Specialist plans effectively and purposefully.

    ### As Evidenced By

    The Media Specialist:

a. Clearly states objectives for lessons.	1 2 3 4
b. Sequences content and/or skills to be taught in relation to student achievement levels.	1 2 3 4
c. Prepares specific written lesson plans. Plans include varied activities during the class period.	1 2 3 4
d. Identifies and sequences components of the lesson.	1 2 3 4
e. Reviews and updates year-to-year unit plans.	1 2 3 4
f. Uses provided preparation time for tasks directly related to the media center program.	1 2 3 4

2. The Media Specialist uses a variety of materials and activities to stimulate and maximize learning.

    ### As Evidenced By

    The Media Specialist:

a. Uses materials and vocabulary appropriate to the achievement level of the students.	1 2 3 4
b. Develops an aesthetically pleasing environment.	1 2 3 4
c. Arranges the media center to facilitate instruction.	1 2 3 4
d. Makes appropriate use of audio visual materials.	1 2 3 4
e. Makes sure students understand expectations before beginning activities or using materials.	1 2 3 4
f. Uses activities that relate directly to the objective of the lesson.	1 2 3 4
g. Has materials and equipment necessary for the lesson available at the beginning of the lesson.	1 2 3 4
h. Actively involves students in the learning process.	1 2 3 4

A.   Teaching Strategies and Methodologies (*continued*)

3.   The Media Specialist delivers instruction in a manner that facilitates and maximizes learning.

As Evidenced By

The Media Specialist:

a.   Teaches to the objective established for the lesson.   1   2   3   4

b.   Presents assignments and directions clearly and concisely.   1   2   3   4

c.   Presents necessary input.   1   2   3   4

d.   Models or demonstrates expected learning for students.   1   2   3   4

e.   Stimulates pupil participation through directed discussion and questioning.   1   2   3   4

f.   Promotes higher level thinking.   1   2   3   4

g.   Provides time for practice and review.   1   2   3   4

h.   Provides opportunity for all students to be successful.   1   2   3   4

i.   Provides opportunity for all students to be successful.   1   2   3   4

4.   The Media Specialist demonstrates mastery of subject matter appropriate to level of students being taught.

As Evidenced By

The Media Specialist:

a.   Makes learning meaningful to students.   1   2   3   4

b.   Develops student's ability to use the media center independently.   1   2   3   4

c.   Keeps the difficulty level of instruction appropriate for each individual student by monitoring and adjusting the level of difficulty.   1   2   3   4

d.   Establishes a series of objectives which are clear and consistent with classroom curriculum.   1   2   3   4

Evaluator Comments:

B. Student Management.

1. The Media Specialist defines school and media center expectations to students.

    ### As Evidenced By

    The Media Specialist:

    a. Informs students of and consistently enforces behavioral expectations.   1 2 3 4

    b. Informs students of emergency procedures.   1 2 3 4

    c. Assumes responsibility for student supervision in all areas of the building.   1 2 3 4

    d. Follows procedures defined in district/building discipline policies.   1 2 3 4

    e. Does not leave students unsupervised.   1 2 3 4

2. The Media Specialist is skilled in management of student behavior.

    ### As Evidenced By

    The Media Specialist:

    a. Reinforces desired student behavior and responds appropriately to disruptive student behavior.   1 2 3 4

    b. Is consistent in the implementation of rules, regulations, and policies.   1 2 3 4

    c. Deals privately with students in discussing behavioral situations.   1 2 3 4

    d. Remains calm and poised in handling behavioral concerns.   1 2 3 4

    e. Informs parents of student behavioral concerns.   1 2 3 4

3. The Media Specialist respects the worth and dignity of each student.

    ### As Evidenced By

    The Media Specialist:

    a. Demonstrates a manner free from cynicism and/or sarcasm.   1 2 3 4

    b. Recognizes conditions which may lead to disciplinary problems and takes appropriate preventive action.   1 2 3 4

    c. Recognizes, analyzes, and works to correct causes of individual student dissatisfaction.   1 2 3 4

    d. Shows warmth and concern for students.   1 2 3 4

    e. Provides encouragement and support.   1 2 3 4

Evaluator Comments:

C. Curriculum

1. The Media Specialist demonstrates knowledge of the building curriculum.

    <u>As Evidenced By</u>

    The Media Specialist:

    a. Selects materials that support the building curriculum.   1 2 3 4

    b. Participates in building curriculum committees, department
        meetings and/or team meetings.   1 2 3 4

    c. Develops a procedure for staff to communicate units taught
        during the year.   1 2 3 4

    d. Initiates communication with staff regarding materials in the
        media center that match units being taught.   2 3 4 5

2. The Media Specialist provides support services and materials for teachers.

    <u>As Evidenced By</u>

    The Media Specialist:

    a. Meets spur-of-the-moment requests for assistance and
        materials.   1 2 3 4

    b. Takes advantage of informal opportunities to recommend
        materials or offer services.   1 2 3 4

    c. Gathers materials in advance of classroom instruction upon
        teacher request.   1 2 3 4

    d. Identifies specific materials/strategies appropriate for the
        teacher's objectives and the students' needs.   1 2 3 4

    e. Schedules times with individual teachers to plan use of media
        center materials in instruction.   1 2 3 4

    f. Plans units cooperatively with teachers and participates in
        the delivery of instruction.   1 2 3 4

    g. Assists teachers/students in use of media equipment.   1 2 3 4

3. The Media Specialist encourages students to read independently.

<u>As Evidenced By</u>

The Media Specialist:

a. Develops activities which promote reading. 1 2 3 4

b. Provides reading guidance to students, considering both student interest and appropriate level of difficulty. 1 2 3 4

c. Communicates with teachers regarding students' reading in terms of quantity, appropriateness of content, and level of difficulty. 1 2 3 4

d. Demonstrates knowledge of literature appropriate for students in his/her building. 1 2 3 4

Evaluator Comments:

D. Media Center Organization

1. The Media Specialist organizes the collection to facilitate use.

    #### As Evidenced By

    The Media Specialist:

    a. Maintains accurate and up-to-date catalogs and records.   1 2 3 4
    b. Arranges the collection systematically.   1 2 3 4
    c. Reviews and weeds the collection to keep it current and
        appropriate.   1 2 3 4
    d. Uses accepted inventory procedures.   1 2 3 4
    e. Works toward building a fully centralized collection of
        instructional materials and equipment.   1 2 3 4
    f. Insures that all equipment is in operating condition.   1 2 3 4

2. The Media Specialist develops circulation procedures.

    #### As Evidenced By

    The Media Specialist:

    a. Cooperates with the principal in developing circulation
        policy and procedures for the school.   1 2 3 4
    b. Implements a system for check-out and return of materials
        and equipment.   1 2 3 4
    c. Informs teaching staff of newly acquired materials.   1 2 3 4
    d. Encourages use of media center and its materials by teachers
        and students.   1 2 3 4
    e. Shares materials and equipment with other buildings in the
        district.   1 2 3 4

3. The Media Specialist implements budgeting procedures.

    #### As Evidenced By

    The Media Specialist:

    a. Cooperates with the principal in planning and managing the
        budget.   1 2 3 4
    b. Allocates media center budget in response to curricular
        needs of the building.   1 2 3 4
    c. Works with support staff to maintain appropriate budget
        records.   1 2 3 4

Evaluator Comments:

E.   Interpersonal Relations

1.   The Media Specialist demonstrates positive interpersonal relations.

<u>As Evidenced By</u>

The Media Specialist:

a.   Demonstrates poise and tactfulness.   1   2   3   4

b.   Is adaptable to change.   1   2   3   4

c.   Demonstrates tolerance for students, parents, staff, and administrators, whose ideas and opinions differ from his/her own.   1   2   3   4

d.   Effectively utilizes principles of reinforcement in working with others.   1   2   3   4

e.   Demonstrates a courteous and helpful attitude toward students, parents, staff and administrators.   1   2   3   4

2.   The Media Specialist works cooperatively with students, parents, staff, faculty, and administration to alleviate concerns and problems.

<u>As Evidenced By</u>

The Media Specialist:

a.   Participates in parent-teacher groups and activities.   1   2   3   4

b.   Respects privileged information.   1   2   3   4

c.   Places value in feelings of students, parents, and staff.   1   2   3   4

d.   Schedules meetings with parents to discuss concerns and problems.   1   2   3   4

e.   Responds to parent inquiries.   1   2   3   4

f.   Informs administrators and supervisors of potential problems.   1   2   3   4

g.   Implements plans developed to resolve problems and provides evidence of such to administrators.   1   2   3   4

Evaluator Comments:

F. Professional Responsibilities.

1. The Media Specialist has demonstrated professional growth.

    <u>As Evidenced By</u>

    The Media Specialist:

    a. Participates in professional growth activities.   1 2 3 4
    b. Shares ideas gained from professional growth activities.   1 2 3 4
    c. Works toward achieving building and district educational
        goals.   1 2 3 4
    d. Is current in learning theory, teaching methods, media
        philosophy, subject matter, and district curriculum.   1 2 3 4

2. The Media Specialist fulfills professional responsibilities.

    <u>As Evidenced By</u>

    a. Takes care of and uses appropriately furniture, equipment,
        materials, and all other school property.   1 2 3 4
    b. Shares district materials willingly with other staff members.   1 2 3 4
    c. Fulfills the conditions of employment according to the
        negotiated agreement.   1 2 3 4
    d. Is on duty at assigned place and time.   1 2 3 4
    e. Has work habits that reflect punctuality, dependability, effi-
        ciency, and accuracy.   1 2 3 4
    f. Outlines schedules, procedures, and daily lesson plans for
        substitute.   1 2 3 4
    g. Makes appropriate use of support personnel.   1 2 3 4
    h. Positively communicates school information within the
        community.   1 2 3 4

Evaluator Comments:

_____   _____
Name of Person Evaluated   Evaluator

_____
Date of Conference

*Your signature indicates that you have received a copy of this document. It does not necessarily indicate agreement with the content. The Media Specialist may submit a written response to be attached to this document.

ATTACHMENTS:

1. Observation records
2. Conference notes
3.
4.

THE TENNESSEE MODEL*

The Tennessee model for evaluating library media specialists and their programs is the most ambitious and the most thorough in the country. The entire program is based on a career ladder system which provides pay incentives to Tennessee teachers who can demonstrate excellence. There are three major career levels for library media specialists, each with a set of criteria and each of which must be earned every ten years.

The entire evaluation system in Tennessee rests upon a set of stated beliefs and principles which have been established in law. These beliefs are worthy of study, for they can serve as guidelines for anyone creating an evaluation system.

FUNDAMENTAL BELIEFS AND PRINCIPLES

The Career Ladder Library Evaluation System is constructed upon fundamental beliefs and principles of the education profession. Below are stated the fundamental beliefs about the evaluation program, library media specialists, evaluators, evaluation process and procedures, and the evaluation instruments.

Some of the stated fundamental beliefs and principles have been established by the Comprehensive Education Reform Act of 1984. Others are based on educational research and the experience of those instrumental in developing the evaluation system.

THE PROGRAM

1. The primary goal of the evaluation program is to identify and reward outstanding performance.

2. Other important goals of the evaluaiton program are library management and instructional improvement.

3. A sound evaluation program focuses on performance rather than credentials.

4. To be most useful, the evaluation program must be coupled with a strong professional development program.

THE LIBRARY MEDIA SPECIALIST

1. The library media specialist wants to be a competent professional.

2. Instruction and management are the primary elements in the overall role of the library media specialist.

---

*"Library Media Specialist Orientation Manual" (Nashville, Tenn.: Tennessee Department of Education, 1986), 4-5, 26.

3. It is possible to assess differences in library media specialist performance.

4. Skills needed and used by outstanding library media specialists do not differ from skills needed by less able library media specialists.

5. All library media specialists can improve performance.

THE EVALUATOR

1. Library media specialists are best able to evaluate the performance of their peers.

2. Rigorous and comprehensive training is essential for an evaluator.

3. Evaluation is best conducted by a team of evaluators rather than a single individual.

4. The evaluator must have a commitment to instructional and library management improvement.

THE PROCESS

1. The evaluation process should not discourage diversity in teaching and management behavior.

2. Multiple observations of teaching are necessary to obtain a reliable picture of teaching behavior.

3. Multiple observations of library management are necessary to obtain a reliable picture of management behavior.

4. Effectiveness of management behavior must be assessed in light of library users, school and/or school system characteristics, needs and organizational structures.

5. The evaluation process should focus on the identification of patterns of teaching and management behavior.

6. Multiple sources of data are essential to the development of a complete picture of teaching and management performance.

THE EVALUATION INSTRUMENTS

1. The evaluation instrument(s) must be developed from the evaluation process.

2. The instrument(s) must be understood by all library media specialists and administrators.

3. The instrument(s) must assess the performance of competencies/skills deemed important to effective teaching and management.

4. Checklists and rating scales are useful only as reflections of *summarized* information.

Using the basic principles as a reference, a checklist was developed which lists the features of the LMC program and the competencies which are to be evaluated. Eight different methods are used to evaluate the checklist. The methods are:

1. Observation done by administrators and peers.

2. Dialogue—a structured interview which allows the library media specialist to document certain program components.

3. A principal questionnaire which rates the library media specialist on each major checklist topic.

4. A student questionnaire which asks about services and the quality of personal assistance.

5. A teacher questionnaire asking the frequency of services.

6. A professional development and leadership summary which documents efforts toward professionalism.

7. A written test covering the management and operation of a library media program.

8. A management observation of operational procedures and services.

The checklist of items to be evaluated, together with the method used, follows:

Method Used		Item
7	I.	Prepares effectively for media center operation.
2,3	A.	Establishes appropriate goals and related objectives for library media programs, including library instruction.
1,2,3,5,8	B.	Prepares instructional plans and materials incorporating principles of effective instruction.
2,3,5	C.	Plans for effective scheduling of the library media center.

Method Used		Item
7	II.	Uses teaching strategies and procedures appropriate to content, objectives and learners.
1,2,3,4,8	A.	Provides a clear description of the learning task and its content.
1,2,3,4	B.	Monitors learner understanding and reteaches as necessary.
1,2,3,4	C.	Provides learners appropriate practice and review.
1,2,3,4	D.	Establishes and maintains learner involvement in the learning task.
	III.	Evaluates and selects appropriate learning materials and equipment for the library media center.
2,3,4,5,8	A.	Develops and administers procedures for previewing, evaluating, and selecting materials and equipment.
2,3,4,5	B.	Evaluates and selects with teacher input resources to support the instructional program(s) of the school.
2,3,5,8	C.	Assists teachers in developing units of instruction using library resources.
7	IV.	Uses evaluation to improve library media center operation and library instruction.
2,3,4	A.	Uses information about learner interest and performance to improve library resources and instruction.
2,3,4,5	B.	Evaluates media center program and services.
	C.	Improves learner performance (Field Test Only)
1,3,4	D.	Reports learner status and progress to learners.
1,7	V.	Manages library media center and instruction effectively.
1,3,4,5,8	A.	Establishes and maintains appropriate learner behavior.
1,3,4,8	B.	Establishes and maintains a climate conducive to learning.
1,2,3,4,5,8	C.	Makes effective use of library media center resources.
2,3,4,8	D.	Systematically acquires, organizes, processes and circulates materials and equipment.

Method Used	Item
7	VI. Establishes and maintains a professional leadership role.
3,5,6	A. Improves professional skills and knowledge.
3,5,6	B. Takes a leadership role in improving education.
3	C. (Screening) Performs professional responsibilities efficiently.
	VII. (Screening) Communicates effectively
3,7	A. Writes clearly and correctly.
3,7	B. Communicates oral information effectively.
3,7	C. Reads professionally relevant literature materials with comprehension.

SARASOTA COUNTY, FLORIDA, MODEL*

This instrument is an example of an evaluation in which job activities expected of the school library media specialist are listed along with the sample evidence that the specialist should provide to demonstrate that the activity is being performed. The evidenced is collected and presented during a performance interview with supervisors and principals depending on the district plan for teacher evaluation.

The instrument contains almost no reference to resource-based teaching, but concentrates on warehousing, some direct services, and library skills as a vertical program feature. Users of the instrument could easily include more direct services and the resource-based teaching role in the same format.

*Sarasota County, Florida, "School Media Specialists Performance Evaluation." (Available from Library Media Services, The School Board of Sarasota County, Florida, 2205 Industrial Blvd., Sarasota, FL 32434.)

090187

SCHOOL BOARD OF SARASOTA COUNTY
SCHOOL MEDIA SPECIALIST PERFORMANCE EVALUATION

Media Specialist _____   Date of Submision _____

School _____

Supervising Visit(s)   Total Minutes Supervision

Election being considered (check one):

Second _____

Third _____

Continuing Contract _____   _____ date   _____ minutes

Date of Pre-Conference _____   _____ date   _____ minutes

Date of Post-Conference _____   _____ date   _____ minutes

JOB ACTIVITY/PERFORMANCE   EFFECTIVE INDICATORS

		Effective	Needs Improvement	Not Effective
1. Provides guidance to students and school staff in the use of library media materials, equipment and services designed to assist in meeting school instructional objectives.	a. ESTABLISHES MEDIA COMMITTEE of teachers, students, and parents. b. MEETS WITH FACULTY GROUPS periodically and/or as the need arises (grade level teachers, departments). c. ORIENTS NEW STAFF to available services and equipment. d. PUBLISHES LIST OF SERVICES AVAILABLE through school media center. e. INSTRUCTS STAFF and STUDENTS in the proper use of equipment.	☐	☐	☐

Evaluator's Comments:

Media Specialist's comments (optional):

		Effective	Needs Improvement	Not Effective
2. With school administration and faculty, develops goals and functions of the media program which support meeting the objectives of the total school instructional program.	a. INVOLVES MEDIA COMMITTEE and SCHOOL ADMINISTRATION in developing goals. b. PUBLISHES SHORT TERM GOALS (1-10 mos.) and LONG TERM GOALS with timeline. c. PROVIDES FOR A METHOD OF EVALUATION of the school media program by students, teachers, administrators and parents. d. INVITES SUGGESTIONS to improve the school media program from students, teachers, administrators, and parents.	☐	☐	☐

Evaluator's Comments:

Media Specialist's comments (optional):

White copy: Personnel   Canary copy: Employee   Pink copy: Evaluator

3. With the cooperation of the staff and students and parents, where appropriate, establishes written policies and procedures which achieve the goals of the media program.

   a. INVOLVES MEDIA COMMITTEE in developing written policy and procedures.
   b. PUBLISHES POLICIES and PROCEDURES in student and teacher handbook.
   c. UPDATES POLICIES and PROCEDURES at least every two years.

   Effective ☐ Needs Improvement ☐ Not Effective ☐

   Media Specialist's comments (optional):

   Evaluator's comments:

4. In cooperation with the students and faculty establishes, builds and maintains a collection of varied types of media, resources, and equipment which meet individual student and teacher needs.

   a. Within budget restrictions, PURCHASES MATERIALS to "FILL GAPS."
   b. SYSTEMATICALLY INVOLVES teachers and students identifying NEEDS.
   c. Within budget restrictions, PURCHASES MATERIALS FOR ALL TYPES OF LEARNERS.

   Effective ☐ Needs Improvement ☐ Not Effective ☐

   Media Specialist's comments (optional):

   Evaluator's comments:

5. Provides specific information and resources in response to requests, using local and/or outside sources.

   a. RESPONDS TO REQUESTS for information and resources not found in the school.
   b. PROVIDES MULTIMEDIA BIBLIOGRAPHIES as needed.

   Effective ☐ Needs Improvement ☐ Not Effective ☐

   Media Specialist's comments (optional):

   Evaluator's comments:

6. Prepares and justifies the annual media program budget request.

   a. PRESENTS to school budget committee ITEMIZED BUDGET related to goals.

   Effective ☐ Needs Improvement ☐ Not Effective ☐

   Media Specialist's comments (optional):

   Evaluator's comments:

7. Plans activities and/or opportunities that motivate students to properly use media.

   a. PRESENTS DISPLAYS for students and teachers showing media application.
   b. MAINTAINS AREA for students and teachers to USE AV EQUIPMENT AND MATERIALS.
   C. COMPUTERS ARE AVAILABLE for student and teacher use.

   Effective ☐ Needs Improvement ☐ Not Effective ☐

   Media Specialist's comments (optional):

   Evaluator's comments:

8. Maintains effective working relationships among district-wide media staff and attends district meetings and participates on district committees.

   a. ATTENDS all regularly scheduled MIIC MEETINGS.
   b. VOLUNTEERS to work on at least one MIIC COMMITTEE.

   Effective ☐ Needs Improvement ☐ Not Effective ☐

   Media Specialist's comments (optional):

   Evaluator's comments:

JOB ACTIVITY/PERFORMANCE — EFFECTIVE INDICATORS

	Effective	Needs Improvement	Not Effective
9a	☐	☐	☐
10	☐	☐	☐
11	☐	☐	☐
12	☐	☐	☐
13	☐	☐	☐

9. Uses accepted inventory procedures and evaluation processes for materials and equipment retention/deletion.

   a. CONDUCTS and REPORTS INVENTORY each year.

      Media Specialist's comments (optional):

   Evaluator's comments:

10. Makes effective use of available media facilities and plans with administration, faculty, and students for growing needs and trends.

    a. MAINTAINS STUDENT CENTERED media center.
    b. Media Center is VISUALLY PLEASING, WELL ORGANIZED.
    c. MEETS WITH SCHOOL ADMINISTRATION at least once yearly to plan for the future.

       Media Specialist's comments (optional):

    Evaluator's comments:

11. Establishes and maintains procedures that assure optimum use of materials and equipment for both students and teachers.

    a. Has equipment USE and TRACKING SYSTEM to provide information on equipment.
    b. Has EFFECTIVE CHECK OUT/IN system.
    c. Has COMMUNICATION SYSTEM with teachers to determine future needs.
    d. Has CARD CATALOG efficiently organized by a standard method.
    e. Has an INTEGRATED CATALOG.

       Media Specialist's comments (optional):

    Evaluator's comments:

12. Assists teachers in motivating students toward developing discriminating reading, viewing and listening habits.

    a. PROVIDES INFORMATION to teachers and students regarding upcoming tv, films, etc.
    b. MAKES SUGGESTIONS to teachers and students regarding BOOK REPORTS, reading grudance, etc.
    c. LOCATES MATERIALS and TECHNIQUES to promote good LISTENING HABITS.

       Media Specialist's comments (optional):

    Evaluator's comments:

13. Assists in the teaching of the program of state developed INFORMATION SKILLS FOR FLORIDA SCHOOLS K-12.

    a. ASSISTS TEACHERS in incorporating INFORMATION SKILLS into the curriculum.
    b. PROVIDES ASSISTANCE to teachers requiring help in teaching the INFORMATION SKILLS.

       Media Specialist's comments (optional):

    Evaluator's comments:

	Effective	Needs Improvement	Not Effective

14. Provides students and faculty with experiences that teach the effective use of media and equipment.

   a. DEVELOPS and MAINTAINS EFFECTIVE WORKING RELATIONSHIPS with school staff. ☐ Effective ☐ Needs Improvement ☐ Not Effective

   b. OFFERS at least one INSERVICE ACTIVITY in the effective use of media to school staff each year.

   c. PROVIDES AN OPPORTUNITY for at least one instructional segment (5 hrs.) to students in MEDIA PRODUCTION (photography, TV, script writing, computer programming, etc.

     Media Specialist's comments (optional):

Evaluator's comments:

15. Keeps up to date with standards, guidelines, emerging practices and innovations in library media programs.

   a. READS at least one MEDIA JOURNAL each month. ☐ Effective ☐ Needs Improvement ☐ Not Effective

   b. ATTENDS FAME, FLA or a COMPUTER CONFERENCE at least once every three years.

     Media Specialist's comments (optional):

Evaluator's comments:

16. Uses authoritative bibliographic sources which provide current reviews and information for the selection of materials.

   a. USES CURRENT REVIEWS in selection of materials. ☐ Effective ☐ Needs Improvement ☐ Not Effective

   b. MAKES CURRENT REVIEWS AVAILABLE to teachers and students.

     Media Specialist's comments (optional):

Evaluator's comments:

17. Participates in curriculum planning on both school and district level.

   a. MAINTAINS ACTIVE MEMBERSHIP on school-wide CURRICULUM COMMITTEE. ☐ Effective ☐ Needs Improvement ☐ Not Effective

   b. PARTICIPATES with CURRICULUM INSTRUCTIONAL DEVELOPMENT COMMITTEES as assigned.

   c. PROVIDES SUGGESTIONS/REVISIONS to improve Information Skills Curriculum.

     Media Specialist's comments (optional):

Evaluator's comments:

18. Makes appropriate recommendations pertaining to needs of the media program and facilities, both physical and environmental.

   a. MAINTAINS FILE of WRITTEN RECOMMENDATIONS to school administrators. ☐ Effective ☐ Needs Improvement ☐ Not Effective

     Media Specialist's comments (optional):

Evaluator's comments:

19. Maintains contact with other library, education, and information agencies.

   a. CONTACTS at least ONE SUCH AGENCY each month. ☐ Effective ☐ Needs Improvement ☐ Not Effective

     Media Specialist's comments (optional):

Evaluator's commments:

JOB ACTIVITY/PERFORMANCE

EFFECTIVE INDICATORS

	Effective	Needs Improvement	Not Effective
20. Provides and maintains an area/method by which students and faculty can select and evaluate materials.	☐	☐	☐

a. SCHEDULES PREVIEW ACTIVITIES at least once yearly.
b. MAINTAINS EVALUATION FILE for SELECTION of materials.
c. INVITES faculty and students by word and written memo TO EVALUATE MATERIALS for possible purchase.
d. PROVIDES SPECIFIC OPPORTUNITIES for students TO EVALUATE MATERIALS for possible purchase.

Media Specialist's comments (optional):

Evaluator's comments:

	Effective	Needs Improvement	Not Effective
21. Participates in the selection and evaluation of the school media center staff.	☐	☐	☐

a. PARTICIPATES IN SELECTION of aides and volunteers.
b. PARTICIPATES IN EVALUATION of aides and volunteers.

Media Specialist's comments (optional):

Evaluator's comments:

	Effective	Needs Improvement	Not Effective
22. Trains, schedules, and supervises aides and/or volunteers.	☐	☐	☐

a. USES SYSTEMATIC TRAINING PROCEDURES with aides and volunteers.
b. SCHEDULES WORK for aides and volunteers.
c. SUPERVISES THE WORK of aides and volunteers.

Media Specialist's comments (optional):

Evaluator's comments:

_____
Evaluator's Signature

I have read and discussed this evaluation with my evaluator.

_____
Media Specialist's Signature

_____
Date

THE WISCONSIN MODEL*

The following instrument is really two combined. The Wisconsin School Library Media Association has produced and published brief job descriptions of the professional library media specialist and support staff. For each of these job descriptions, a brief evaluation checklist has been constructed. The observer (presumably the principal) rates the quality of each of the major responsibilities. The major problem with the job descriptions is that resource-based teaching is not viewed as a responsibility of the library media specialist. Many warehouse functions are listed and a role in the reading program is emphasized. A revision of the role statements would be easy if the form appeals to you.

---

*Wisconsin School Library Media Association, "School Library/Media Specialists in the 80's; School Library/Media Support Staff in the 80's" (Madison, Wis.: The Association, 1983).

SCHOOL LIBRARY/MEDIA SPECIALISTS IN THE 80'S

— This job description and evaluation instrument has been produced by the Wisconsin School Library Media Association —

The Wisconsin School Library Media Association is a division of the Wisconsin Library Association. It serves as a professional organization for school library media specialists in the state of Wisconsin. The general purpose of the association is the improvement of education through effective use of print and non-print materials, technology, and instructional methods.

The job description and evaluation form was created by the Professional Development and Public Relations Committees. We hope these materials will be helpful to building level school library media specialists and administrators in clarifying the role of library media specialists in Wisconsin schools. If you would like more information, or additional copies of this form, please contact the Wisconsin School Library Media Association, c/o the Wisconsin Library Association, 1922 University Avenue, Madison, Wisconsin 53705 (Telephone 608-231-1513).

JOB DESCRIPTION FOR SCHOOL LIBRARY MEDIA SPECIALIST

Position:

Head of School Library Media Center

Reports to:

Building Principal

Supervises:

Clerical Staff
Technical Staff
Student Assistants
Adult Volunteers

Mission:

All responsibilities listed here are essential to an adequate library media program. Administrators and the library media specialists should determine the degree to which these components can be implemented in the local situation.

The school library media specialist's responsibilities can be categorized as administrative, educational, technical, and professional.

I. Administrative Responsibilities include:

A. Planning the school library media program
   — planning hours of operation
   — establishing circulation procedures
   — scheduling classes
   — establishing rules, disciplinary policies, and attendance procedures
   — planning use of resources by students and teachers
   — planning a program for teaching library media skills
   — preparing orientation and inservice activities
   — planning for integration with total educational program
   — evaluating the program with representatives of faculty and student body

B. Preparing and administering the budget
   — authorizing orders and payments
   — maintaining records of expenditures

C. Supervising public relations activities
- developing bulletin boards and displays
- announcements, brochures and newspaper publicity
- special activities

D. Planning, designing and arranging school library media centers

E. Cooperating with school and local libraries and library systems

F. Participating in recruiting, hiring, training, and supervising clerical help, student assistants, and volunteers

II. Educational Responsibilities include:

A. Providing services, resources, and guidance to students and teachers
- evaluating and selecting new materials
- evaluating the collection for obsolete materials
- answering reference questions
- supplying students and teachers with needed materials and equipment
- supervising students
- preparing bibliographies
- preparing individual or group instruction in library skills and media production
- providing guidance in the use of materials and special equipment such as microcomputers
- working with individual teachers in planning learning activities
- developing programs to motivate reading, listening, viewing, and communications skills

B. Creating an atmosphere conducive to learning
- teaching effective use of library resources
- teaching students responsibility in the care of materials, equipment, and environment
- arranging the library media center to support a variety of learning activities

C. Promoting professional reading for staff
- reading and scanning professional journals
- routing materials of interest to staff members
- selecting and organizing materials for the professional collection
- keeping current with educational trends
- circulating materials for professional growth of teachers

D. Acquiring knowledge of the educational program and of student needs
- becoming familiar with courses of study
- conversing with students to determine interests
- surveying faculty and students to determine needed resources
- examining student reading scores
- collaborating with teachers in special projects

E. Participating in departmental, faculty, curriculum, and special meetings
- attending faculty and department meetings
- serving on committees whose activities directly affect the instructional media program

III. Technical responsibilities include:

A. Acquiring and organizing materials
- ordering, cataloging, and classifying media
- supervising physical preparation of materials
- supervising check in, stamping, labeling, filing, etc.

B. Supervising withdrawal of obsolete and damaged items
- removing catalog cards
- adjusting inventory records
- preparing materials for discard
- reclassifying to other areas of the library

C. Planning circulation policies and procedures
- directing assistants in charging and discharging materials, writing notices, counting, filing, and keeping circulation records

D. Maintaining records of materials ordered
- keeping circulation statistics
- inventorying materials regularly
- compiling records of library holdings for annual report

IV. Professional responsibilities include:

A. Participating in professional organizations and activities relating to both education and librarianship

B. Continuing to acquire knowledge through inservice education and academic courses

SCHOOL LIBRARY/MEDIA SUPPORT STAFF IN THE 80'S

– This job description and the related evaluation instrument have been produced by the Wisconsin School Library Media Association –

The Wisconsin School Library Media Association is a division of the Wisconsin Library Association. It serves as a professional organization for school library media specialists in the state of Wisconsin. The general purpose of the association is the improvement of education through effective use of print and non-print materials, technology, and instructional methods.

The job description and evaluation forms were created by the Professional Development and Public Relations Committees. We hope these materials will be helpful to building level school library media support staff in Wisconsin schools. If you would like more information, or additional copies of this form, please contact the Wisconsin School Library Media Association, c/o the Wisconsin Library Association, 1922 University Avenue, Madison, Wisconsin 53705 (Telephone 608-231-1513).

JOB DESCRIPTION
FOR
SCHOOL LIBRARY MEDIA SUPPORT STAFF

Position:
Library Media Support Staff

Reports to:
Library Media Specialist

Mission:
All responsibilities listed here are essential to an adequate library media program. Library media specialists should have primary responsibility for determining the degree to which these components can be implemented in the local situation.

The school library media support staff's responsibilities can be categorized as clerical and technical.

1. Clerical Responsibilities include:

    A. Assuming general secretarial responsibilities
       – Types
       – Files
       – Duplicates materials
       – Assists with financial records
       – Operates computers

    B. Compiling statistics
       – Records circulation and other service information
       – Assists with annual reports

    C. Ordering and processing print and nonprint materials
       – Maintains consideration and order files
       – Follows processing procedures established by library media specialist

D. Maintaining inventory of and ordering supplies
- Checks supplies
- Prepares order list

E. Circulating print and nonprint materials
- Assists with circulation processes
- Shelves materials
- Assists with Interlibrary Loan process
- Compiles overdue records

F. Performing other library media center duties as assigned

II. Technical Responsibilities include:

A. Assisting students and staff with location and use of materials and equipment
- Answers directional questions
- Demonstrates proper use of equipment and software
- Operates audiovisual and production equipment

B. Maintaining library media catalogs
- Adds enteries
- Withdraws entries

C. Performing preventive maintenance and minor repairs on equipment
- Changes lamps and other easily replaceable parts
- Cleans and lubricates equipment parts

D. Preparing displays
- Gathers necessary materials
- Displays materials appropriately

E. Scheduling use of and delivering materials and equipment
- Maintains records of rental materials and equipment
- Coordinates use of building materials and equipment

F. Assisting with preparation of bibliographies
- Organizes bibliographic information
- Prepares information in appropriate format

G. Maintaining media collection
- Reads shelves and files
- Withdraws items as directed by the library media specialist
- Mends and repairs items
- Assists with inventory

H. Performing other library media center duties as assigned

JOB EVALUATION
FOR
SCHOOL LIBRARY MEDIA SPECIALIST

Instructions:

This is designed to be used with the local evaluation procedure. It is correlated to the school library media specialist job description developed by the Wisconsin School Library Media Association in 1982.

Legend:

O - Outstanding
C - Commendable
S - Satisfactory
NI - Needs improvement
NO - Not observed
NA - Not applicable

ADMINISTRATIVE

	O	C	S	NI	NO	NA
1. Develops policies to implement the school library media program.	___	___	___	___	___	___
2. Prepares the budget.	___	___	___	___	___	___
3. Administers the budget.	___	___	___	___	___	___
4. Plans and evaluates the school library media program.	___	___	___	___	___	___
5. Organizes public relations activities.	___	___	___	___	___	___
6. Develops functional library media center arrangements.	___	___	___	___	___	___
7. Cooperates with other school library media centers.	___	___	___	___	___	___
8. Cooperates with local libraries and library system.	___	___	___	___	___	___
9. Participates in recruiting, training and supervising supportive staff.	___	___	___	___	___	___

EDUCATIONAL

	O	C	S	NI	NO	NA
1. Provides students and faculty with media services and resources.	___	___	___	___	___	___
2. Creates an atmosphere conducive to learning.	___	___	___	___	___	___
3. Builds a collection of materials appropriate to the educational program and student needs.	___	___	___	___	___	___
4. Provides materials for the professional growth of faculty.	___	___	___	___	___	___
5. Assumes an active, responsible role in departmental, faculty, curriculum, and special activities.	___	___	___	___	___	___

	O	C	S	NI	NO	NA

6. Provides instruction in the use of media services and resources. —— —— —— —— —— ——

7. Works closely with faculty to promote effective use of media services and resources. —— —— —— —— —— ——

TECHNICAL

1. Establishes efficient acquisition procedures. —— —— —— —— —— ——

2. Establishes efficient processing procedures. —— —— —— —— —— ——

3. Provides an up-to-date collection of materials. —— —— —— —— —— ——

4. Keeps the collection in good condition. —— —— —— —— —— ——

5. Compiles and maintains essential records and statistics of library media center operations. —— —— —— —— —— ——

6. Assures easy access to the collection. —— —— —— —— —— ——

PROFESSIONAL

1. Assumes an active role in professional organizations and activities. —— —— —— —— —— ——

2. Continues to acquire knowledge through inservice and academic courses. —— —— —— —— —— ——

3. Maintains an effective relationship with students, staff, and the community. —— —— —— —— —— ——

OTHER PROJECTS

_____

_____

_____

_____

_____

Signature of evaluator   Date

Signature of library media specialist   Date

JOB EVALUATION
FOR
SCHOOL LIBRARY MEDIA SUPPORT STAFF

Instructions:

This is designed to be used with the local evaluation procedure. It is correlated to the school library media support staff job description developed by the Wisconsin School Library Media Association in 1983.

Legend:

O - Outstanding
C - Commendable
S - Satisfactory
NI - Needs improvement
NO - Not observed
NA - Not applicable

CLERICAL

	O	C	S	NI	NO	NA
1. Performs general secretarial responsibilities.	___	___	___	___	___	___
2. Compiles statistics.	___	___	___	___	___	___
3. Orders and processes print and nonprint materials.	___	___	___	___	___	___
4. Maintains inventory of and orders supplies.	___	___	___	___	___	___
5. Circulates print and nonprint materials.	___	___	___	___	___	___
6. Performs other library media center duties as assigned.	___	___	___	___	___	___

EDUCATIONAL

	O	C	S	NI	NO	NA
1. Assists students and staff with locating and using materials and equipment.	___	___	___	___	___	___
2. Maintains library media catalogs.	___	___	___	___	___	___
3. Performs preventive maintenance and minor repairs on equipment.	___	___	___	___	___	___
4. Prepares displays.	___	___	___	___	___	___
5. Schedules use of and delivers materials and equipment.	___	___	___	___	___	___
6. Assists with preparation of bibliographies.	___	___	___	___	___	___
7. Maintains media collection.	___	___	___	___	___	___
8. Performs other library media center duties as assigned.	___	___	___	___	___	___

OTHER PROJECTS

_____

_____

_____

_____

_____
Signature of evaluator   Date

_____
Signature of library media specialist   Date

PASCO COUNTY, FLORIDA, MODEL*

The Pasco County model was developed as a part of an in-service program by library media specialists in the district. The first step was to create a set of mission statements and goals. This was followed by the creation of a media specialist job responsibility checklist. Finally, an evaluation form based on the checklist was created. This form was then used by a district-level team consisting of the department director, a media supervisor, and a selected school media specialist. The data for the form are collected through observation and through interview of the media specialist and any other persons in the school.

*Fred C. Pfister, Joyce P. Vincelette, and Jonnie B. Sprimont, "An Integrated Performance Evaluation and Program Evaluation System," *School Library Media Quarterly* 14, no. 2 (Winter 1986): 61-66.

LIBRARY MEDIA SERVICES

GRADES K-12

PROGRAM DESCRIPTION

The library media program's prime responsibility is to facilitate the teaching-learning process by providing resources and services which satisfy both individual and instructional needs of students. The program is designed to assist learners to grow in their ability to find, generate, evaluate and apply information that helps them to function effectively as individuals and to participate successfully in society. Students are provided opportunities to acquire and strengthen skills in reading, observing, listening and communicating ideas.

MISSIONS AND GOALS

I. <u>Mission</u>

To plan with others in the school, the district, and the community for the most effective use of available resources.

<u>Goals</u>

Media specialists in cooperation with educators, students and parents, where appropriate, will:

a. Establish written policies and procedures for the school library media program.

b. Provide an on-going evaluation of the library media program and make modifications, as needed.

c. Participate in curriculum planning on both the school and district level.

d. Prepare an annual library media budget based on the objectives of the school library media program.

e. Participate in the selection, training and supervision of media support personnel, student aides and volunteers.

f. Participate in the planning, arrangement, utilization and development of media facilities.

II. <u>Mission</u>

To assure optimum use of facilities, materials, and equipment in support of district curriculum objectives.

<u>Goals</u>

The media staff in cooperation with educators, students and parents, where appropriate, will provide:

a. Interpretation of the collection to students and educators.

b. Opportunities for students to discover and explore library media resources, independent of or beyond the stated curriculum.

Missions and Goals - Continued

    c. Media skills instruction that is coordinated with the classroom curriculum.

    d. Assistance to students and educators in the use of materials and equipment.

    e. Assistance to students and educators in developing audio-visual production skills such as audio and video taping, slide/tape presentations, photographic displays, etc.

    f. For the motivation of students toward discriminating reading, viewing, and listening habits.

    g. Educators with information about new media materials and recent media developments in their instructional area.

    h. Library media centers that are open and staffed throughout the school day and at other times as needed.

III. Mission

To build and maintain library media collections consistent with the current and anticipated instructional and personal needs of students and educators within the limitations of available resources; and to provide access to needed information located elsewhere.

Goals

The media staff will:

a. Follow approved district policies for selection, evaluation and disposition of materials and equipment.

b. Obtain educator and student suggestions for the improvement of the library media collection.

c. Provide expertise in and facilities for the production of a variety of educational materials by students and educators.

d. Identify and provide access to sources of information outside the library media center.

IV. Mission

To organize and bring under bibliographic and inventory control the schools' non-consumable instructional materials and equipment.

Goals

The media staff will:

a. Follow district approved procedures for inventory control so that all non-consumable materials and equipment for instruction are accounted for:

Missions and Goals - Continued

    b. Follow district approved standards for providing bibliographic control so that accepted methods of cataloging, classifying, and indexing are provided for the non-consumable instructional materials owned by the school.

    c. Provide for an effective circulation system for instructional materials and equipment.

V. Mission

To provide for the continued professional growth of library media center staff.

Goals

The media staff will:

a. Engage in self-evaluation to identify the areas of need for continuing education and professional growth.

b. Show evidence of professional growth by participating in such activities as inservice, workshops and meetings, college classwork, and membership and activity in professional organizations.

PASCO COUNTY SCHOOLS, K-12
LIBRARY MEDIA SERVICES
PROGRAM EVALUATION CHECKLIST

MIS #662

PLANNING

	YES	NO
Educators, students and parents have been involved in the planning process.	☐	☐

How?_____

_____

	YES	NO
A written statement of annual and long-range objectives to support district goals is available.	☐	☐
Written policies are available. (for faculty & students)	☐	☐
Written procedures are available.	☐	☐
Program evaluation has been conducted within the last year by school staff.	☐	☐

How?_____

_____

Curriculum planning is evidenced by:

	YES	NO
Media Center staff on school planning committee(s)	☐	☐
Media center staff on district planning committee(s)	☐	☐
Other: _____	☐	☐

Comments:_____

_____

_____

_____

_____

BUDGET

	YES	NO
Department heads or grade level chairpersons and school media committee(s) provide input for budget planning.	☐	☐
Media Center budget requests have been submitted to principal for his/her consideration during preliminary budget planning.	☐	☐
The Media Specialist constructs a detailed budget for allocated funds based on program objectives.	☐	☐

Comments: _____

_____

_____

_____

PERSONNEL

	YES	NO
Specific responsibilities and duties of clerk, student aides, and volunteers are available.	☐	☐
Media Specialist participates in selection of support staff.	☐	☐
A plan for training support personnel is available.	☐	☐
A systematic plan of work for support staff is available (schedules, duty roster, etc.).	☐	☐

Comments: _____

_____

_____

MEDIA FACILITIES

	YES	NO
The location of the center is appropriate.	☐	☐
The facilities for group use of resources are adequate.	☐	☐
The facilities for individual use of resources are adequate.	☐	☐
The provisions for staff work areas are adequate.	☐	☐
The facilities for production of resources are adequate.	☐	☐
The storage space for materials is adequate.	☐	☐
The storage space for equipment is adequate.	☐	☐
The provisions for security are adequate.	☐	☐
The arrangement and appearance of the Media Center is appropriate.	☐	☐
The Media Center is equipped with adequate electrical and plumbing, temperature, humidity and accoustical controls, telephone, lighting and the like.	☐	☐
The facilities are adequately maintained.	☐	☐

Comments:_____

_____

_____

_____

USE OF FACILITIES, MATERIALS & EQUIPMENT

	YES	NO
Media Center is interpreted to students and educators.	☐	☐

How? (Handbooks, orientation sessions, learning stations, etc.)

_____

_____

	YES	NO
Students have an opportunity to use the Media Center resources for personal reasons outside the curriculum requirements.	☐	☐
Pasco Media Information Skills Curriculum is coordinated with classroom curricula.	☐	☐

How? (Elementary level - teaming with teachers on specific skills lessons/units.)

(Secondary level - teaming with teachers on reference units, literature/media appreciation.)

_____

Media Center staff provides assistance in the use of materials and equipment to:

	YES	NO
(a) Students	☐	☐
(b) Educators	☐	☐

How?_____

_____

USE OF FACILITIES, MATERIALS & EQUIPMENT (continued)

	YES	NO
Media Center provides assistance in developing audio-visual production skills to:		
(a) Students	☐	☐
(b) Educators	☐	☐

How?_____

_____

	YES	NO
Media Center staff provides for the motivation and guidance of students in reading, viewing and listening.	☐	☐

How?_____

_____

	YES	NO
Media Center staff provides educators with information about new media materials and recent media developments in their instructional area.	☐	☐

How?_____

_____

The Library Media Center is open and staffed throughout the school day and at other times as needed.

Comments:_____

_____

_____

_____

COLLECTION BUILDING

	YES	NO
Appropriate school-wide process for the selection of materials and equipment has been established.	☐	☐
Teachers are involved in the selection/evaluation of materials and equipment.	☐	☐
Students are involved in the selection /evaluation of materials.	☐	☐
Administrators are involved in the selection/evaluation of materials and equipment.	☐	☐
The District process for removing obsolete materials and equipment has been followed.	☐	☐
Provisions are available for the production of new instructional materials.	☐	☐
Access to sources of information outside the school's library media center is provided.	☐	☐

How?_____

_____

	YES	NO
The quality and quantity of school library media resources are adequate.	☐	☐

Comments:_____

_____

_____

_____

BIBLIOGRAPHIC & INVENTORY CONTROL

	YES	NO
All media of permanent value are classified, cataloged, and processed for central distribution according to district approved procedures.	☐	☐
All materials and equipment are organized for easy accessibility and effective use.	☐	☐
District approved procedures for inventory control are followed.	☐	☐
An effective circulation system for materials and for equipment is used.	☐	☐

Comments:_____

_____

_____

_____

PROFESSIONAL GROWTH

	YES	NO
Media center staff shows evidence of continued professional growth.	☐	☐

How?_____

_____

Comments:_____

_____

_____

_____

_____

THE ILLINOIS MODEL*

The Illinois Association for Media in Education (IAME) and the International Association of School Librarianship (IASL) worked together to create an evaluation tool which would concentrate on the quality of the program. Their document was based on one created earlier by the Palatine Community Consolidated School District 15 in Palatine, Illinois. Like other evaluative instruments, a checklist of program statements is presented, but the instrument allows each local school to first accept whether the item is a goal of the library media program; if it is, a rating is made on how that item is implemented. The idea is that a person should not be judged against a criteria list which is not applicable. Like other instruments, this one ignores resource-based teaching as a service of the LMC program, but it could be easily added.

No detailed directions are given on who should conduct the evauation or how the data should be analyzed if a team of persons were to conduct it, but the directions do hint that a local and/or regional staff would presumably visit the center and through observation and interview fill in the form.

---

*Illinois Association for Media in Education and the International Association of School Librarianship, *Indicators of Quality for School Library/Media Programs.* International ed. (Springfield, Ill.: The Associations, 1985).

DIRECTIONS FOR USE

This document was designed to measure quality **not** quantity. Each of the items listed must be judged only in terms of the **local** library/media center program.

The document contains two scales. **Scale 1** measures the **Degree of Acceptance** (the degree to which the item is accepted as in indicator of a quality program). **Scale 2** measures the **Degree of Implementation** (the degree to which the indicator is perceived to be present).

Descriptors for the numerical scale used in the document are as follows:

Degree of Acceptance	**Degree of Implementation**
1. Unacceptable	1. Not implemented
2. Questionable	2. Weakly implemented
3. Accept with reservations	3. Average implementation
4. Accept in general	4. Strongly implemented
5. Endorse completely	5. Fully implemented

The local and/or regional staff will perform the following tasks when using **Indicators of Quality** to evaluate the local library/media program. The involvement of administration will strengthen the evaluation process and validate the development and implementation of priorities to improve the library/media program.

1. Analyze each item in the seven categories using only the **Degree of Acceptance** scale. Accept all indicators that appear to be desirable goals even if they have not been accepted prior to the evaluation.

2. Rewrite any indicators which are unacceptable.

3. Write additional indicators necessary to meet specific local needs.

4. Analyze each accepted item in all categories using the **Degree of Implementation** scale.

5. Develop regional and local standards for facilities, materials and equipment, and personnel using the quantitative worksheet found in the appendix and appropriate local standards.

6. Determine priorities in the areas of personnel, services, facilities, materials and equipment.

7. Develop long-range plans and estimate costs necessary to achieve the goals of a quality library/media program as they are perceived at the local and/or regional level.

8. Present the long-range plan and cost estimates to the administrator and the Board of Education for final approval.

	Degree of Acceptance	Degree of Implementation

I. LIBRARY/MEDIA CENTER STAFF

A. Local Level

Professional Staff

1. Each Library/Media Center will be administered by adequate professional staff[1].......................

    Degree of Acceptance: 1 2 3 4 5   Degree of Implementation: 1 2 3 4 5

2. Each Library/Media Center professional staff member will be certified as a teacher and have adequate training in library science/instructional media including course work in administration, organization (cataloging and classification), reference, and selection of materials at either the elementary or secondary level..................................

    Degree of Acceptance: 1 2 3 4 5   Degree of Implementation: 1 2 3 4 5

3. Each Library/Media Center staff member will acquire and demonstrate a broad general knowledge of the curriculum in all content areas.............

    Degree of Acceptance: 1 2 3 4 5   Degree of Implementation: 1 2 3 4 5

4. Each Library/Media Center staff member will be employed only after the Director of Library/Media Services or appropriate equivalent has interviewed the candidate and consulted with the Director of Personnel and Principal..........................

    Degree of Acceptance: 1 2 3 4 5   Degree of Implementation: 1 2 3 4 5

5. Each Library/Media Center staff will include a professional who is trained in the preparation, use and maintenance of materials and equipment......

    Degree of Acceptance: 1 2 3 4 5   Degree of Implementation: 1 2 3 4 5

6. The professional members of the Library/Media Center staff will be an integral part of the teaching-learning process.................................

    Degree of Acceptance: 1 2 3 4 5   Degree of Implementation: 1 2 3 4 5

Supportive Staff

1. Each Library/Media Center staff will include adequate supportive staff[1]..........................

    Degree of Acceptance: 1 2 3 4 5   Degree of Implementation: 1 2 3 4 5

2. Supportive staff is employed, trained and supervised in relation to an appropriate job description..

    Degree of Acceptance: 1 2 3 4 5   Degree of Implementation: 1 2 3 4 5

3. Supportive staff will be employed only after interviews with both the professional Library/Media staff and the Principal...........................

    Degree of Acceptance: 1 2 3 4 5   Degree of Implementation: 1 2 3 4 5

4. Volunteers (both adult and student) are recruited, trained, and supervised by the professional Library/Media Center staff................................

    Degree of Acceptance: 1 2 3 4 5   Degree of Implementation: 1 2 3 4 5

[1]See appropriate local standards.

	Degree of Acceptance	Degree of Implementation

LIBRARY/MEDIA CENTER STAFF (continued)

B. Regional Level

1. Each regional level Library/Media professional staff member will be certified as a teacher with adequate training in library science/instructional media, including course work in administration, organization (cataloging and classification), reference, selection of materials for both the elementary and secondary levels, and production 1 2 3 4 5   1 2 3 4 5

2. Each regional level Library/Media Coordinator/Director will hold an appropriate certificate with professional preparation in administration, curriculum and supervision 1 2 3 4 5   1 2 3 4 5

3. Each regional level Library/Media program will include adequate support staff including secretarial, clerical and technical, required to implement all of the regional program elements, e.g. centralized processing, television production, etc............. 1 2 3 4 5   1 2 3 4 5

4. The regional level support staff will be trained, supervised and evaluated by the regional Library/Media coordinator according to specific job descriptions 1 2 3 4 5   1 2 3 4 5

II. PROGRAM OF SERVICES

A. Local Level

1. The professional Library/Media Center staff will develop and administer a program of services which reflect the needs of the school community.. 1 2 3 4 5   1 2 3 4 5

2. The goal of the Library/Media instructional program will be to develop functional skills in research and retrieval that will serve the student throughout his/her lifetime 1 2 3 4 5   1 2 3 4 5

3. The Library/Media instructional program for students will be described by a skills continuum written in behavioral objective form 1 2 3 4 5   1 2 3 4 5

4. The teaching of Library/Media skills will be an integral part of the total curriculum and will be planned by the classroom teacher and the Library/Media Center professional staff.................. 1 2 3 4 5   1 2 3 4 5

5. The Library/Media professional staff will assume major responsibility for teaching the skills continuum... 1 2 3 4 5   1 2 3 4 5

	Degree of Acceptance	Degree of Implementation

PROGRAM OF SERVICES (continued)

6. Formal and informal instruction in the use of the Library/Media Center will be provided for both individuals and small groups by the Library/Media Center professional staff.......................... 1 2 3 4 5   1 2 3 4 5

7. Professional guidance will be offered to students and staff for the purpose of selecting, evaluating, and utilizing those resources appropriate to individual interest and academic needs.............. 1 2 3 4 5   1 2 3 4 5

8. Professional guidance will be offered in the development of competencies in research and inquiry, literary appreciation, and equipment utilization..... 1 2 3 4 5   1 2 3 4 5

9. All resources and equipment to meet a variety of interests, needs and abilities will be available for use both in the center and for circulation.......... 1 2 3 4 5   1 2 3 4 5

10. The services and resources of the Library/Media Center will be available to all users during the school day (including lunch hour) as well as before and after school when possible.................... 1 2 3 4 5   1 2 3 4 5

11. The Library/Media Center philosophy and the scheduling of students will permit flexible use of the Library/Media Center............................. 1 2 3 4 5   1 2 3 4 5

12. Opportunities will be provided for students and staff to design and produce media-related materials for educational purposes......................... 1 2 3 4 5   1 2 3 4 5

13. The Library/Media Center professional staff will assist the teaching staff and students in obtaining appropriate resources from other sources such as the public library system, other schools, and other community sources............................... 1 2 3 4 5   1 2 3 4 5

B. **Regional Level**

1. The regional Library/Media Coordinator will be actively involved in curriculum planning to determine the role of the Library/Media program in achieving the goals and objectives of the regional's instructional program and will coordinate the efforts of all the Library/Media Centers to the end......... 1 2 3 4 5   1 2 3 4 5

2. The regional Library/Media Coordinator provides leadership in the areas of:

    a. instructional program development............ 1 2 3 4 5   1 2 3 4 5

—4—

	Degree of Acceptance	Degree of Implementation

PROGRAM OF SERVICES (continued)

    b. Library/Media Center staff development and evaluation 1 2 3 4 5   1 2 3 4 5

    c. position classification for media personnel 1 2 3 4 5   1 2 3 4 5

    d. public relations 1 2 3 4 5   1 2 3 4 5

3. The regional Library/Media Coordinator will be responsible for the development, coordination and implementation of a long-range plan for the achievement of a quality Library/Media program for the region..   1 2 3 4 5   1 2 3 4 5

4. A collection of instructional films, videotapes and other appropriate non-print resources will be provided at the regional level to support the regional program..   1 2 3 4 5   1 2 3 4 5

5. A professional library to meet administrative and curricular development needs will be provided at the regional level..............................   1 2 3 4 5   1 2 3 4 5

6. The regional level Library/Media professional staff will facilitate and coordinate the interlibrary loan of regional resources...........................   1 2 3 4 5   1 2 3 4 5

7. Exhibits of commercially prepared print and non-print resources will be provided for teacher evaluation by regional staff personnel...................   1 2 3 4 5   1 2 3 4 5

III. INSERVICE PROGRAM

A. Local Level

1. Inservice programs will be provided in the production and utilization of curriculum related materials and the operation of equipment 1 2 3 4 5   1 2 3 4 5

2. Planned visitations by the Library/Media Center professional staff to other Library/Media Centers both within and outside the region will be arranged yearly...   1 2 3 4 5   1 2 3 4 5

3. The Library/Media Center professional staff will acquaint the local staff with available resources relevant to the current instructional program.......   1 2 3 4 5   1 2 3 4 5

4. The Library/Media Center professional staff will assist the local staff in the design, development, and production of media resource units and special materials..   1 2 3 4 5   1 2 3 4 5

	Degree of Acceptance	Degree of Implementation

INSERVICE PROGRAM (continued)

5. The Library/Media Center professional staff will identify and design media-related services to meet a variety of teaching strategies................... 1 2 3 4 5   1 2 3 4 5

B. **Regional Level**

1. The regional coordinator will involve the local level Library/Media professional staff in the development of a program of Library/Media services to achieve the goals and objectives of the region's instructional program................................. 1 2 3 4 5   1 2 3 4 5

2. The regional coordinator will plan and implement a staff development program for local level Library/Media staff...................................... 1 2 3 4 5   1 2 3 4 5

3. The regional coordinator will encourage and facilitate the local level Library/Media professional staff's participation in Library/Media related workshops... 1 2 3 4 5   1 2 3 4 5

4. Inservice training in the production and utilization of media-related materials will be initiated and conducted according to individual and local needs by regional Library/Media personnel................. 1 2 3 4 5   1 2 3 4 5

5. The regional coordinator will provide professional and technical assistance to the instructional staff in the design and development of media-related materials....................................... 1 2 3 4 5   1 2 3 4 5

IV. **MATERIALS AND EQUIPMENT**

A. **Local Level**

1. The Library/Media Center materials collection will reflect the regional standards in both quality and quantity... 1 2 3 4 5   1 2 3 4 5

2. The Library/Media Center professional staff will review the materials and equipment collections annually and recommend new acquisitions........ 1 2 3 4 5   1 2 3 4 5

3. Print and non-print materials will correlate with and support all curriculum areas..................... 1 2 3 4 5   1 2 3 4 5

4. Print and non-print materials including realia will be selected using approved selection aids and will reflect the interests, ability levels, and learning styles of the users............................... 1 2 3 4 5   1 2 3 4 5

	Degree of Acceptance	Degree of Implementation

MATERIALS AND EQUIPMENT (continued)

5. Print and non-print collections will be reviewed and "weeded" annually........................... 1 2 3 4 5   1 2 3 4 5

6. The collection will include materials in formats most appropriate to learning activities and abilities of learners....................................... 1 2 3 4 5   1 2 3 4 5

7. Materials will be cataloged, arranged and administered so that students and staff can use them efficiently to achieve their learning objectives...... 1 2 3 4 5   1 2 3 4 5

8. The Library/Media Center professional staff will plan and coordinate the circulation of media-related equipment to insure its availability................ 1 2 3 4 5   1 2 3 4 5

9. Current professional periodicals, journals, and books will be purchased annually and made available in each Library/Media Center........................ 1 2 3 4 5   1 2 3 4 5

10. Library/Media Center professional staff with the help of the building staff, will select the professional materials to be ordered for each building Library/ Media Center..................................... 1 2 3 4 5   1 2 3 4 5

B. Regional Level

1. The region will establish quantitative standards for materials and equipment based on regional needs and the standards of professional library associations.. 1 2 3 4 5   1 2 3 4 5

2. The region will provide specialized production equipment which is not feasible at the local level.. 1 2 3 4 5   1 2 3 4 5

3. Exhibits of commercially prepared print and non-print resources will be provided for teacher evaluation by regional staff personnel.................... 1 2 3 4 5   1 2 3 4 5

V. FACILITIES

A. Local Level

1. Space will be provided to accommodate a minimum of _____% of the students at any one time in the Library/Media Center............................. 1 2 3 4 5   1 2 3 4 5

2. Space will be provided in the Library/Media Center for the following activities:

	Degree of Acceptance	Degree of Implementation

FACILITIES (continued)

		Degree of Acceptance	Degree of Implementation
a.	reading	1 2 3 4 5	1 2 3 4 5
b.	viewing and listening	1 2 3 4 5	1 2 3 4 5
c.	investigating	1 2 3 4 5	1 2 3 4 5
d.	instruction	1 2 3 4 5	1 2 3 4 5
e.	individual and group activity	1 2 3 4 5	1 2 3 4 5
f.	processing of materials	1 2 3 4 5	1 2 3 4 5
g.	production of materials	1 2 3 4 5	1 2 3 4 5

3. Sufficient shelving and storage space for materials/ equipment will be provided in the Library/Media Center as described in the quantitative regional standards 1 2 3 4 5   1 2 3 4 5

4. A readily accessible central card catalog of all resources, based on standardized cataloging procedures, will be provided in the Library/Media Center 1 2 3 4 5   1 2 3 4 5

5. Space will be provided in the Library/Media Center for diverse activities, quiet and active, individual and group in an atmosphere conducive to learning 1 2 3 4 5   1 2 3 4 5

B. Regional Level

1. The region will provide space and equipment for the production of materials which cannot technically or economically be produced at the local level 1 2 3 4 5   1 2 3 4 5

2. The region will provide space for the storage, retrieval, and exhibit of instructional materials including the film library and videotape library 1 2 3 4 5   1 2 3 4 5

3. The region will provide space and equipment for other regional wide services, e.g. centralized purchasing, centralized cataloging and processing.... 1 2 3 4 5   1 2 3 4 5

4. The region will provide space for a professional library to meet administrative and curricular needs... 1 2 3 4 5   1 2 3 4 5

VI. EVALUATION

A. Local Level

1. Students, staff, parents, and administrators will be involved in the formal and informal evaluation of the Library/Media Center program 1 2 3 4 5   1 2 3 4 5

	Degree of Acceptance	Degree of Implementation

EVALUATION (continued)

2. Informal evaluations of the program will be conducted throughout the year via conferences with the Library/Media Center professional staff, building administrators, and the regional Library/Media coordinator...................................... 1 2 3 4 5   1 2 3 4 5

3. **Indicators of Quality** will be used annually to (1) evaluate the Library/Media Center program of each local level and (2) analyze progress toward established goals and prepare recommendations for future Library/Media development................. 1 2 3 4 5   1 2 3 4 5

B. **Regional Level**

1. **Indicators of Quality** will be used annually to evaluate the total regional Library/Media program...... 1 2 3 4 5   1 2 3 4 5

2. The region will establish a Library/Media Services Planning and Development Committee to be composed of representative local level and regional level personnel to (1) review the results of the quality indicator analysis at both the local level and regional level and (2) analyze progress toward established goals and prepare recommendations for future regional Library/Media development......... 1 2 3 4 5   1 2 3 4 5

VII. **BUDGET**

A. **Local Level**

1. Teaching staff, principals, supervisors, department chairpersons, and other appropriate regional resource personnel will be involved in budget recomdations for the Library/Media program............. 1 2 3 4 5   1 2 3 4 5

2. The Library/Media Center annual budget requests will reflect a consensus of both regional and staff priorities within the approved standards........... 1 2 3 4 5   1 2 3 4 5

B. **Regional Level**

1. The regional Library/Media budget will be developed to implement the region's long-range plan which reflects the standards and priorities determined through the application of **Indicators of Quality**.... 1 2 3 4 5   1 2 3 4 5

2. The regional coordinator will be responsible for providing leadership in the development, adoption and administration of the total Library/Media program budget (regional and local level).............. 1 2 3 4 5   1 2 3 4 5

Appendix B: PSES
Purdue Self-Evaluation System
for School Media Centers*

PSES was developed by the author and Janet G. Stroud as an outgrowth of two dissertation studies and a research study done by the author and Phyllis Land of the Indiana State Department of Public Instruction. It has been used as the basis of many dissertation studies and at the local level to probe the services of the library media centers. *PSES* contains eight service areas which roughly correspond to this book's model in the following ways:

Loertscher's Taxonomy Model	PSES Service Categories
Warehouse Services	Accessibility Services Professional Services (Some) Acquisition Services Production Services (Most)
Direct Services	Awareness Services Professional Services (Some) Utilization Services (Some) Activity Services
Resource-based Teaching	Planning Services
Vertical Program Features	Utilization Services (Some) Production Services (A few)

PSES is reprinted here in its entirety with permission of the Purdue Research Foundation which assisted in partially funding its original development. Copyright © 1976, Purdue Research Foundation (West Lafayette, IN 47907). Additional copies may be obtained from Hi Willow Research and Publishing (P.O. Box 3988, Englewood, CO 80155-3988).

INSTRUCTIONS

There are many facets of a library media center program that can be measured. These might include facilities, staffing, budget, collection, circulation, etc. But many professionals agree that one of the more effective measures is to evaluate the services provided by the library media staff to the users.

The *Purdue Self-Evaluation System (PSES) for Media Centers* offers library media specialists a technique for involving teachers, students, and administrators in the evaluation of library media center services. The unique feature of *PSES* is that the library media specialist may tailor-make the evaluation instrument to the service program of a specific library media center. It may constitute a portion of a comprehensive planning and evaluation system or it may simply be exploratory in nature.

The catalog encompasses nine broad service categories: Accessibility, Awareness, Professional, Utilization, Planning, Acquisition, Production, Evaluation and Activity. The library media specialist may wish to concentrate on a few categories or do a broad survey over all categories. The library media specialist also may query one user group or several to include administrators, library media staff, teachers and students.

PSES measures the user's perception of both frequency and variety of services offered by the library media center. The technique can also be used to compare the library media staff's perception of the service program with any of the user group's perceptions. Library media specialists are advised to select those items which match their own program objectives.

The catalog was developed originally in cooperation with the Indiana Department of Public Instruction in a survey of elementary school library media centers during the 1974-75 school year. It has also been used as a source for many doctoral dissertations. There is a certain amount of bias represented in this instrument toward services emphasized in the *Media Programs: District and School* (AASL & AECT: 1975); that is, both library and audiovisual services as well as instructional development services have been included. Library media specialists can select items from the main catalog to use in local questionnaires for teachers and administrators. They can then select matching items using student-oriented language for use with students. These student questions are printed in the student catalog.

Item Selection

Several reasons could influence a library media specialist's choice of a particular item. For example, one might wish to offer a service and would like to "educate" the user to its possible implementation. The service chosen may be relatively new and the library media staff wishes to check the awareness of the users as to its existence. The library media specialist may also want to find out what segments of the user groups are taking advantage of a particular service; for example, what percentage in each grade level takes advantage of a particular service.

The adult catalog contains services in nine different categories (Accessibility, Awareness, etc.). Three columns for media staff, teachers, and students, are beside each service statement. An "x" in a column indicates which group the statement may be used for; let us look at item #7, for example.

<u>M</u> <u>T</u> <u>S</u>

<u>x</u> _ <u>x</u>   The media center is used for meetings of
student organizations.

This item may be selected to be answered by either the library media staff, the students, or both. The item should not be put on a teacher questionnaire. For item #7, the question would be used from the main catalog for the library media staff questionnaire. The student question, however, would be #7 listed in the student catalog. The student item should match the main question, but would contain simpler language.

The authors do not recommend more than 150 items for the library media staff, 75 items for teachers, or 50 for students. Creating longer questionnaires will curtail the response rate and may affect the accuracy of the responses because of fatigue. The authors recommend the following scale for all responses: A = Regularly; B = Occasionally; C = Rarely or never; D = Don't know. A,B,C,D has been used here if optical scanning sheets are used. If locally printed answer sheets are used, the scale might be: 3 = Regularly; 2 = Occasionally; 1 = Rarely or never; X = Don't know.

To analyze the questionnaire data, the authors recommend that a mean (average) response of each group be computed for each question using the numbered scale above. Means can be compared across groups. If a .5 difference or more exists betweeen the means, then a disagreement is said to have occurred. For example, if the library media specialists rate a service as 3.00 (regular) and the average response of the teachers is 2.50, then the two groups do not agree on the frequency of that service.

Patterns of agreement and disagreement can be analyzed. For example, compare means of student responses across grade levels. Does agreement decline as the grade level rises?

For in-depth suggestions on item analysis, consult Janet G. Stroud, *Evaluative Case Studies of School Library Media Services: The PSES Approach* (Idaho Falls, Idaho: Hi Willow Research and Publishing, 1978). Available from Libraries Unlimited.

ELEMENTARY SCHOOL ADULT CATALOG

ACCESSIBILITY SERVICES

M T S

The media center is used for

1. X X _   scheduled class visits (weekly, semi-weekly, etc.)
2. X X _   class use upon teacher request (other than scheduled visits)
3. X X _   small groups upon teacher request
4. X X _   individual student research
5. X X _   individual student enjoyment

The media center is used for meetings of

6. X X _   faculty
7. X _ X   student organizations
8. X _ _   administrators or school boards
9. X _ _   school-related parent groups

The media center provides books for

10. X X _   temporary reserve collections for instructional units
11. X X _   temporary room collections for instructional units
12. X X _   permanent room or department collections

The media center provides AV materials for

13. X X _   temporary reserve collections for instructional units
14. X X _   temporary room collections for instructional units
15. X X _   permanent room or department collections

The media center provides AV equipment for

16. X X _   loan to teachers (1 day or less)
17. X X _   loan to teachers (less than 30 days)
18. X X _   temporary loan to department
19. X X _   permanent loan to teachers
20. X X _   permanent loan to department

Students use the media center

21. X _ X   before school
22. X _ X   after school

Teachers use the media center

23. X X _   before school
24. X X _   after school

Students take home from the media center

25. X _ X   books
26. X _ X   AV materials
27. X _ X   AV equipment

Students check out for building use

28. X _ X   books
29. X _ X   AV materials
30. X _ X   AV equipment

ACCESSIBILITY SERVICES (cont.)

M T S

31. X X _ Teachers *have time* to come to the media center.
32. X _ X Students *have time* to come to the media center.
33. X X _ Teachers have time to consult with the media staff.
34. X X X Books are kept in repair.
35. X X X AV materials are kept in repair.
36. X X X AV equipment is kept in operating condition.
37. X _ X Students use AV equipment in the media center.

AWARENESS SERVICES

M T S

Teachers are given information about
38. X X _   new AV equipment in the building
39. X X _   new books and AV materials in the media center
40. X X _   services available from the district media center (library)
41. X X _   services available from other libraries in the area
42. X X _   community resources (guests, field trips, etc.)
43. X X _   existing media center services
44. X X _   newly added media center services

Students are given information about
45. X _ X   new AV equipment in the media center
46. X _ X   new books and AV materials in the media center
47. X _ X   services available from the district media center (library)
48. X _ X   services available from other libraries in the area
49. X _ X   community resources (guests, field trips, etc.)
50. X _ X   existing media center services
51. X _ X   newly added media center services

The media staff sponsors special programs for
52. X X _   National Library Week, Book Week, etc.
53. X X _   local events of importance
54. X X _   national events
55. X X _   school-public library cooperative efforts

The media staff promotes the media program via
56. X X _   news releases
57. X X _   radio or TV
58. X X _   displays or bulletin boards
59. X X _   programs for parents
60. X X _   programs for administrators
61. X X _   presentations to the school board
62. X X _   presentations to community groups

PROFESSIONAL SERVICES

M T S

The *school* media staff acquires for the professional collection

63. X X _   books
64. X X _   periodicals
65. X X _   AV materials
66. X X _   research reports
67. X X _   curriculum guides

The *district* media staff acquires for the professional collection

68. X X _   books
69. X X _   periodicals
70. X X _   AV materials
71. X X _   research reports
72. X X _   curriculum guides

In-service topics for teachers include

73. X X _   integrating media center materials into instruction
74. X X _   utilizing media center services effectively
75. X X _   producing AV materials
76. X X _   utilizing AV equipment
77. X X _   existing media center services
78. X X _   newly added media center services

The media staff works with teachers/counselors to help

79. X X _   improve student progress in learning
80. X X X   students with their personal problems
81. X X· _   students make career decisions

UTILIZATION SERVICES

M T S

Teachers are helped to locate materials in

82. X X _   the media center collection
83. X X _   the various classroom collections

The media staff assists teachers by

84. X X _   suggesting various uses of media center materials
85. X X _   locating materials of various difficulty and interest levels
86. X X _   demonstrating the versatility of AV equipment
87. X X _   aiding in the use of equipment and accessories

Reference service in the media center is given *teachers* by

88. X X _   answering simple questions (e.g., who wrote *Charlotte's Web*?)
89. X X _   answering more complex questions
90. X X _   requiring teachers to try to answer their own questions
91. X X _   referring teachers to resources not in the media center

UTILIZATION SERVICES (cont.)

M T S

Reference service in the media center is given *students* by

92. X _ X		answering simple questions (e.g., who wrote *Charlotte's Web*?)
93. X _ X		answering more complex questions
94. X _ X		requiring students to try to answer their own questions
95. X _ X		referring students to resources not in the media center

Instruction in the use of the media center is

96. X X _		given as a unit of instruction
97. X X _		integrated into classroom instructional units
98. X X _		given informally upon request

Instruction in the use of the media center is given *to*

99. X X _		individual students
100. X X _		small groups
101. X X _		classes and/or large groups
102. X X _		new students

Instruction in the use of the media center is given *by*

103. X X _		teacher and media staff in a team approach
104. X X _		the teacher
105. X X _		the media staff

Group guidance is given by the media staff through

106. X X X		book or media talks on recreational materials
107. X X X		book or media talks on materials for classwork
108. X X X		distribution of materials lists
109. X X X		displays, exhibits and/or bulletin boards

Individual guidance is given by the media staff through

110. X X X		individualized materials lists
111. X X X		help in the location of materials
112. X X X		help in the selection of materials

The media staff engages in a program of

113. X X _		reading guidance
114. X X _		viewing guidance (visual literacy)
115. X X _		listening guidance
116. X X _		improvement of study habits
117. X X _		development of critical thinking

118. X X X Help is given when AV equipment problems arise.

PLANNING SERVICES

M T S

Media center staff assists teachers in unit planning by

119. X X _   consulting *in advance* of unit presentation
120. X X _   assisting in analysis of learning tasks
121. X X _   helping formulate behavioral objectives
122. X X _   gathering materials
123. X X _   preparing bibliographies
124. X X _   suggesting materials of appropriate difficulty
125. X X _   suggesting materials of varying *interest levels*

126. X X _   The media specialist consults with the curriculum committee

ACQUISITION SERVICES

M T S

Inter-library loans for *teachers* are provided from

127. X X _   the district center collection
128. X X _   other school media centers in the district
129. X X _   public libraries in the area
130. X X _   academic libraries in the area
131. X X _   rental libraries
132. X X _   regional libraries

Inter-library loans for *students* are provided from

133. X _ X   the district center collection
134. X _ X   other school media centers in the district
135. X _ X   public libraries in the area .
136. X _ X   academic libraries in the area
137. X _ _   rental libraries
138. X _ _   regional libraries

The media staff purchases materials

139. X X _   on recommendation of the teachers
140. X _ X   on recommendation of the students

The media staff provides for the purpose of purchasing

141. X X _   teacher previewing
142. X X _   student previewing
143. X X _   producers' catalogs
144. X X _   published evaluations of materials
145. X X _   published evaluations of equipment

The media staff orders

146. X X _   materials only at specified times
147. X X _   individual orders upon request

PRODUCTION SERVICES

M T S

Which are produced by your *school* media staff?

148. X X X   graphics (lettering, poster making, etc.)
149. X X X   slides
150. X X X   videotapes
151. X X X   tape recordings
152. X X X   8mm films
153. X X X   radio programs
154. X X X   16mm films
155. X X X   puppets
156. X X X   models and dioramas
157. X X X   transparencies
158. X X X   kits
159. X X X   games
160. X X X   filmstrips
161. X X X   learning packages
162. X X X   photocopies
163. X X X   mounted materials
164. X X X   laminated materials
165. X X X   printed or duplicated materials
166. X X X   computer-assisted instruction
167. X X X   programmed instruction
168. X X X   computer programing

Which are produced by your *district* media staff?

169. X X _   graphics (lettering, poster making, etc.)
170. X X _   slides
171. X X _   videotapes
172. X X _   tape recordings
173. X X _   8mm films
174. X X _   radio programs
175. X X _   16mm films
176. X X _   puppets
177. X X _   models and dioramas
178. X X _   transparencies
179. X X _   kits
180. X X _   games
181. X X _   filmstrips
182. X X _   learning packages
183. X X _   photocopies
184. X X _   mounted materials
185. X X _   laminated materials
186. X X _   printed or duplicated materials
187. X X _   computer-assisted instruction
188. X X _   programmed instruction
189. X X _   computer programing

PRODUCTION SERVICES (cont.)

M T S

Teachers who want locally produced AV materials are provided

190. X X _   facilities and equipment
191. X X _   supplies
192. X X _   help from the media staff
193. X X _   the finished product from the media staff

Students who want locally produced AV materials are provided

194. X _ X   facilities and equipment
195. X _ X   supplies
196. X _ X   help from the media staff
197. X _ X   the finished product from the media staff

EVALUATION SERVICES

M T S

The media center collection provides

198. X X X   a variety of media to meet user needs
199. X X X   current material
200. X X X   enough material for the number of users
201. X X X   quality materials

Together, teachers and media staff evaluate the success of

202. X X _   class projects involving the media center
203. X X _   small group projects involving the media center
204. X X _   individual projects involving the media center
205. X X _   library skills training for students
206. X X _   jointly planned units of instruction

The media staff provides *students* opportunities to evaluate

207. X _ X   the materials collection
208. X _ X   media center services
209. X _ X   media center facilities
210. X _ X   media center policies

The media staff provides *teachers* opportunities to evaluate

211. X X _   the materials collection
212. X X _   media center services
213. X X _   media center facilities
214. X X _   media center policies

ACTIVITY SERVICES

M T S

In the media center, students

215.	X _ X	read or look at books
216.	X _ X	read magazines and newspapers
217.	X _ X	look at AV materials in large groups
218.	X _ X	look at AV materials in small groups
219.	X _ X	look at AV materials as individuals
220.	X _ X	listen to recordings in large groups
221.	X _ X	listen to recordings in small groups
222.	X _ X	listen to recordings as individuals
223.	X _ X	make puppets and have puppet shows
224.	X _ X	listen to stories
225.	X _ X	play games
226.	X _ X	find materials and information for school subjects
227.	X _ X	make AV materials
228.	X _ X	make printed materials
229.	X _ X	tutor other students
230.	X _ X	observe animals or plants
231.	X _ X	meet, talk, or listen to community resource persons
232.	X _ X	select materials to borrow
233.	X _ X	learn to operate AV equipment
234.	X _ X	study with other students
235.	X _ X	discuss materials
236.	X _ X	participate in library clubs or media organizations
237.	X _ X	use computer-assisted instruction
238.	X _ X	view displays and exhibits

In the media center, teachers

239.	X X _	have access to recreational materials
240.	X X _	socialize with colleagues
241.	X X _	have a place to 'get away from it all'
242.	X X _	engage in unit planning with colleagues
243.	X X _	eat and drink

ELEMENTARY SCHOOL STUDENT CATALOG

ACCESSIBILITY SERVICES — Student Catalog

The media center is used for
7. club or student meetings

I use the media center
21. before school
22. after school

I take home from the media center
25. books
26. AV materials
27. AV equipment

For use in school, I check out
28. books
29. AV materials
30. AV equipment

32. I *have time* to go to the media center.

34. The media center's books are in good condition.

35. The media center's AV materials are in good condition.

36. The media center's AV equipment is in good condition.

37. I use AV equipment in the media center.

AWARENESS SERVICES — Student Catalog

The media staff tells me about
45. new AV equipment in the media center
46. new books and AV materials in the media center
47. materials I can get from the district media center (library)
48. materials I can get from other libraries in my city
49. people and places I can visit near my home
50. things I can do in the media center
51. new things I can do in the media center

PROFESSIONAL SERVICES — Student Catalog

The media staff helps me
80. with my problems

UTILIZATION SERVICES — Student Catalog

The media staff helps me by
92. answering easy questions (e.g., who wrote *Charlotte's Web*?)
93. answering harder questions
94. asking me to try to answer my own questions
95. sending me to people or places outside the media center

The media staff helps my group by
106. talking about fun things to read or look at
107. telling me about things I can use for class
108. giving me a list of books or AV materials
109. having bulletin boards

The media staff helps me
110. by giving me a list of books or AV materials
111. find books and AV materials
112. choose books or AV materials

118. I receive help when AV equipment will not work.

ACQUISITION SERVICES — Student Catalog

The media staff will get me books or AV materials from
133. the district media center
134. other school media centers
135. the public library
136. the college library

The media staff will
140. buy things I ask for

PRODUCTION SERVICES — Student Catalog

Our school media center makes
148. graphics (lettering, signs, posters, etc.)
149. slides
150. videotapes (television programs)
151. tape recordings
152. 8mm films
153. radio programs
154. 16mm films
155. puppets
156. models and dioramas
157. transparencies
158. kits
159. games
160. filmstrips
161. learning packages
162. photocopies

PRODUCTION SERVICES — Student Catalog (cont.)

Our school media center makes
- 163. mounted materials
- 164. laminated materials
- 165. printed or duplicated materials
- 166. computer-assisted instruction
- 167. programmed instruction
- 168. computer programs

If I want AV materials *made,* the media staff
- 194. gives me space and equipment
- 195. gives me supplies
- 196. gives me help
- 197. does it for me

EVALUATION SERVICES — Student Catalog

The media center collection has
- 198. many kinds of things to help me
- 199. new material
- 200. enough books and AV materials for everybody to use
- 201. good books and AV materials

The media staff gives me a chance to say what I like or don't like about
- 207. the books or AV materials in the media center
- 208. the things I can do in the media center
- 209. media center chairs, tables, shelves, places to work, etc.
- 210. media center rules

ACTIVITY SERVICES — Student Catalog

In the media center, I
- 215. read or look at books
- 216. read magazines and newspapers
- 217. look at AV materials in large groups
- 218. look at AV materials in small groups
- 219. look at AV materials by myself
- 220. listen to recordings in large groups
- 221. listen to recordings in small groups
- 222. listen to recordings by myself
- 223. make puppets and have puppet shows
- 224. listen to stories
- 225. play games
- 226. find materials and information for school subjects
- 227. make AV materials
- 228. make printed materials
- 229. help other students
- 230. see animals or plants

ACTIVITY SERVICES — Student Catalog (cont.)

In the media center, I

231. meet, talk, or listen to visitors
232. select materials to borrow
233. learn to operate AV equipment
234. study with other students
235. discuss materials
236. meet with library or media clubs
237. use computers for school work
238. look at bulletin boards or displays

JUNIOR-SENIOR HIGH SCHOOL
ADULT CATALOG

ACCESSIBILITY SERVICES

M T S

The media center is used for
1. X X _   class use upon teacher request
2. X X _   small groups upon teacher request
3. X X _   individual student research
4. X X _   individual student enjoyment

The media center is used for meetings of
5. X X _   faculty
6. X _ X   student organizations or activities
7. X _ _   administrators or school boards
8. X _ _   school-related parent groups

The media center provides books for
9. X X _   temporary reserve collections for instructional units
10. X X _   temporary room collections for instructional units
11. X X _   permanent room or department collections

The media center provides AV materials for
12. X X _   temporary reserve collections for instructional units
13. X X _   temporary room collections for instructional units
14. X X _   permanent room or department collections

The media center provides AV equipment for
15. X X _   loan to teachers (1 day or less)
16. X X _   loan to teachers (less than 30 days)
17. X X _   temporary loan to department
18. X X _   permanent loan to teachers
19. X X _   permanent loan to department

Students use the media center
20. X _ X   before school
21. X _ X   after school

Teachers use the media center
22. X X _   before school
23. X X _   after school

Students take home from the media center
24. X _ X   books
25. X _ X   AV materials
26. X _ X   AV equipment

Students check out for building use
27. X _ X   books
28. X _ X   AV materials
29. X _ X   AV equipment

30. X X _   Teachers *have time* to come to the media center.

ACCESSIBILITY SERVICES (cont.)

M T S

31. X _ X Students *have time* to come to the media center.
32. X X _ Teachers have time to consult with the media staff.
33. X X X Books are kept in good condition.
34. X X X AV materials are kept in good condition.
35. X X X AV equipment is kept in good condition.
36. X _ X Students use AV equipment in the media center.

AWARENESS SERVICES

M T S

Teachers are given information about
37. X X _   new AV equipment in the building
38. X X _   new books and AV materials in the media center
39. X X _   services available from the district media center (library)
40. X X _   services available from the regional media center (library)
41. X X _   services available from other libraries
42. X X _   community resources (guests, field trips, etc.)
43. X X _   existing media center services
44. X X _   newly added media center services

Students are given information about
45. X _ X   new AV equipment in the media center
46. X _ X   new books and AV materials in the media center
47. X _ X   services available from the district media center (library)
48. X _ X   services available from the regional media center (library)
49. X _ X   services available from other libraries in the area
50. X _ X   community resources (guests, field trips, etc.)
51. X _ X   existing media center services
52. X _ X   newly added media center services

The media staff sponsors special programs for
53. X X _   National Library Week, Book Week, etc.
54. X X _   local events of importance
55. X X _   national events
56. X X _   school-public library cooperative efforts

The media staff promotes the media program via
57. X X _   news releases
58. X X _   radio or TV
59. X X _   displays or bulletin boards
60. X X _   programs for parents
61. X X _   programs for administrators
62. X X _   presentations to the school board
63. X X _   presentations to community groups

PROFESSIONAL SERVICES

M T S

The *school* media staff acquires for the professional collection
64. X X _   books
65. X X _   periodicals
66. X X _   AV materials
67. X X _   research reports
68. X X _   curriculum guides

The *district* media staff acquires for the professional collection
69. X X _   books
70. X X _   periodicals
71. X X _   AV materials
72. X X _   research reports
73. X X _   curriculum guides

The *regional* media staff acquires for the professional collection
74. X X _   books
75. X X _   periodicals
76. X X _   AV materials
77. X X _   research reports
78. X X _   curriculum guides

In-service topics for teachers include
79. X X _   integrating media center materials into instruction
80. X X _   utilizing media center services effectively
81. X X _   producing AV materials
82. X X _   utilizing AV equipment
83. X X _   existing media center services
84. X X _   newly added media center services

The media staff works with teachers/counselors to help
85. X X _   improve student progress in learning
86. X _ X   students with their personal problems
87. X _ X   students make career decisions

UTILIZATION SERVICES

M T S

Teachers are helped to locate materials in
88. X X _   the media center collection
89. X X _   the various classroom collections

The media staff assists teachers by
90. X X _   suggesting various uses of media center materials
91. X X _   locating materials of various difficulty and interest levels
92. X X _   demonstrating the versatility of AV equipment
93. X X _   aiding in the use of equipment and accessories

UTILIZATION SERVICES (cont.)

M T S

Reference service in the media center is given *teachers* by

94. X X _   answering simple questions (e.g., who wrote *Street Rod*)
95. X X _   answering more complex questions
96. X X _   requiring teachers to try to answer their own questions
97. X X _   referring teachers to resources not in the media center

Reference service in the media center is given *students* by

98. X _ X   answering simple questions (e.g., who wrote *Street Rod*)
99. X _ X   answering more complex questions
100. X _ X   requiring students to try to answer their own questions
101. X _ X   referring students to resources not in the media center

Instruction in the use of the media center is

102. X X _   given as a unit of instruction
103. X X _   integrated into classroom instructional units
104. X X _   given informally upon request

Instruction in the use of the media center is given *to*

105. X X _   individual students
106. X X _   small groups
107. X X _   classes and/or large groups
108. X X _   entering grade-level students
109. X X _   new students

Instruction in the use of the media center is given *by*

110. X X _   teacher and media staff in a team approach
111. X X _   the teacher
112. X X _   the media staff

Group guidance is given by the media staff through

113. X X X   book or media talks on recreational materials
114. X X X   book or media talks on materials for classwork
115. X X X   distribution of materials lists
116. X X X   displays, exhibits and/or bulletin boards

Individual guidance is given by the media staff through

117. X X X   individualized materials lists
118. X X X   help in the location of materials
119. X X X   help in the selection of materials

The media staff engages in a program of

120. X X _   reading guidance
121. X X _   viewing guidance (visual literacy)
122. X X _   listening guidance
123. X X _   improvement of study habits
124. X X _   development of critical thinking

125. X X X Help is given when AV equipment problems arise.

PLANNING SERVICES

M T S

Media center staff assists teachers in unit planning by

126. X X _   consulting *in advance* of unit presentation
127. X X _   assisting in analysis of learning tasks
128. X X _   helping formulate behavioral objectives
129. X X _   gathering materials
130. X X _   preparing bibliographies
131. X X _   suggesting materials of appropriate difficulty
132. X X _   suggesting materials at varying *interest levels*

133. X X _ The media specialist consults with the curriculum committee.

ACQUISITION SERVICES

M T S

Inter-library loans for *teachers* are provided from

134. X X _   the district center collection
135. X X _   other school media centers in the district
136. X X _   public libraries in the area
137. X X _   academic libraries in the area
138. X X _   rental libraries
139. X X _   regional media centers (libraries)

Inter-library loans for *students* are provided from

140. X _ X   the district center collection
141. X _ X   other school media centers in the district
142. X _ X   public libraries in the area
143. X _ X   academic libraries in the area
144. X _ _   rental libraries
145. X _ X   regional media centers (libraries)

The media staff purchases materials

146. X X _   on recommendation of the teachers
147. X _ X   on recommendation of the students

The media staff provides for the purpose of purchasing

148. X X _   teacher previewing
149. X X _   student previewing
150. X X _   producers' catalogs
151. X X _   published evaluations of materials
152. X X _   published evaluations of equipment

The media staff orders

153. X X _   materials only at specified times
154. X X _   individual orders upon request

PRODUCTION SERVICES

M T S

Which are produced by your *school* media staff?

155.	X X X	graphics (lettering, poster making, etc.)
156.	X X X	slides
157.	X X X	videotapes
158.	X X X	tape recordings
159.	X X X	8mm films
160.	X X X	radio programs
161.	X X X	16mm films
162.	X X X	models and dioramas
163.	X X X	transparencies
164.	X X X	kits
165.	X X X	games
166.	X X X	filmstrips
167.	X X X	learning packages
168.	X X X	photocopies
169.	X X X	mounted materials
170.	X X X	laminated materials
171.	X X X	printed or duplicated materials
172.	X X X	computer-assisted instruction
173.	X X X	programmed instruction
174.	X X X	computer programs

Which are produced by your *district* media staff?

175.	X X _	graphics (lettering, poster making, etc.)
176.	X X _	slides
177.	X X _	videotapes
178.	X X _	tape recordings
179.	X X _	8mm films
180.	X X _	radio programs
181.	X X _	16mm films
182.	X X _	models and dioramas
183.	X X _	transparencies
184.	X X _	kits
185.	X X _	games
186.	X X _	filmstrips
187.	X X _	learning packages
188.	X X _	photocopies
189.	X X _	mounted materials
190.	X X _	laminated materials
191.	X X _	printed or duplicated materials
192.	X X _	computer-assisted instruction
193.	X X _	programmed instruction
194.	X X _	computer programs

PRODUCTION SERVICES (cont.)

M T S

Which are produced by your *regional* media staff?

195. X X __   graphics (lettering, poster making, etc.)
196. X X __   slides
197. X X __   videotapes
198. X X __   tape recordings
199. X X __   8mm films
200. X X __   radio programs
201. X X __   16mm films
202. X X __   models and dioramas
203. X X __   transparencies
204. X X __   kits
205. X X __   games
206. X X __   filmstrips
207. X X __   learning packages
208. X X __   photocopies
209. X X __   mounted materials
210. X X __   laminated materials
211. X X __   printed or duplicated materials
212. X X __   computer-assisted instruction
213. X X __   programmed instruction
214. X X __   computer programs

Teachers who want locally produced AV materials are provided

215. X X __   facilities and equipment
216. X X __   supplies
217. X X __   help from the media staff
218. X X __   the finished product from the media staff

Students who want locally produced AV materials are provided

219. X __ X   facilities and equipment
220. X __ X   supplies
221. X __ X   help from the media staff
222. X __ X   the finished product from the media staff

EVALUATION SERVICES

M T S

The media center collection provides

223. X X X   a variety of media to meet user needs
224. X X X   current material
225. X X X   enough material for the number of users
226. X X X   quality materials

EVALUATION SERVICES (cont.)

M T S

Together, teachers and media staff evaluate the success of

227. X X _   class projects involving the media center
228. X X _   small group projects involving the media center
229. X X _   individual projects involving the media center
230. X X _   library skills training for students
231. X X _   jointly planned units of instruction

The media staff provides *students* opportunities to evaluate

232. X _ X   the materials collection
233. X _ X   media center services
234. X _ X   media center facilities
235. X _ X   media center policies

The media staff provides *teachers* opportunities to evaluate

236. X X _   the materials collection
237. X X _   media center services
238. X X _   media center facilities
239. X X _   media center policies

ACTIVITY SERVICES

M T S

In the media center, students

240. X _ X   read or look at books
241. X _ X   read magazines and newspapers
242. X _ X   look at AV materials in large groups
243. X _ X   look at AV materials in small groups
244. X _ X   look at AV materials as individuals
245. X _ X   listen to recordings in large groups
246. X _ X   listen to recordings in small groups
247. X _ X   listen to recordings as individuals
248. X _ X   play games (educational, chess, etc.)
249. X _ X   find materials and information for school subjects
250. X _ X   make AV materials
251. X _ X   make printed materials
252. X _ X   tutor other students
253. X _ X   meet, talk, or listen to community resource persons
254. X _ X   select materials to borrow
255. X _ X   learn to operate AV equipment
256. X _ X   study with other students
257. X _ X   discuss materials
258. X _ X   participate in library clubs or media organizations
259. X _ X   use computer-assisted instruction
260. X _ X   view displays and exhibits

ACTIVITY SERVICES (cont.)

M T S

In the media center, teachers
261. X X __ have access to recreational materials
262. X X __ socialize with colleagues
263. X X __ have a place to 'get away from it all'
264. X X __ engage in unit planning with colleagues
265. X X __ eat and drink

JUNIOR-SENIOR HIGH SCHOOL
STUDENT CATALOG

ACCESSIBILITY SERVICES — Student Catalog

The media center is used for
      6. student meetings and activities

I use the media center
      20. before school
      21. after school

I take home from the media center
      24. books
      25. AV materials
      26. AV equipment

For use in the building, I check out
      27. books
      28. AV materials
      29. AV equipment

  31. I *have time* to come to the media center.

  33. The media center's books are kept in good condition.

  34. The media center's AV materials are kept in good condition.

  35. The media center's AV equipment is kept in good condition.

  36. I use AV equipment in the media center.

AWARENESS SERVICES — Student Catalog

I am given information about
      45. new AV equipment in the media center
      46. new books and AV materials in the media center
      47. services available from the district media center (library)
      48. services available from the regional media center (library)
      49. services available from other libraries in the area
      50. community resources (guests, field trips, etc.)
      51. existing media center services
      52. newly added media center services

PROFESSIONAL SERVICES — Student Catalog

The media staff helps me
      86. with my personal problems
      87. make career decisions

UTILIZATION SERVICES — Student Catalog

The media staff helps me by
      98. answering simple questions (e.g., who wrote *Street Rod*)
      99. answering harder questions

UTILIZATION SERVICES — Student Catalog (Cont.)

The media staff helps me by

100. asking me to try to answer my own questions
101. sending me to people or materials outside the media center

The media staff helps my group by

113. discussing recreational materials with us
114. giving talks on materials for classwork
115. handing out lists of materials
116. making displays and bulletin boards

The media staff helps me

117. by giving me lists of materials
118. find materials
119. choose materials

125. I receive help when AV equipment problems arise.

ACQUISITION SERVICES — Student Catalog

I receive inter-library loans from

140. the district center collection
141. other school media centers in the district
142. public libraries in the area
143. college libraries in the area
145. regional media centers (libraries)

The media staff will buy materials

147. I ask for

PRODUCTION SERVICES — Student Catalog

Our school media center makes

155. graphics (lettering, poster making, etc.)
156. slides
157. videotapes
158. tape recordings
159. 8mm films
160. radio programs
161. 16mm films
162. models and dioramas
163. transparencies
164. kits
165. games
166. filmstrips
167. learning packages
168. photocopies
169. mounted materials

PRODUCTION SERVICES — Student Catalog (Cont.)

Our school media center makes

170. laminated materials
171. printed or duplicated materials
172. computer-assisted instruction
173. programmed instruction
174. computer programs

If I want AV materials *made,* the media staff
219. gives me space and equipment
220. gives me supplies
221. gives me help
222. does it for me

EVALUATION SERVICES — Student Catalog

The media center collection has
223. a variety of media to meet my needs
224. current material
225. enough material for the number of users
226. quality materials

The media staff gives me a chance to evaluate
232. the materials collection
233. media center services
234. media center facilities
235. media center rules

ACTIVITY SERVICES — Student Catalog

In the media center, I
240. read or look at books
241. read magazines and newspapers
242. look at AV materials in large groups
243. look at AV materials in small groups
244. look at AV materials by myself
245. listen to recordings in large groups
246. listen to recordings in small groups
247. listen to recordings by myself
248. play games (educational, chess, etc.)
249. find materials and information for school subjects
250. make AV materials
251. make printed materials
252. help other students
253. meet, talk, or listen to visitors
254. select materials to borrow
255. learn to operate AV equipment

ACTIVITY SERVICES — Student Catalog (Cont.)

In the media center, I

256. study with other students
257. discuss materials
258. participate in library clubs or media organizations
259. use computer-assisted instruction
260. view displays and exhibits

Appendix C:
Additional Readings

INSTRUCTIONAL INVOLVEMENT

Callison, Daniel. "School Library Media Programs & Free Inquiry Learning." *School Library Journal* 32, no. 6 (February 1986): 20-24.
    Callison provides a method for doing resource-based teaching as a cooperative activity between the teacher and the library media specialist which will encourage growth and development of inquiry learning (student questioning and discovery of information).

Didier, Elaine K. "An Overview of Research on the Impact of School Library Media Programs on Student Achievement." *School Library Media Quarterly* 14, no. 1 (Fall 1985): 33-36.
    Didier pulls together evidence from research that a sound library media program has the potential to affect the quality of a student's education.

Loertscher, David V. "Computer Coordinator Involvement in Instruction." In *The Microcomputer Facility and the School Library Media Specialist*, edited by Blanche Woolls and David V. Loertscher, 152-55. Chicago: American Library Association, 1986.
    The resource-based teaching planning form is adapted for use by a computer specialist who is on the library media staff.

McDonald, Frances Beck. *The Emerging School Library Media Program: Readings*. Englewood, Colo.: Libraries Unlimited, 1988.
    McDonald has collected a number of articles about resource-based teaching. Included are:

    Oberg, Antoinette. "The School Librarian and the Classroom Teacher: Partners in Curriculum Planning." *Emergency Librarian* 14 (September/October 1986): 9-14.

    Patrick, Retta. "School Library Media Programs Today: The Taxonomy Applied." *Wilson Library Bulletin* 56 (February 1982): 422-27.

    Stripling, Barbara. "What Price ID? A Practical Approach to a Personal Dilemma." *School Library Media Quarterly* 12 (Summer 1984): 290-96.

    Stroud, Janet. "Library Media Center Taxonomy: Future Implications." *Wilson Library Bulletin* 56 (February 1985): 428-33.

Thurman, Glenda. "Strategy for Change: Implementing the ID Process in Your School." *School Learning Resources* 2 (December 1982): 5-7.

Vandergrift, Kay E. *The Teaching Role of the School Library Media Specialist*. Chicago: AASL, 1979.
The best of early explorations of curricular involvement.

INSTRUCTIONAL DESIGN

Cleaver, Betty T., and William D. Taylor. *Involving the School Library Media Specialist in Curriculum Development*. School Media Centers: Focus on Trends and Issues, no. 8. Chicago: American Library Association, 1983.
Provides a step-by-step guide to planning instructional units.

Dick, Walter, and Lou Carey. *The Systematic Design of Instruction*. 2nd ed. Glenview, Ill.: Scott Foresman, 1985.
A basic text used by many graduate professors in teaching instructional development.

Kemp, Jerrold E. *The Instructional Design Process*. New York: Harper & Row, 1985.
A basic text which describes systematic instructional planning. Each chapter contains an overview, contains illustrations, and prints review exercises.

Rosenfield, Sylvia. *Instructional Consultation*. Hillsdale, N.J.: Lawrence Erlbaum Associates, 1987.
Instructional development from the point of view of the school psychologist.

Turner, Philip. *Case Studies for Helping Teachers Teach*. Englewood, Colo.: Libraries Unlimited, 1988.
Actual case studies from school library media specialists around the country exemplify the principles of Turner's method of instructional design.

Turner, Philip. *Helping Teachers Teach*. Littleton, Colo.: Libraries Unlimited, 1986.
Turner translates the formal instructional design process into a practical method for school library media specialists.

Turner, Philip. "Research on Helping Teachers Teach." *School Library Media Quarterly* 15, no. 4 (Summer 1987): 229-31.
Turner reviews research dealing with the library media specialist's role in instructional development and outlines the direction of future research.

CURRICULUM

Saylor, J. Galen. *Who Planned the Curriculum?: A Curriculum Plans Reservoir Model with Historical Examples*. West Lafayette, Ind.: Kappa Delta Pi Press, 1982.
An excellent overview of how curriculum is formulated in the United States by textbook publishers, national voluntary agencies, universities and accrediting agencies, the federal government, states, and local school districts.

PLANNING

Liesener, James W. *A Systematic Planning Process for School Media Programs*. Chicago: American Library Association, 1976.

ROLES

Anderson, Pauline H. *Library Media Leadership in Academic Secondary Schools*. Hamden, Conn.: Library Professional Publications/Shoestring Press, 1985.
Discusses the role of the library media specialist working in the private or academically oriented high school.

Baker, Phil. *The Library Media Program and the School*. Littleton, Colo.: Libraries Unlimited, 1984.
Baker's view of the function of the library media program in the school.

Craver, Kathleen W. "The Changing Instructional Role of the High School Library Media Specialist: 1950-84." *School Library Media Quarterly* 14, no. 4 (Summer 1986): 183-92.
Craver provides the best summary of the research literature which documents the change of role for the library media specialist.

Haycock, Ken. "Services of School Resource Centers." *Emergency Librarian* 13, no. 1 (September/October 1985): 28-29.
Haycock advocates that the library media center should be an integral part of the curriculum processes in the school.

Haycock, Ken. "Strengthening the Foundations for Teacher-Librarianship." *School Library Media Quarterly* 13, no. 2 (Spring 1985): 102-9.
Ken's keynote address to the 1984 conference of the International Association of School Librarianship in Honolulu, Hawaii. An important statement on the role and change of directions for the library media center.

Liesener, James W. "Learning at Risk: School Library Media Programs in an Information World." *School Library Media Quarterly* 14, no. 1 (Fall 1985): 11-20.
This paper was presented for a series of seminars, held January through March 1984, sponsored by the U.S. Department of Education. It was one of the papers in response to "A Nation at Risk."

Vandergrift, Kay E., and Jane Anne Hannigan. "Elementary School Library Media Centers as Essential Components in the Schooling Process: An AASL Position Paper." *School Library Media Quarterly* 14, no. 4 (Summer 1986): 171-73.
An important and succinct statement about the purpose of the elementary school library media center backed up with an extensive bibliography.

FACILITIES

Hannigan, Jane A. "Charette: Media Facilities Design." *School Media Quarterly* 2, no. 3 (Spring 1974): 185-294.
   Articles by twenty contributors that cover a wide spectrum of facilities design problems.

Lamkin, Bernice. "A Media Center for the 21st Century." *School Library Journal* 33, no. 3 (November 1986): 25-29.
   Lamkin provides a description of the total process of building a new high school library media center from architectural plans through establishing a program in the facility.

Media Center Facility Design for Maryland Schools. Baltimore, Md.: Maryland State Department of Education, Division of Library Development and Services, 1975. ERIC ED 107 297.
   One of the best of the state documents covering facilities design and specifications.

Patrick, Retta Ball. *Facilities for School Library Media Centers: A Guide for Designing and Remodeling.* Englewood, Colo.: Libraries Unlimited, 1988.
   A major source for planning, writing specifications, designing, and arranging facilities for the support of curricular activities.

ADMINISTRATION

Topical

Biagini, Mary K. *A Model for Problem Solving and Decision Making: Managing School Library Media Programs.* Englewood, Colo.: Libraries Unlimited, 1988.
   A major case study with many situations and problems to assist the library media specialist in making decisions and confronting real-life issues. A companion to Woolls's *Managing School Library Programs.*

Craver, Kathleen W. "Use of Academic Libraries by High School Students: Implications for Research." *RQ* 27, no. 1 (Fall 1987): 53-66.
   Reviews both the professional and research literature dealing with the topic.

Eisenberg, Michael B., and Robert E. Berkowitz. *Curriculum Initiative: An Agenda and Strategy for Library Media Programs.* Norwood, N.J.: Ablex Publishing Corp., 1988.
   A conceptual framework and practical approach to meeting the curriculum-related responsibilities of school library media specialists, including curriculum support services and library and information instruction skills. Includes an accompanying workbook.

Hart, Thomas L., ed. *Behavior Management in the School Library Media Center*. Chicago: American Library Association, 1985.

A useful guide to understanding the problem and solutions gleaned from practitioners around the country.

Mancall, Jacqueline C., and M. Carl Drott. *Measuring Student Information Use: A Guide for School Library Media Specialists*. Littleton, Colo.: Libraries Unlimited, 1983.

Miller, Marilyn L., and Barbara Moran. "Expenditures for Resources in School Library Media Centers FY '85-'86." *School Library Journal* 33, no. 10 (June-July 1987): 37-45.

The third in a series of research studies not only of expenditures, but also of staffing and technology.

Woolls, Blanche. *Grant Proposal Writing: A Handbook for School Library Media Specialists*. Westport, Conn.: Greenwood Press, 1987.

A manual for obtaining money not a part of regular district budgets.

Woolls, Blanche. *Managing School Library Programs*. Englewood, Colo.: Libraries Unlimited, 1988.

Starting with the first day on the job, this manual covers program, organization, budgeting, facilities, equipment, collection development, and networking.

Manuals

Nickel, Mildred L. *Steps to Service: A Handbook of Procedures for the School Library Media Center*. Chicago: American Library Association, 1975.

The most well-known library media manual on the market.

Procedures Manual for School Library Media Centers. Oklahoma City, Okla.: Oklahoma State Department of Education, 1982.

One of the best procedure manuals available. It is an amalgamation of many available manuals from all parts of the country.

Technology

Casciero, Albert J., and Raymond G. Roney. *Audiovisual Technology Primer*. Englewood, Colo.: Libraries Unlimited, 1988.

A basic text which covers most of the forms of technology that a library media specialist will have to know. It provides an excellent review for those who think they are familiar with technology but who desire a little more technical approach.

Costa, Betty, and Marie Costa. *A Micro Handbook for Small Libraries and Media Centers*. 2nd ed. Littleton, Colo.: Libraries Unlimited, 1986.

The most popular introductory work for computers in the school library media program.

Murray, William, ed. *A Guide to Basic Media Materials and Equipment Operations Training*. Aurora, Colo.: Aurora Public Schools, 1985. Order address: 875 Peoria St., Aurora, CO 80011, $8.53.

An excellent handbook and training guide for simple repair and maintenance of audiovisual equipment.

Woolls, Blanche, and David V. Loertscher. *The Microcomputer Facility and the School Library Media Specialist*. Chicago: American Library Association, 1986.

A collection of original articles from practitioners providing guidance on the management of the microcomputer as a part of both teaching and administrative functions.

REVIEWS OF RESEARCH
(in order of publication)

Woodworth, Mary Lorraine. *The Identification and Examination of Areas of Needed Research in School Librarianship*. Washington, D.C.: U.S. Department of Health, Education, and Welfare, 1967. ERIC ED 018 243 LI 000 372.

Lowrie, Jean E. "A Review of Research in School Librarianship." In *Research Methods in Librarianship*, edited by Herbert Goldhor, 51-53. Urbana, Ill.: University of Illinois Graduate School of Library Science, 1968.

Aaron, Shirley L. "A Review of Selected Research Studies in School Librarianship 1967-1971: Part I." *School Libraries* 21, no. 4 (Summer 1972): 29-46.

Aaron, Shirley L. "A Review of Selected Research Studies in School Librarianship 1967-71: Part II." *School Media Quarterly* 1, no. 1 (Fall 1972): 41-48.

Schlachter, Gail, and Dennis Thomison. *Library Science Dissertations, 1925-1972: An Annotated Bibliography*. Littleton, Colo.: Libraries Unlimited, 1974.

Freeman, Patricia. *Index to Research in School Librarianship, 1960-1974*. Syracuse, N.Y.: ERIC Document Reproduction Service, 1976. ED 119 741.

Barron, Daniel D. "A Review of Selected Research in School Librarianship: 1972-76." *School Media Quarterly* 5, no. 4 (Summer 1977): 271-89.

Wilkinson, Gene L. *Media in Instruction: 60 Years of Research*. Washington, D.C.: Association for Educational Communications and Technology, 1980.

Aaron, Shirley L. "A Review of Selected Doctoral Dissertations about School Library Media Programs and Resources, January 1972-December 1980." *School Library Media Quarterly* 10, no. 3 (Spring 1982): 210-45.

Schlachter, Gail, and Dennis Thomison. *Library Science Dissertations, 1973-1981: An Annotated Bibliography*. Littleton, Colo.: Libraries Unlimited, 1982.

Aaron, Shirley L. "A Review of Selected Research Studies about School Library Media Programs, Resources, and Personnel: January 1972-June 1981." In *School Library Media Annual* 1, 303-85. Littleton, Colo.: Libraries Unlimited, 1983.

Aaron, Shirley L. "Selected Research Studies about School Library Media Programs, Resources, and Personnel: June 1981-December 1982." In *School Library Media Annual* 2, 362-80. Littleton, Colo.: Libraries Unlimited, 1984.

Minor, Barbara B. "ERIC Research Studies Dealing with School Library Media Programs: June 1981-June 1984." In *School Library Media Annual* 3, 348-71. Littleton, Colo.: Libraries Unlimited, 1985.

Aaron, Shirley L. "Selected Research Studies about School Library Media Programs, Resources, and Personnel: January 1983-January 1984." In *School Library Media Annual* 3, 372-82. Littleton, Colo.: Libraries Unlimited, 1985.

Minor, Barbara B. "Research Studies Dealing with School Library Media Programs from the ERIC Files: July 1984-June 1985." In *School Library Media Annual* 4, 394-408. Littleton, Colo.: Libraries Unlimited, 1986.

Aaron, Shirley L. "Selected Research Studies about School Library Media Programs, Resources, and Personnel." In *School Library Media Annual* 4, 409-18. Littleton, Colo.: Libraries Unlimited, 1986.

Minor, Barbara B. "Research Studies Dealing with School Library Media Programs from the ERIC Files: July 1985-June 1986." In *School Library Media Annual* 5, 294-308. Littleton, Colo.: Libraries Unlimited, 1987.

Aaron, Shirley L. "Selected Research Studies about School Library Media Programs, Resources, and Personnel." In *School Library Media Annual* 5, 309-22. Littleton, Colo.: Libraries Unlimited, 1987.

Barron, Daniel D. "School Library Media Program Research: Review of 1986." In *Library and Information Science Annual* 3, 36-43. Littleton, Colo.: Libraries Unlimited, 1987.

EDITIONS OF NATIONAL STANDARDS AND GUIDELINES

Certain, C. C. *Standard Library Organization and Equipment for Secondary Schools of Different Sizes.* National Education Association, Department of Secondary Education, 1920.

Certain, C. C. *Elementary School Library Standards.* Prepared under the supervision of a Joint Committee of the National Education Association and the American Library Association. Chicago: American Library Association, 1925.

Committees on Post-War Planning of the American Library Association, *School Libraries for Today and Tomorrow, Functions and Standards*. Chicago: American Library Association, 1945.

American Association of School Librarians. *Standards for School Library Programs*. Chicago: American Library Association, 1960.

American Association of School Librarians and the Department of Audiovisual Instruction of the National Education Association. *Standards for School Media Programs*. Chicago: American Library Association, 1969.

American Association of School Librarians and Association for Educational Communications and Technology. *Media Programs District and School*. Chicago: American Library Association, 1975.

American Association of School Librarians and Association for Educational Communications and Technology. *Information Power: Guidelines for School Library Media Programs*. Chicago: American Library Association, 1988.

Index